The 7th Planet
Mercury Rising

Gerald R. Clark

GERALD CLARK

All referenced images obtained via license-free public sources

ISBN-13:
978-1505531886

ISBN-10:
1505531888

DEDICATION

I would like to dedicate this book to my twin flame Christa J. Clark. She inspires my days with love and beauty and fearlessly probes unseen dark places filling them with effervescent light. Without my soul mate by my side everyday on this holographic journey towards our mutual destiny, it is doubtful you would be reading these words today.

In addition to the loving support I receive at home, time must be taken to acknowledge the community that has formed in response to both of our missions, both Artistic Vegan and Anunnaki of Nibiru fans alike. There has been fan crossover which has been fun for both of us. Thanks to all of you and your kind support for our individual and joint missions. Because of your love and support, Christa and I have responded to the community needs and provided both Star Fire Gold and the immunity bolstering Colloidal Silver that is now available.

Last but not least, I would like to dedicate this book to all the truth seekers in the world. Your willingness to go beyond the normal script has led you to an important and interesting puzzle piece in your archetypal path towards the ultimate goal, a homecoming! Enjoy the book and share the wisdom...

Christa Clark, my wife and twin flame living her personal legend helping mankind purify their consciousness and live in the LIGHT!

So proud of her fearless dedication to her mission!

See www.artisticvegan.com for all that she does for humanity!

TABLE OF CONTENTS

GERALD CLARK

FIGURES AND TABLES

ACKNOWLEDGMENTS

There are so many names that come to mind when deciding who to acknowledge for positively impacting the writing of this book. Every man must think that he has the best mother on the block, as do I. My mother was always a trusted source of support in all my endeavors. We all owe sincere gratitude to the sacred feminine archetypal goddess that gave life to mankind; Ninharsag to her peers, Isis to the Egyptians.

I would also like to acknowledge the profoundly brave scientist and pioneering ancient astronaut, Lord Enki. His mission was very difficult here on Earth, and like us all on the ascendency path returning to the source of ALL, he too received lessons to facilitate his soul path progressing always toward the LIGHT, venerating the CREATOR OF ALL. His profound ponderings over fate and destiny forever changed my definition of interesting. As mankind's father and Lord of the Seas, Poseidon is a true man's hero.

Speaking of heroes, the magic of Hermes is alluring. His wisdom is as profound as to leave one electrified during a mere probe into the map to ascension he authored: The Emerald Tablets

GERALD CLARK

of Thoth the Atlantean.   His wise counsel is the key to life and death. May the spirit of Thoth visit you daily, illuminating your way and lighting your path to your destiny, where we all return to the source of ALL.

Last but most significantly, I would like to acknowledge the CREATOR OF ALL for the opportunity to take on a human form being an eternal flame, to progress in my soul's path where truth-seeking and a reflective consciousness coupled with intelligence, integrity, and the realization that the source of CAUSE and EFFECT lead us home to the Light!

Also wanted to give honorable mention to my deceased father, Donald L. Clark, the artist and gentle spirit that painted my mother shown here when I was 3 months old. Thanks Dad for the memory!

GERALD CLARK

INTRODUCTION

This is the book you and I have been waiting for since authoring my first book The Anunnaki of Nibiru released August 4th, 2013. The issues and questions that this research raised with the readers was carefully studied to determine where the link was between the past disclosures concerning humanity's South African genesis account and today. How does one proceed after discovering that modern man was fashioned by the Anunnaki to supplant the labor force they brought to Earth from Nibiru? This knowledge changes all that we have been coerced into believing as the truth.

A theme began to emerge given the lessons garnered from sacred writings accessed. The profound nature of the material provided in this book took time to study, understand, process the lessons and assimilate them into a coherent message that picks up where the reader left off in the Anunnaki of Nibiru.

Questions were posed by the readers such as "If the Anunnaki created mankind, then who created them?" The answer takes one back to the SOURCE of our reality. Are we evolving physically and consciously towards an archetype used in our biological design?

Where are we headed as a species and to what extent are our genetic creators shaping the outcome? Are the Anunnaki remnants attempting to establish a one world government, revealing the severe oppressive nature of some malignant entity that animates the Dark Lords? Evil forces appear to be having their way with the primitive worker populace as destruction reigns in the headlines.

In my quest to find the trail that leads to ascension out of the prison planet conditions we find ourselves in, no map was found. The truth, as it always has been for participants on the stage of life, is a pathless land. Only through deep seeking, vetting the lessons at a spiritual level, could the sought after wisdom be accessed.

Profound and timely guidance, inscribed as character building law codes from the twin pillars of Enki-Poseidon's legendary city of Atlantis, holds the key to our ascension. It is now time to explode the glass ceiling of oppression, rising in consciousness from our lowly primitive worker state, unaware of the intervention that turned a hairy barbarian from the land of Khem to a Mystery School Graduate, opening the guarded portal on Earth to return to the Source of All creation. Mystery Schools along the Nile, established by the first Al-Khemist, Thoth the Atlantean, instructed highly qualified candidates in the ancient science of continuous creation. Some well-known graduates include Plato and Pythagoras. Thoth, also known as Ningishzida in the Sumerian cuneiform records, had many names in cultures separated by thousands of years. Also known as names (AKA) for him cause great consternation in the Abrahamic religions. Ningishzida, Thoth the Atlantean, Thrice Great Hermes, Yehoshua (Biblical Jesus) and Melchizedek are just a few. Thoth was one of the immortals that chose to participate in helping mankind out of his quarantined perception prison.

Combining genealogy studies, biblical theology, ancient astronaut theory, geopolitical developments, and a deep scientific understanding of the properties and nature of light led to an unexpected outcome, a profound unveiling intended for my supporters. The message and detailed criteria on how to participate in the Great Year ascension is presented to the reader in a manner that is easy to understand, given the complex nature of our reality. The unveiling re-invigorated me to write this book, simultaneous to the timing of the great culling planned for WW3.

The reader will undoubtedly put the book down, zealously seeking to share the wisdom with family and friends, arming them with the knowledge that removes any remaining ideas or fear about the sting of death as we understand it.

Overcoming our fear of death is part of the process to embrace the transformation we experience during aging. What if you knew that death was an illusion and conducted your life to achieve the goals that were determined by the Creator of All to lead you to the reflective consciousness that is the source of space-time and our reality here on the 7th Planet, where Mercury-Ningishzida's role to raise mankind's consciousness during the ascension window is reaching a crescendo. Join me on this profound life-altering journey where the reader will encounter the mystical process that leads to the knowledge and reality of immortality if one chooses it. May the soul of the universe be with you and provide unmatched peace and comfort holding thy form through the transition to a new reality. I look forward to meeting you all at the SOURCE. Thank you for your support!

CHAPTER 1: Background

Access to higher consciousness has always been a significant factor to consider for those who govern. Intellectuals, dissidents, and anti-government militias share some common goals. Intellectuals compare and contrast systems of governance with the potential to resist any current regime that exercises control by inhibiting free thinking that leads to revolutionary ideology. Next, the free thinker's ideas spread to those rebels who exhibit dissent in the public arena, perhaps arm in arm with the intellects. Once the disenfranchisement among the populace reaches a crescendo, critical mass if you will, more serious members begin to fill the ranks and files of the resistance, to potentially include armed militias.

Thus, governments exert significant effort to anticipate and detect unrest among the populace. The police, lawyers, judges, and prison systems represent the enforcement and penalty arm of the government, being licensed agents of the state. These permitted agents and government elements are in place to enforce laws or norms of behavior and to punish those that do not comply with the powers that be (PTB), especially dissidents and revolutionaries.

Viewing the subservient worker from the standpoint of its creator or its governor is significantly different. How much access to higher consciousness-energy would a meta-creator make available to a subservient "primitive worker"? Would the being be provided with intelligence and a consciousness that could use memory and therefore, with the application of comparative thinking and reflection, assess their own state as enslaved? Could the circumstances of the subservient be created in such a way that they were not aware of their enslavement?

For instance, suppose a large swath of land was allocated to a primitive workforce that was free to operate within the boundaries of the permitted area, but was restricted from approaching the borders within some specified distance? As long as the populace operates in accordance with the prescribed laws, to include respecting the border boundary rules, all is well and the perception of freedom remains intact. It is a matter of the perceived degree of freedom that governors allow in order to prevent the populace feeling they are in a cage versus the level of measures that can be used to re-establish control in the event of a rebellion.

Each form of government uses the primal instincts all humans possess to provide a common national identity, a sense of security in one's own homeland, and stimulus as was used in Roman times down at the sports stadium, I mean coliseum, to prevent boredom. I give you professional sports like NFL, AFL, and other prolific governing tactics used to placate the populace and provide a pressure relief valve for pent up aggression. State-sponsored events and entertainment modalities provide an aggressive emotional outlet for pent up slave anger, while amusing them with comedy and stimulus.

Boundaries establish mankind's primitive need to have a designated hunting-gathering territory. Separation also leads to labels such as *us* and *them*. Promoting a national identity is in the governments best interest as this sponsored "pride" can be used to enroll young heroes into the war machine, targeting an enemy beyond the territorial limits or defending one's homeland. Other governments simply mandate national military service using a draft or a simple age trigger, cutting out the advertising cost of attracting unsuspecting "support our troops at any cost" ads that mislead young warriors. Those overlords that run effective media advertising campaigns have been successful at luring war volunteers as is done in the United States and other countries complete with glamorizing military recruitment ads and commercials on television.

Governments can implement extreme measures to control the consciousness of their serfs. Regulating what the populace can purchase in the marketplace is an easy first step to prevent products that can change consciousness from being consumed. Most class 1 "drugs" listed as illegal in the United States are categorized as such in order to prevent humans from experimenting with alternative consciousness levels, which have now been documented and attributable to their mind-expanding use by millions of people around the world. Thus, the black market exists in spite of prohibition, just as was the case with alcohol bans earlier in American history.

Control measures used by governments that target consciousness have now been shown to extend beyond mere consumable items like food, spices, herbs and "illegal drugs". The human body is electric and is significantly affected by externally generated frequencies. Some frequencies can make us happy, others can scramble mental functions or even cause death. For example, the household microwave oven utilizes a 2.4 GHz whose frequency is significantly absorbed by water. This transfer of energy from the microwave frequency to the water molecule via induced motion creates heat subsequently cooking the item. Clearly humans, composed mostly of water, would be negatively affected if exposed to high powered microwave frequencies.

More subtle use of less damaging frequencies and signal amplitudes can be used in an unseen manner. Modulated data like voice may be placed onto a carrier wave in the extreme low frequency (ELF) range. Human brain waves operate in this same range, specifically from about 0.5 Hz to 20 Hz. Any device used by a government or its representatives that is broadcasting in the ELF is highly suspect, especially if it is operating in the human brain wave region previously cited. HAARP is just such an example of such technology, disguised as a high amplitude acousto-auro atmospheric research project owned and operated by the military or its research arm. How can the people's money be used to construct devices secretly destined to suppress or even kill massive numbers of people? Progressively, iteratively, and intentionally the Constitution of the United States has been shredded. All the while, the government has expanded to an incredulous and burgeoning behemoth ready and willing to show its fangs to any and all who question its authority. In the book "Ishmael" [26] written by Daniel Quinn, the evolved guerrilla comments that "if mankind knew how to live, then their laws would not be changing continuously". If we stop to assess our present legal morass, we are forced then to concede that the eight hundred pound gorilla in the room is correct.

What governments cannot control is what catalyzes them to irrational action. Suppose that some new illegal drug were to be smuggled into the consumer market by the notorious Mexican cartel. Further suppose that the drug had the ability to change human consciousness by activating latent DNA and when exposed to full-spectrum energy from the sun, began integrating gravity with the human energy body represented by the Chakras. This integration process acts as the freight train to human consciousness evolution by rapidly awakening the Chakras and subsequently integrating the human energy body. The result: physical body-enlightened and sleeping serfs no more.

Suddenly, the government would be faced with a new front on the drug war to stem the tide of the consciousness altering chemicals deemed responsible for the sudden uprisings. Next a regional or national public announcement would be formulated to scare the populace about the ills of the new drug simultaneous with eliminating the source. Next, those who were partaking of the drug would be watched for behavioral modification impact that could be potentially seen as a threat to the government. This stage of crisis management activities could potentially be more rapidly concluded using a live subject, studying them while under the influence of the drug, most certainly under three-letter agency supervision. Finally, based on the government's findings, new laws could potentially be levied in the war on drugs and the class 1 drug listing would be appended with a new addition. Arrests and undercover operations might follow in order to locate the supply lines and have them interdicted, confiscated, publicized for agency funding justification. These drugs would likely be redistributed in some illegal profiteering scheme, possibly with an agency-formulated toxic debilitating drug additive for those that dare cross the class 1 legal line. The effects of the additive can also be studied by the government to determine its effectiveness at curbing any public interest in pursuing the drug given the negatively hedged risk-reward ratio, coupled with the public service announcement (PSA) and new laws to make it so.

Taking our imagination one step further, consider an unstoppable external catalyst that automatically begins to increase human consciousness. Suppose further that the escalating consciousness change in humans is potentially an energy-based catalyst, versus the Mexican cartel chemical origin as hypothesized in the previous paragraphs.

Recall that the human body was modeled as an antenna in my first book, "The Anunnaki of Nibiru" [3, Ch. 6]. In this model, it was postulated that the human structure, having significant electro-magnetic interactions, can be represented as a modulator-demodulator (MODEM) system. Working with this model in mind, variations in the electro-magnetic spectrum (EMS) can have significant effects on the bio-energetic state of humans. For those who study the principles of Astrology, it should be clear that the position of the various planets in the Zodiacal Houses have the potential to change the EMS received on the surface of the Earth.

These energetic relationships between the spherical masses in our solar system and their EMS resultant energy are now monitored by scientific instrumentation. Solar coronal mass ejections (CME) and the subsequent impact on the Earth's electro-magnetic field and its atmosphere are fairly well understood. Radiated energy from the sun, the basis for the EMS, fluctuates over time. Solar maximums occur cyclically every eleven years at which point the radiated energy from the sun can be disastrous for life in the solar system.

Often times the solar maximum results in large storms and CMEs. Twenty two years ago, the Canadian electrical grid was knocked offline by a CME. The most recent solar maxima occurred in the year 2013 as shown in Figure 1 below. The sun did not produce damaging CMEs and oddly resulted in two South poles versus an expected flip in the North-South poles. [http://www.space.com/21937-sun-solar-weather-peak-is-weak.html. Credit: Hathaway/NASA/MSFC] North-south flows carry magnetic elements from sunspots to the sun's poles, building up the polar magnetic fields until they eventually flip around the time of the solar maximum, Hathaway explained.

The sun emitted two X-grade solar flares on the morning of

Tuesday, July 12th 2013 at 7.42am and 8.52am - X being the most powerful kind of solar flare - and a third X-class flare early yesterday. Solar flares are largely harmless, as Earth's atmosphere absorbs most of the harmful particles they emit. However they can cause satellites to malfunction, and disrupt the layer of atmosphere some communications pass through, causing interruptions.

Could this be the same environmental catalyst that spawned the Anunnaki to leave Nibiru some 450,000 years ago, in search of an atmospheric radiation reflective material like gold? The Sumerian records indicate that the Anunnaki were here on Earth, specifically in South Africa mining gold as told to us by the Atrahasis account [2]. We share the same sun with all inhabitants of this solar system and thus they too must have wrestled with the same issues regarding radiation threatening terrestrial life forms, including the Anunnaki themselves.

Because the last major CME occurred in the year 1859, long before the planet was dependent on electronics for our day-to-day lives, little is known about what the real impact would be if a similar event occurred today. It is proffered that perhaps large electronics would be badly affected, causing long disruptions to power supplies, phone networks and the internet. Small electronics, such as mobile phones and computers, would likely be unaffected, but would be rendered almost useless with large networks knocked out [27]

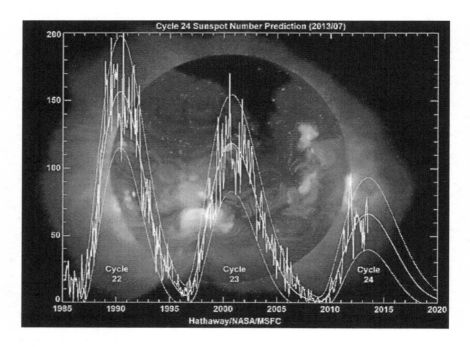

Figure 1: Solar Maxima 11-Year Repeating Cycle

As can be readily seen from Figure 1, the sun took a siesta in 2013 and appears to be headed towards an even lower maxima during cycle 25 due to occur in the year 2024. Thus, theories of a cooling cycle, a new ice age, should be atop the world's top weather change concerns as the diminishing energy solar cycle proceeds.

It is noteworthy that the founder of the Weather Channel, [28]

John Coleman, has become a staunch contrarian to the supposition that man is causing the global climate change.   For the thinking person, carbon dioxide is exhaled by humans and is supposedly the same concern for burning carbon based fuels.   The fact of the matter is that as the CO_2 level increases, plant life flourishes feeding off the excess levels. Newly forested terrain then becomes covering on the ground decreasing temperatures reflected and re-radiated into the atmosphere by the Earth.   Additionally, the radiated photons from the sun are absorbed by the plants during the photosynthesis process, transforming them into a useable chemical fuel when impacting chlorophyll containing leaves.   They crave $CO_2.$

So, if man is not responsible for global climate changes, who or what is?   And how are those changes, known by the governments around the world for many years, related to the statement *Ordo ab Chao* (*order out of chaos*)? What do the secret societies know about the coming changes to both the physical Earth and the political realities sought by a New World Order so often spoken of by purveyors of the deceived, the marionettes of influence,   and   the   secret   power   behind   the   presidential puppeteering seats of power, worldwide?

In this book, *"The Seventh Planet, Mercury Rising"*, the reader is taken on a journey whose perspective is conveyed from one of the original Anunnaki scientists mentioned in the Sumerian records, detailing the cosmogony and genetic origins of mankind. This progenitor was given the responsibility by the Niburian king, Anu, to be mankind's teacher. Could it be that the lessons imparted to the Anunnaki primitive workers, written on clay and emerald tablets by this benevolent being towards mankind, stayed here on planet Earth when many of the pioneering astronauts returned to Nibiru when given the chance?

His goal was to complete the mission he was assigned. His mission is our reality and the sooner we figure out the rules of the game, our destiny if you will, the quicker responsibility can be taken for our thoughts and actions coalescing our efforts toward making our fated forks in the road weave together toward our communal spiritual destiny. Each soul's pathway must traverse this material simulator with humble beginnings as a primitive worker barbarian, genetically designed to break out of the downtrodden enslavement, a Phoenix rising crescendo evolving toward the Utopian ideal state of co-existence and Galactic Brotherhood.

An iterative rollout of technology, civilizing capabilities, and knowledge conveyed to mankind essentially defines the developmental ages for cultural anthropology. Consider the Bronze Age, the Iron Age, the Industrial Revolution, and Information Ages which are in full exponential proliferation since the transistor was invented by ATT-Bell Labs on November 17, 1947.

Each of these ancient astronaut how-to capabilities were provided to primitive man at key points in history around the world. Was this the highly coveted knowledge the cuneiform documents termed the ME Tablets? These MEs were protected by Enki himself. This story of civilizing mankind is memorialized in many tales, including that of Prometheus stealing fire from the gods for mankind's benefit, for which he suffered negative consequences from higher ranking members of the Anunnaki Council. Azazel, the Watcher from the Lost Book of Enoch taught humans metallurgy and other forbidden knowledge, including alchemical secrets.

Highly civilized society features and functions were pervasive in the culture of old Sumer, including mathematics, law codes, astronomy, physical sciences and metallurgy. Society-changing dispensations to mankind caused significant paradigm shifts in history, leading to a more sophisticated culture. I give you the Space Age we live in now!

Pragmatic acts performed by the Anunnaki to civilize the primitive workers and their systems of government are captured in an early painting on the ceiling of the United States Capital Building rotunda. Why is Ningishzida-Hermes shown providing a bag of gold as funding for the American Revolutionary War in Figure 2? Are the ancient astronauts interacting with the founding fathers of the United States as part of an agenda they had for this country? The funds being handed to Robert Morris by Hermes as depicted, imply direct involvement by the Anunnaki in predicating the infrastructure for war and Enki shown establishing the Trans-Atlantic telecommunications infrastructure intended for his New Atlantis, Washington DC.

Could it be true that some of the Anunnaki were willing to facilitate benevolent changes in governing styles like those indicated by a revolutionary war against the British? Could their help with communications capabilities for the New Atlantis being established, have been memorialized by Masonic rituals, symbols, and writings as the evidence shows? Would it also stand to reason that the same powers or higher ranking council members that smote Prometheus for helping mankind are still active today? What if Prometheus was on the same world governing council as the Being who was angered by him helping mankind?

It was Enlil that headed the Anunnaki council of twelve in the Sumerian records, deemed the Lord of the Command. He was the chief deity housed in one of several temples in the Mesopotamian city of Ur and Nippur circa 2900 BCE. Holding the Anunnaki Council of Twelve rank of 50 out of 60 in a sexagesimal number system meant that Enlil was fully in charge on Earth. Anu, Enki and Enlil's father on Nibiru, held the highest rank on the Council, that of 60. Is it significant that Enki and his son Ningishzida-Thoth are both shown together helping establish America?

Enki and Ningishzida, US Capital

Ningishzida-Mercury, god of commerce, with his winged cap and sandals and caduceus, hands a bag of gold to Robert Morris, financier of the Revolutionary War.

Enki-Neptune, god of the sea, holding his trident and crowned with seaweed, rides in a shell chariot drawn by sea horses. Venus, goddess of love born from the sea, helps lay the transatlantic cable.

Figure 2: Poseidon and Hermes Start America?

Ningishzida-Mercury funds freedom for the new civilizing colonial experiment. His father, Enki-Poseidon, Lord of the Waters, is shown holding his Trident while directing naval forces to establish a trans-Atlantic cable line for future high tech communications. This painting atop the United States Capital building rotunda was commissioned during the presidential reign of George Washington.

Could these important historical events, painted hundreds of years ago on the United States Capital dome, be recording direct interactions between ancient astronauts substantively influencing American civilization, which have actually have taken place? What other interactions have the Anunnaki been concocting behind the wizard's curtain, shaping the world we live in? Are other countries and governments similarly influenced by the hidden hand of Anunnaki Gods?

During the last Zodiacal age of Pisces, perpetual wars and destruction have reigned supreme. Consider WWI, WW2, Korea, Vietnam, Iraq, Afghanistan, Syria, and others. Each country on Earth has a similar warring past. Even with the massive human death that ensued during this period, the populace reported by various census sources indicates there are approximately 7 billion folks occupying this spherical prison planet as of the year 2014.

Given the fact that the Anunnaki created mankind as a slave species, allocating workers to replace the Igigi miners in South Africa, a labor quota was most likely specified. Did the proliferation of mankind happen as planned by the Anunnaki, or, while the cat was not looking did the mouse population explode and now needs a haircut? Why would our creators allow massive population growth just to cull it destructively at some future point in time?

Or could it be that the overpopulation was intentional, causing a form of evolution of the species, competing for resources just like the creatures in nature must do daily to survive? Animals are exposed to natural selection forces, whereas humans have insulated themselves for the most part from the rigors involved in natural survival and selection, leading to massive population numbers.

One could think of the rat maze analogy posited earlier. Mankind's urban behavior is quite similar to a rat population that becomes overcrowded. Infighting over feeding terrain and resources leads to mortal combat. This is not unique to rats; many predatory species have the inbred genetic propensity to defend their territorial imperative by marking boundaries and defending it with their lives. Forcing the human populace to move from rural farms into urban mega cities has a devastating effect on the communal consciousness.

Simply consider the difference in how you feel when stuck in gridlock traffic, playing the slave species game of making a living in the fast lane, versus your relaxed state when you get out of town for a hiatus. There is no comparison for city life to the feeling of solitude in a vast expansive beauty of a painted desert or the tranquil remote beaches untouched by pollution and overcrowding. The biologic and energetic constructs designed into our DNA shares some of the same primitive inclinations demonstrated in nature.

Enki, the premier Niburian scientist, initially brought fifty subservient workers from Nibiru with him to set up Eridu. This home far away, Earth Station One if you will, is located where the Tigris and the Euphrates rivers empty into the Persian Gulf. Once the Anunnaki allowed mankind to "be fruitful and multiply" (Genesis 1:28) it seems that the primitive workers most certainly did proliferate over the planet.

The question arises, given the obvious means used by the ancient astronauts to control the population, how many of the primitive workers are actually needed as various assigned milestones are accomplished? Think GANNT chart here in terms of resource planning. More specifically, what happens when the Anunnaki get an ionizable transition metal like gold to spray in their atmosphere or make gold cities out of it for all we know. How many primitive workers were suddenly expendable given the completion of mining tasks in Africa? Were food supplies and the management required to accommodate the slaves a burden to maintain?

That brings us to the question that affects you and me, now knowing that we are in the same enslaved condition that our primitive gold mining progenitors found themselves in, as pointed out in the Atrahasis. During Atrahasis-Noah's time, after six hundred years of the slave primitive breeding program, mankind was assaulted by many of the same deadly culling series of manufactured extinction level events facing us all over the world, here and now, November 20th, 2014.

It is interesting to note 666 years ago, the Black Death swept over Europe and then the rest of the world killing 75-200 million folks. As of this writing, the Ebola pandemic is raging in West Africa (Ghana, Liberia, Sierra Leone and now Mali) and no quarantine measures are being implemented in the United States. Over 160 West Africans from the pandemic hot zone are being allowed to fly into major U.S. cities daily, relying on thermal screening and an honor system questionnaire to prevent the pandemic from spreading. This is a recipe for certain disaster when dealing with a bio-terrorism weapon of mass destruction, a bio-weapons defense level 4 (BDL4) hazard according to the CDC and the USAID Army researchers tasked with the implementation of New World Order destructive agendas. Are we once again living in the days of Noah? The Bibliography contains a link to a YouTube video I made to discuss this matter further. [29]

In my first book the ceremonial term limits allocated to the "Lord of the Earth" title, Anunnaki Rank 50 on the twelve person council, change hands every 2160 years, an equivalent house model for each Zodiacal sign. We are transiting from Pisces to Aquarius at this time. Accordingly, the Anunnaki incumbent Zodiacal leader(s) and staff are cleaning up their ruler ship remnants and culling their followers as the scepter of power changes hands. The massive culling of the population is underway in a more accelerated fashion in anticipation of meeting the alien mandates. These shady alien contracts were established in the early years of the American governing experiment, whose military mongrels agreed to trade anonymity and facilities to the ancient astronauts, still alive on Earth, for advanced killing machines in order to force the New World Order. Reports and evidence suggest that some Greek God venerating Anunnaki remnants are running the policy decision in America and have been in charge puppeteering us all since 1945. Is there any hope of intervention by benevolent forces (Enkiites) powerful enough to smite the dark forces in charge? There is real hope, disclosed in this book, a brilliant light at the end of our struggles, so take heart!

The primitive workers left in the dark through the ages in this prison planet operation are now waking up to their obvious enslavement due to many factors. In my first book, the concept of latent genetic programs in our DNA sensitive to frequency and energy were explored. External energy triggers, among other factors are responsible for influencing the mass consciousness. Information accessibility, electronic lingual translators, and in general the digital era are all evidence of a thinning veil. Additionally, what we consume and the environment we live in is also under scrutiny. The legalization of marijuana in the United States, forced by a grass roots movement among the populace, is an indication that the consciousness suppression veil is being lifted ever so gently with no end in sight. Consider that the brain wave altering THC contained in the plant's flower bud were sought out by the Igigi miners, the subservient workers of their day, to gain access to the telepathic communications of their Anunnaki taskmasters. Does the plant still have the same effect today? What is your experience?

Monsanto, the GMO-plant pushing world tyrant, is vying to control the global seed bank and a small number of companies are cornering the fresh water supply ownership rights worldwide. As the Atrahasis described, as in the days of Noah many engineered events are unfolding, such as plagues, pestilence, famine, disease, and war. In response, as the onslaught is recognized, movements arise to thwart the destructive forces aimed at their collective craniums.

Through it all, carnage and chaos, some of the ancient astronauts who were seminal and responsible for our creation have not lost sight of our plight. Yes, it may seem that we have been abandoned by our Creator(s) but is that really true? The Anunnaki referred to planet Earth using the Sumerian term *KI*. To them *KI* was the seventh planet counting from the outer planets, including Nibiru, toward the sun.

This book attempts to lift the veil on the controlling forces running this prison planet and take the reader on a simulator busting excursion, taking apart the electromagnetic constructs which comprise the holographic reality within which the primitive workers were designed to operate. Interestingly, those who designed the primitive workers also embedded hidden latent capabilities in the DNA code as a mechanism which could be activated in order to transcend the frequency and genetic dumbing down and ultimate enslavement of modern man. In other words, our creators provided us with a narrow gate to escape the entrapment of their slave design. You and I were not told about this feature nor is there a definitive manual issued among Americans describing any semblance of how to play the Earth graduate game and win.

It is like creating a maze for a rat and starting the stopwatch to see how long it takes it to find an escape route. To make the game more fun and interesting for the potentially demented observer, adding hidden trap doors, death chambers filled with noxious fumes or contaminated food, would reduce the likelihood of the unfortunate slave rat getting out alive. This hypothetical maze of life is precisely the circumstances many are waking up to. Malevolent beings are currently active on planet Earth, along with some benevolent ones like Enki and Ningishzida, all operating in secret to influence the world stage.

Taking the world's temperature relative to uprisings, both peaceful and violent, one is forced to ask what's going on here. Why the worldwide dissatisfaction with the simulator constructs? As the timing of the New World Order trestle board predicates change is due, the temperature rises among the primitive workers while those benevolent Niburians sensitive to our plight are taking notice.

Mercury is rising as a barometric response to the culling onslaught facing mankind at this time. The planet Mercury is aptly named due to the high content of the mystery liquid metal Hg contained therein. Another name for Mercury is *MUMU* as told to us in the Anunnaki creation account for our solar system. Ningishzida-Mercury is affiliated with the planet Mercury as he obviously chose the cultural name as well as the names other Anunnaki rulers took on such as Zeus and Poseidon, during stints on the Olympian ruling Roman Council of Gods. Zeus (Enlil) took on the name of the planet Jupiter for the Romans and Enki-Poseidon adopted the name of his planetary affiliation given in the Enuma

Elish, Neptune.

Mercury (Hg) is a very special element in that it can occupy various matter states to include a vapor form, as if existing in a liquid metal form was not strange enough already. Alchemy gives special credence to Hg and recognizes Thoth as the first alchemist, another name for Ningishzida as you may recall from the God Table proffered in my first book. Recall the fact that names which appeared in the Sumerian account for the Anunnaki members had also-known-as names (AKA) which spanned many cultures to include Sumer, Egypt, Greece, Rome, and many others. Modified Table 1 shown below, first published in *"The Anunnaki of Nibiru"* [3], showed the AKA name list for some of the most influential members of the Anunnaki council across multiple cultures. Ningishzida-Thoth-Hermes-Mercury had many AKA names, some of which are very controversial in religious communities. See Table 1 for the Anunnaki god table which provides the reader with a quick reference and correlation of these AKA names.

Rank	Nibiru	Sumer	Egypt	Greece	Rome
60	Anu	Anshar	Geb/Seb	Cronus	Saturn
55	Antu	Nintu	Nut/Neith	Rhea	Ops
50	Enlil	Ashur		Zeus	Jupiter
45	Ninlil	Nammu	Ma'at	Maia	Majesta
40	Ea	Enki	Ptah	Poseidon	Neptune
30	Gizida	Ningishzida	Thoth	Hermes	Mercury
15	Inanna	Ishtar	Hathor	Diana	Venus
05	Ninharsag	Ninmah	Isis	Aphrodite	Juno

Table 1: Anunnaki God Table

As we humans face the transition to a new state in the simulator, which is an alchemical transformation if you will, we can find hope in the knowledge that as the world grumbles and extinction level events abound, here on the Seventh Planet, Mercury is rising just in time to facilitate order out of chaos. Wade with me through the ashes of a destructive Zodiacal cycle ruled by Enlil-Zeus, the great destroyer. Investigate the narrow gate simulator constructs designed by our ancient astronaut creators, viewed through modern lenses, in which paradise awaits the holographic simulator Archetypal Hero. The primitive workers are being awakened energetically by genetically specified, somewhat dormant DNA code. These enslaved beings here on the Seventh planet are being made ready to join Mercury's rising influence as we witness the new Zodiacal house of Aquarius arrive. Will you join me on the journey through the narrow gate?

CHAPTER 2: In the Beginning

In my first book, *"The Anunnaki of Nibiru: Mankind's Forgotten Creators, Enslavers, Destroyers, Saviors and Hidden Architects of the New World Order"[3]*, evidence was presented from the Sumerian culture that a race of ancient astronauts came to Earth to obtain valuable natural resources like the precious metal gold. Due to life-threatening radiation exposure warnings, an augmentation to Nibiru's atmospheric shielding was needed.

The Anunnaki of Nibiru

Each time the Anunnaki home planet Nibiru, operating in a 3,600 year retrograde orbit with its aphelion residing beyond Pluto, comes to its closest point to the sun, resultant atmospheric damage can potentially occur. The most precious prizes sought out by the Anunnaki on Earth were gold and other metals like orichalcum, purported to be more precious than all metals. The name has Greek origins meaning literally "Copper Mountain". **Orichalcum** or **aurichalcum** is a metal mentioned in several ancient writings, including a story of Atlantis in the *Critias* dialogue, recorded by Plato. According to Critias, orichalcum was considered second only to gold in value, and was found and mined in many parts of Atlantis in ancient times. By the time of Critias, however, it was known only by name.

Given the proximity to the oil-rich Middle East which contained Sumer, petroleum and natural gas were also prized. Many of their temporary building and infrastructure projects required a variety of supplemental resources from the planet. Large trees culled from the Cedar Forest in Lebanon, and decorative stones were quarried in distant lands destined for a foundation, wall, or statue in the Ziggurat temples that lined the two great rivers in Mesopotamia, the Tigris and the Euphrates. King Gilgamesh hailing from Uruk, mentioned in his famous epic that he visited Lebanon to gather Cedar wood and other materials for his beloved city.

Sumerian Cosmogony and Mercury

The story of a primary celestial battle begins when Enki learns of a plot by the Sun and Mercury to destroy Tiamat. In other words, the orbital paths monitored by the Anunnaki indicate that if something was not done with the orbital paths of the inner planets, a future collision event was inevitable. The collision with Tiamat with some unspecified planetary object, (most likely an Anunnaki claimed resource on a moon, meteor, or outer planet) would cause destruction of both.

The Sumerian Seven Tablets of Creation, also referenced as the *Enuma Elish* [2, Pg. 233] clay tablets on display at the University of Pennsylvania Museum, is told as an allegory of celestial battle involving warriors (Anunnaki affiliated names with planets) whose skirmishes and exploits lead to the planets and their hosts circuits around the sun. The Old Babylonian Version (OBV) of the clay tablets which record the Cuneiform inscribed tale were dated to approximately 1936-1901 BCE. According to the Sumerian records, Marduk, first born son of Enki, was the national deity of Babylon, and at the height of his reign at approximately 2000 BCE. This piece of historical chronology linking Babylon's chief deity Marduk to the creation tablets adds validity to the Sumerian records which Zecharia Sitchen also cites as the same account. Marduk required that the seven tablets of creation be read every Spring during a ceremony in his honor.

It is highly probable that a much older version of the creation tale is in existence, in which Nibiru was named as the home planet. The name Nibiru, which was replaced by the name Marduk in the OBV. The names of the planets and their orbital distance from the sun are accurately depicted, with a few exceptions. What is amazing about the Babylonian creation account is the advanced knowledge of our solar system that has only recently been verified by modern science. Is it possible that current scientific knowledge is only now maturing to the point that we can validate the Babylonian Epic of Creation?

The account specifies ten versus nine planets and includes the sun and moon among the hosts. Table 3 below depicts the solar system planets and the Niburian names assigned to them. Note also that the Anunnaki elite each have planets associated with their namesake according to the Sumerian records.

Rank	Celestial Body	Epic of Creation Name
11	Sun	Apsu
10	Moon	Qingu
9	Mercury	Mummu
8	Venus	Lahamu
7	Earth	Ki
6	Mars	Lahmu
5	Jupiter	Kishar

4	Saturn	Anshar
3	Neptune	Nudimud
2	Uranus	Anu
1	Pluto	Gaga
12	Nibiru	Marduk

Table 2: Babylonian Epic of Creation Planets

Below is a summarized accounting of the Epic of Creation. The story begins with the Sun and Mercury conspiring to destroy Tiamat. *Enki learns of the plot and shields Mercury by quelling the Sun's radiation*. Enki then puts Mercury to "sleep" [2, Pg. 235] as well as the sun. Mercury, the counselor was in a sleepless daze. Ea (yet another name for Enki) unfastened his belt, removed his crown, then took away Mercury's mantel of radiance and put it on himself. *Note that Enki's planet is Neptune and this account could be inferring that Mercury's orbit was temporarily changed while dealing with the solar radiation issue from the Sun.* Nibiru rested on top of the sun for 900 years (captured in the sun's orbit?) [2, Pg. 233]. The sun's solar radiation disturbs Tiamat, Ea and his wife Damkina have offspring, naming their firstborn son Marduk. Herein, Marduk takes liberty with the account as the progeny of the high ranking members of the Anunnaki Council, establishing his birthright spawned in the heavens. Marduk took over the Council Rank of 50 from Enlil, while at the height of his rule in Babylon, circa 2000 BCE.

The signs of the Zodiac in the Heavens are described to include Taurus, Pisces, and Capricorn. *Qingu (currently the Earth's moon) was aligned with Tiamat, which held the Tablet of Destinies*. Neptune attempts to quell Tiamat's fury, stirred by the Sun, turning back and reporting to Anshar (Saturn). This forces Tiamat to stray from its orbital path. Ea recommends disbanding Tiamat's forces and volunteers Marduk (Nibiru) to help. *Nibiru is drawn into Saturn's orbit, providing a calming effect. A satellite or moon of Saturn is sent to both Mercury and Venus as a probe, whereby Mercury and Venus are alluded to as ancestors of Saturn.*

A Radiation weapon termed inhullu-wind is alluded to as an evil wind, the tempest, the whirlwind that releases seven winds against Tiamat, then advances behind in Tiamat's path. A flood weapon is used against Tiamat, as an asteroid (arrow) which hits Tiamat splitting it open. Subsequently, Qingu (Earth's moon) is destroyed. A constellation of planets, stars, and remnants of Tiamat are captured in Nibiru's orbit. The lower part of Tiamat is trampled, sending one half of its mass to the roof of the sky, drawing a bolt across it and a guard to hold it (Enki reference here). Then the waters were arranged so they coagulated as an ocean.

Nibiru's course was then corrected, and the location affixed to the stand of Enlil (planetary affiliation is Jupiter, Zodiac symbol of Taurus) and the stand of Enki (Zodiac affiliation Pisces, planetary affiliation is Neptune). The Earth's moon was previously a moon of Tiamat, Qingu in the account.

The reader is encouraged to read all of the "Seven Tablets of Creation" AKA the Enuma Elish, in full to get a sense of the detailed creation epic [2, 233]. Having the decoded epic provided herein using the table of names and planets in English and the Niburian names, side by side, really aids understanding of this complex story. I will now put the account into a more coherent story, versus the blow by blow interpretation previously as it is very detailed and complex. Here is my go at telling the Anunnaki creation account specifying how our solar system came into being.

From this allegorical account at the point of creation in our solar system, Tiamat, a planet the size of Uranus, had an established orbit between Mars and Jupiter and held the all-important Tablets of Destiny which Enki controls all throughout the Sumerian written accounts. Earth had not come into existence at that time. Nibiru was captured into our solar system's orbit by Neptune and Uranus' gravitational pull. Nibiru, an intruder planet from another Galaxy (adjacent?) got trapped in our Milky Way Galaxy, with various hypotheses about the planet's origins.

Nibiru's retrograde orbit and sharply different solar ecliptic crossing angle distinguishes it from the other nine planets, all essentially aligned in the same orbital plane around the sun. Thus, just by examining our nine planets compared to Nibiru makes one question whence it came? It is like driving your car down the highway in the wrong lane with oncoming traffic. This going against the traffic flow creates a significantly higher probability of planetary impact collisions.

Nibiru's orbital deviation event initiated the celestial battle for planetary position if you will, making Nibiru the focal point of the Anunnaki story, not Earth like our own cosmogony story tells.

When Nibiru entered its orbital path around the sun (aphelion), as it passed the outer planets, a gravitational force tilted Uranus on its side. *This dislodged Pluto from its orbit around Saturn which promoted it to planet status, only to be recently demoted recently by our current scientific community.*

One of Nibiru's satellites strikes Tiamat enroute to solar Perihelion and on its next orbital path Nibiru hits Tiamat directly. A large part of Tiamat broke off and became the Earth, with the leftover debris becoming the asteroid belt, currently located between Mars and Jupiter. The Earth congealed into a solid planet in its current orbit capturing a moon of Nibiru as its own. Some modern scientific analysis of the earth's deep rifts in the Pacific as well as its unusually large size moon have been corroborated with the Sumerian creation account, again which was read every Spring in Babylon. An impact from Nibiru could also have transferred the seeds of life to Earth, a form of accidental Panspermia versus the intentional one proposed by Dr. Jonas Salk of San Diego, suggesting that intelligent beings intentionally seeded planet Earth with alien life forms.

The *most important* part of the Epic of Creation specifies this one additional planet in our solar system, the Anunnaki's home planet of Nibiru, whose aphelion is positioned beyond Pluto in a 3,600 year retrograde orbit around the sun.   Corroborating evidence was provided by the former chief of the U.S. Naval Observatory, Dr. Robert S. Harrington. A gent named Tombaugh discovered Pluto in 1930 and its moon Charon was found in 1978. Planetary wobbles in the orbital paths of Uranus and Neptune spawned the use of an infra-red astronomical satellite, IRAS in 1983 to locate the suspected planet that induced the wobbles. *The IRAS produced results indicating a large brown dwarf, four times the size of the Earth, had been located, without question, which we now know as Nibiru.*

A newspaper article was published in 1992 by Harrington and Van Flandern of the Naval Observatory, working with all the information they had at hand, publishing their findings and opinion that a tenth planet had been located in our solar system, even calling it an intruder planet. [34] Zecharia Sitchin and Dr. Harrington, who was familiar with all Sitchin's writings concerning a tenth planet, met to correlate the IRAS findings with the account from the Babylonian Epic of Creation, the Enuma Elish. Given the evidence reported by the IRAS, other space probes like Pioneer 10 and 11, Voyager, and the corroborating orbital path, planet size, and retrograde characteristics of the tenth planet, Harrington agreed with Sitchin that it was Nibiru [34].

The passage of a planet as large as Nibiru between Mars and Jupiter would certainly have a noticeable impact every 3,600 years. *It is highly probably that Nibiru's passage may be responsible for pole shifts and reversals, changes in the Earth's precession about its axis, and potentially dangerous meteors and space debris dragged along from the asteroid belt inbound to Perihelion.*

As mentioned in my previous book and on many radio shows, an attempt has been made to ignore the various names of the main characters composing the Anunnaki Council of Twelve, like Enki and Ningishzida, and Ninmah-Isis. In the Atrahasis account, the Igigi miners were riled up by Alla(h), who told them to burn their tools and to revolt. They surrounded Enlil's command headquarters near the gold mining operation, South Africa. Enlil demonstrates his severe nature by offering to kill one of the workers to get them back to work. Anu (his father) and Enki (his brother) object, taking the side of the overworked miners. The point that I wish to point out is that by simply testing and analyzing the extremely brutal personality that Enlil exhibits, this is not an isolated case. Recall that after 600 years of the primitive worker program, he called a council meeting to push his genocidal agenda. Disease and famine were ordered along with a global flood as a finishing touch. A similar spirit ruled when Uruk and Ur were occupied by the Enlilites who were given the region by Anu.

Enki Seeks Gold

It should be no surprise that Enki, Anu's first born scientific son on Nibiru, was sent to spearhead the pioneering planetary exploration mission to Earth. His name appears along with many other major Anunnaki players in their cosmogony. The Enuma Elish, is among many other recovered documents recorded in the alien wedge-shaped cuneiform language utilized all over the region. Enki's mission began approximately 360-450,000 years ago when Anu directed him to go to the Earth and help the Niburian inhabitants stave off another solar perihelion atmospheric assault.

Enki's mission objective was to acquire enough of the

radiation-shielding non-corroding metal gold, with symbol of *Au*. Gold has an atomic number of 79, a standard atomic weight of 199.966569, and is categorized as [Xe]$4f^{14}5d^{10}6s$ with ionization energy of 9.2256 electron volts. See the Periodic Table Atomic Properties of the Elements shown in Table 2 below to get the details on other interesting precious resources sought by mining companies the world over.

Element 51, called Antimony or Stibium by some Alchemists, should be of interest to those seeking to understand the composition for the famed Philosopher Stone. Correct proportioning and processing of a mixture of Stibium *(Sb)* and Gold *(Au) smelted together at the right temperature* produces the desired stone. The longevity-boosting, neural pathway super conductor produces DMT from dormant pineal glands described as the *spirit molecule* by Dr. Rick Strassman [35]. This is the famed Star Fire gold discussed many times by me for my book and listening fans, whose consistency and appearance resembles a white talcum powder and has a milky white appearance when stored as a colloidal solution. See http://www.artisticvegan.com/starfire-gold-liquid/ for the product variations that my alchemist wife Christa offers on her website www.artisticvegan.com and available on Amazon.com.

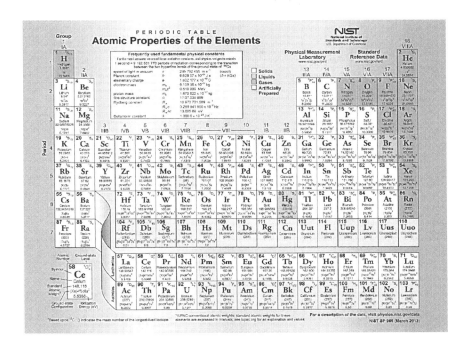

Table 3: Periodic Table of the Elements

See www.nist.gov for more details on the table of elements.

Before one sets up a command structure to locate and mine a resource like a precious metal, the claim must first be prospected to verify how much of the arduously-obtained prize is present in the buried ore. Thus, the Lord of the Command and Enki's half-brother Enlil was not to become involved in the prospecting portion of the operation. The planned utilization was to be an atmospheric shield against excess solar radiation. Enlil, as we saw in the Atrahasis account, had a fortress close enough to the gold mines such that the Igigi were able to surround his house, however, we are not told the distance from the mines to the oppressor Enlil's fort.

Tools versus Slaves

The Anunnaki pondered whether it was more beneficial for their planetary mining mission to use biological workers or machines. A short dialog between Enki and Enlil surfaces in which Enlil specifies his preference for tools versus slaves. We are not told what the pros and cons were for choosing one or the other difficult mining tasks. It seems evident that if they had brought large scale mining tools then the Council would not have to debate the issue. Thus, it was an easy choice to replace one slave force for another, potentially re-allocating the functional responsibilities assigned to the newly freed Igigi miners. In order to help clarify the meat versus machine decision, consider the same issue as it applies to exploring the planet Mars. Should a manned craft be sent for measurements, or would it be more prudent and effective to send a rover to explore the Martian surface? Consider the current Mars rover mission. Pros for using mining machinery tools include the ability to operate in extreme environments. Some of the negative features include machine malfunctions and loss of communications. Put yourself on the surface of the planet. Having a human, not only in the loop, but on the surface of the planet, would be far more effective as an exploration option versus remote telemetry. Consider the obstacles encountered when commanding an unmanned Martian rover remotely, potentially blinded by debris obscuring a rover camera lens, or perhaps experiencing an energy loss due to a charge capacitor electrical shortage which subsequently drains the solar energy reserve power from the onboard battery. From my graduate research involving Evolvable Hardware, I discovered that we humans, as meat-based entities exhibit adaptive control using endemic survival capabilities which are shown to be highly effective. Maintenance and sustainability for machines is problematic. Meat reproduces and is easily replaced. Machines are far more sensitive to failure than meat is. It looks like the Anunnaki used both, but were more capable of producing meat slaves under the remote outpost circumstances on Earth. If one needed to mass produce an item, a factory or assembly line would be required. The Anunnaki appear to have come unprepared for the labor intensive change in plans which required them to mine gold from ore in Africa versus obtaining it as originally planned from the waters of the Persian Gulf.

Evolution is slow and therefore adaptive algorithms planned for use on remote rovers still need a human in the loop to be effective. Imagine trying to codify the ruleset needed to keep the rover on mission schedule and avoid environmental calamities, like a broken solar panel or failed mechanical probe due to temperature fluctuations or high winds. Genetic algorithms are sometimes used to address adaptive problems like teaching an unmanned autonomous vehicle survival skills. These algorithms model evolution, and sometimes in machinery, do not collapse quickly or at all, relegating them useless in complex environments that mandate updating decisions in real time. Use of the life fit function rewards or punishes an offspring based on some required performance parameter, **in real-time**. The iterative nature of the genetic algorithm may take too long to come up with a solution fast enough to deal with an unanticipated minimal warning collision avoidance hazard like an alien version of a territorial gargantuan reptile or an attack without notice from an airborne raptor. These technical difficulties were most likely discussed among the lead Anunnaki Council members, including Anu. The conclusion was that meat wins against machines in an environment where each can operate. Thus, Enki and his half-sister Ninharsag got the green light to find or create a biological primitive worker replacement for the mutinying Igigi miners.

The Anunnaki already had demonstrated their propensity to use the Igigi slave labor in the same manner, and given the fact that the Igigi had been working in the mines for many Niburian years, they had plenty of time to replace slaves with tools, had that been their preference. Instead, they preferred biological agents to do their bidding, most certainly augmented with the tools they could muster or were allowed to disclose.

Consider using primitive workers on site versus remotely operating an agent (biological or machine) remaining in the control loop. The being in the control loop is the weak link, whereas true autonomy specifies operating without biological agents involved. If during mining operations, a worker for whatever reason was absent, the possibility existed that the machine would not be operable autonomously and would need an operator controlling the mining tools as is done still today. The final obvious reason to use biological workers is that they are very successful at self-replicating and expendable. Here we are still doing the same meat MODEM work to eak out a living while our slave overlords live in palaces and abuse the workers who make their lives a breeze comparatively.

African Genetics and Procreation

Given the detailed Sumerian genetic account previously specified in my research, I wanted to focus on Ningishzida's role in Africa as it relates to the primitive workers. Let's discuss the role that Ningishzida played in Africa, augmenting the primitive workers' DNA so they could procreate. He discusses finding the genetic issue and comes up with a plan to "splice" the reproductive second chromosome which is clearly evident in modern man.

It all started in Africa, for mankind that is, and we now that we know it was Enki, the scientist's domain. The First Dynasty god table provided to us by the Egyptian historian Manetho supports that Ptah-Enki and Thoth-Ningishzida together ruled the land of Khem for 9,000 and 3,000 years respectively. One should be stunned, much as I was at seeing the first Sumerian Kings ruler ship term of 28,800 years or 8 shars, (3,600 Earth years) that Ningishzida and Enki could still be around since the creation of man approximately 220,000 years ago up until 10,500 BCE. This was the Age of Leo, the time when Thoth built the Great Sphinx and the Giza Pyramids.

According to studies tracing the mitochondrial DNA and Y-chromosome back to our genetic Adam and Eve, humans showed up in the Homo Sapiens Sapiens bodies circa 220,000 years ago. It is simply astounding that a being that was in South Africa was meddling with primitive worker reproductive chromosomes. Ningishzida carried his Caduceus all the way forward in time to the beginning of the Egyptian dynasties along with his father Ptah-Enki. Lifespans that appear immortal to us and are hard to fathom.

Telomeres and Aging

The discovery of aging tied to decaying DNA caps at the end of the double helix strand have been shown by scientists to be the cause of aging. Below is a press release naming the scientists who received the award for finding the link between Telomeres and the chemical Telomerase.

Press Release   2009-10-05

The Nobel Assembly at Karolinska Institute
has today decided to award

**The Nobel Prize in Physiology or Medicine
2009**

jointly to

**Elizabeth H. Blackburn, Carol W. Greider and
Jack W. Szostak**

for the discovery of

**"how chromosomes are protected
by telomeres and the enzyme telomerase"**

Chimeras, Abominations, and the Adapa

So, if mankind is a genetic mixture of a Niburian Astronaut and
that of a bipedal hominid ovum from the likes of Cro-Magnon or

Neanderthal, we as their human offspring are by definition chimeras. Chimera is a term used in Greece which conjures up images of a half bull half, man minotaur hunting for humans in an underground rat maze.

According to the creation account given to us in the Atrahasis records, there were several mishaps and iterations necessary in order to obtain the primitive worker template designated for manual labor, Adamu.

Genetic Upgrade by Ningishzida

We all know the Biblical story of creating Eve from Adam's rib so that he would have a mate. How did the Anunnaki discover that their proud creation could not procreate? Was it a known problem like breeding a horse with a donkey to produce a mule, whose offspring is impotent? Is this what happened leading to the genetic upgrade evidenced in the splicing of our second chromosome? We recall the genetic upgrade account in which Ningishzida is summoned to analyze the first Adapa's chromosomes to assess why the being was not able to procreate. He locates the genetic problem, upgrading the Adapa DNA so that procreation was possible, the second act of creation involving genetic knowledge. Where did Ningishzida get the serpent code? The Hebrew word for serpent in Genesis is *Nahash*. Two other possible meanings for the word include *He who knows or solves secrets* and *He of the copper*, derived from a seldom used name for Enki, BUZUR. This AKA name for Enki meant both *He who solves secrets* and *He of the metal mines* [36, Pg. 14]. We know that the snake in the Garden of Eden account was the geneticist Enki, having Ningishzida-Thoth as his son to whom all Enki's knowledge was imparted. Enki has also been shown with figures of entwined serpents from which the healing arts absconded symbol of the Caduceus originates. The tree of life depictions found in Enki's city of Eridu clearly identify the entwined snakes with the life giving genetic code for a Creator-God knowing the DNA makeup of his primitive work force.

Enki taught Ningishzida the genetic engineering discipline and passed on to him the alchemical symbol represented by the Caduceus. This symbol is commonly seen in strip malls adorning the commercial chiropractor's shop window symbolically misguiding the populace using it in affiliation with the American Medical Association (AMA) and their approved insurance dispatchers, all agents of the fallen state of man. True knowledge of what the symbol means has for the most part been lost, just as the knowledge about our true creators has been smeared, demonized, occluded, and assaulted on many battlefronts. Namesake substitution, falsifying historical records, and affiliating a symbol of Light with a Roman death sentence ritual is a quintessential example of how an an enemy can be smeared or erased from history. Perhaps this cycle of creation and destruction, even of the innocent, is permitted by the Creator of All to push us all to the Faustian cliff early in our paths, discovering that all matter is of the same source and is transient.

Could the mixing of two disparate species like the Anunnaki and a primitive bi-pedal hominid have produced impotent offspring? We know this to be the result when breeding a male donkey (Jack) and a female horse producing an impotent mule? Similarly, mixing the Neanderthal female ovum with Enki's reproductive genetic material may have initially resulted in primitive workers that could not procreate! So much for replacing the rebellious Igigi miners who could only be placated so long before more violence erupts due to prolonged design iterations prolonging the back-breaking manual labor of mining gold ore in Southern Africa.

This is where the genetic genius of Enki's son Ningishzida is on display, beaming brilliance from behind closed doors of his on-loan African laboratory referred to as the House of Shimti. Ningishzida is portrayed by Sitchin as a brilliant technical researcher and geneticist who performed the problematic DNA analysis to determine what the actual problem was with Enki's chimera non-reproduction status. The higher ranking Anunnaki Council members got all the credit once the issue was identified and remedied by Ningishzida-Thoth. This lack of recognition for one's own good deeds is now the normal state of affairs, as you nod your head in agreement at the fallen state of the simulator. If this has not happened to you, it should sound familiar based on the self-promoting antics running rampant in academia and business these days. How many times have you performed an important task to subsequently have a sycophantic self-promoter take credit for your deeds? It is familiarly disgusting behavior run amok in the congested metropolitan rat maze.

Metropolitan Rat Maze

For those who have never lived in a big city like Los Angeles or San Diego, it is common practice for primitive workers to act like overcrowded rats, biting each other's limbs and pushing aggressively through crowds, operating on what appears to be pure animal instinct. When resource gathering opportunities arise or it is time for the next meal, the savages leave the security of their guarded cave dwellings, destined to hunt down and kill the resource they desire, hauling home the 65 inch LED-LCD flat screen monitor, protected from arrows, spears, and knives in its enshrouded and RFID tagged secure cardboard container filled with impact resistant Styrofoam.

After all, Thanksgiving occurs in the fall football season. It has become a tradition for Americans to spend their Thanksgiving holiday engrossed in mindless hours watching national football league (NFL) games on their big screen TV. That means you had to participate in Black Friday the past year to have your game viewing device in place for the next season. Consider the infamous chaos that occurs on Black Friday, promoted by the history-subverting United States government during its sponsored holiday, egregiously labeled Thanksgiving. This holiday has become an open consumer-catalyzing endorsement of gluttonous over-consumption. Rats caught in the desire for more stuff participate in the annual shopping fiasco endorsed by the likes of the retail giant Walmart. Shoving, pushing, grabbing, stealing, and all manner of bad rat maze behavior is on dishonorable display on this special day. Some go just to see the carnage like a sporting event.

Was the genetic upgrade provided by Ningishzida, enabling the Adapa to procreate, the source of this bad behavior? Or could it be that the original god chosen to slaughter on mankind's behalf is the source of our striving against our brothers? Is this a nature or nurture problem? Is the violation of our territorial need for space, shared by most critters in the animal kingdom including rats, the catalyst for our insecure encroached-upon aggressive defensive behavior? Or does the problem reside in our primitive worker genetics, sporting a dumbed-down subset of Enki's DNA such that we were destined for perpetual enslavement by the Great Anunna?

What if it were the case that Ningishzida secretly added

programming hidden *"back door"* algorithms to the primitive worker DNA that allowed for future upgrades as necessary. Even more amazing would be discovering that latent time or energetically triggered events turned on the hidden feature?

Mayan Calendar and DNA

Consider the amazing knowledge that was brought to bear crafting the Mayan Calendar, with its count down date commemorating our solar system passage through the Milky Way Galaxy center at least once every 25,920 years. This fantastic processional wheel event recently occurred during the Winter Solstice 2012. Was this an energetic event timed by Thoth-Ningishzida-Quetzalcoatl, who, as a scientist, was keenly aware of the energetic design the primitive workers were endowed with his father Enki's genetic code? Thoth knew this code had the light-born link that enabled mankind to eventually become one of the Anunnaki, sons of God if you will. This is advanced energy-matter understanding held by the Mayan priests, allowing them to achieve an elevated consciousness triggered by external frequencies and energy experienced during the dark rift transit. What if the latent DNA activation event, known a priori by the geneticist Ningishzida, was factored into the timing of the unveiling of this hidden feature set?

Alternatively stated, could the desired DNA function be

activated in the primitive worker populace temporally coinciding with a recognizably significant heavenly event like the cyclical Great Year? This seems obvious in retrospect, imparting the most significant knowledge to a populace when it is most awake to receive it. That time occurs in the sign of Ophiuchus, the hidden thirteenth sign of the Zodiac. The fact that the sign of Ophiuchus depicts a man holding a serpent is telling; an Enkiite for sure.

Greek legends state that the Zodiacal man is Asclepius, a healer who was killed by Zeus-Enlil for disclosing healing remedies to others, possibly one or more primitive workers. Perhaps the real issue was breaking the holographic simulation rules not to interfere in the affairs of man, unless a committee approves of a sponsor to intervene on behalf of the Hero under development as depicted with the protagonist Katniss Everdeen, starring in the movie "The Hunger Games."

Holidays in ancient times were chosen based on celestial events whose significance was recorded by historians and celebrated by the masses. Planetary orbits provide the long-term cyclical stopwatch used by the Anunnaki for this Calendrical designated special event. My premise here is that the connection between the processional Great Year and the activation of latent DNA seem to be occurring suspiciously at the same time. Recall that in the Mayan 5th sun, mankind is slated to achieve *Universal*

Consciousness according to the Tzolkin calendar, which in my humble opinion is a mental state taught by Thoth in the Egyptian Mystery Schools that shared the same goal for its graduates. The teachings derived from the twin pillars of Poseidon's Atlantean temple made their way to the land of Khem. We find out later that Ningishzida took the information from his father's law codes, ornately inscribed on the orichalcum red pillars outside of Poseidon's temple, eventually writing the inherited sacred wisdom on his own impervious thirteen *Emerald Tablets of Thoth the Atlantean.* Chapter 5 fully details Thoth's role in Egypt, where he also was depicted carrying the alchemical symbol of the Caduceus as he did in Sumer as well as in Greece and Rome.

Now that we know that Thoth was intimately involved in mankind's fashioning and upgrade process, one must consider the idea that perhaps Ningishzida also wanted to share in his father Enki's notorious genetic primitive worker creation event by being involved. Anything to get help for the Igigi who were demanding relief while working day and night shifts on their gold mining enslavement jobs.

Could it be that Thoth-Ningishzida utilized part of his own genetic material when he participated in the procreation-enabling upgrade process? This idea occurred to me as I was studying the Emerald Tablets, pondering the method or capabilities a being would have to possess in order to manifest in various forms and make such profound claims about the electromagnetic spectrum, as witnessed in the writings.

In the Tablets, Thoth indicates that when he descends to the Halls of Amenti, his soul is able to roam the Earth co-occupying the mankind's container suit which he was intricately involved with designing. *How could Thoth use the electromagnetic spectrum to simultaneously have his soul visit multiple containers located anywhere on planet Earth?* Alchemists throughout history have insinuated this very possibility stating "May Thoth be with you daily" [1].

Futants Anyone?

For those who are not familiar with the future mutant acronym (Futant), Timothy Leary coined the term in the 1960s to denote a human that had enhanced DNA, programmed to function differently than most, formulated to be an example of how the Anunnaki benevolent game masters desire mankind to play in the game of life. We are faced with a choice in our paths, often generically categorized as love or fear. A fearful being accumulates material items to enhance their sense of security, often at the expense of community isolation. Alternatively, the Hero or Heroine who chooses to risk their own security by sharing the acquired knowledge gleaned from their personal truth quest is on the right road to travel. This is the path for Futants, living in a minimalistic way in concert with the teachings of Ningishzida-Jesus in the New Testament.

Was this the method in which Thoth created a back door access to the primitive worker design? Is his ability to access the primitive workers using his soul energy, untethered from his body, to roam freely among his budding alchemy student populace, choosing a being to have intermittent close contact with? Is this the manner in which he directly provides power (read carefully the salvation doctrine Protestant verse John 1:12) subsequently inspiring his followers to achieve their archetypal destiny by finding a way out of the enslaved consciousness simulator imposed in the construction of our perceived holographic reality? Does it appear to be the case that ascension knowledge has been hidden from planet Earth's inhabitants caught in an illusion, having an enslaved primitive human experience, as part of their evolutionary path to higher consciousness?   Narrow are the gates to higher consciousness as ascended masters. Broad is the gate to energetic transformation and the concept of reincarnation and the Karmic wheel, back to the dark void (black hole) to be recycled makes sense to me now in the big scheme of things.

A fascinating opportunity exists for beings operating out of love and not fear. By overcoming the fear of one's own death (security), we are freed to empower those in our communities and achieve our communal destinies, meeting up once more at the SOURCE of ALL CREATION. Given the communications infrastructure in existence today, news broadcasts may be tuned in by a variety of receivers. It could be a radio, television, or an Android mobile smart phone, each perusing alternative information venues seeking to know the actual versus propagandized state of the simulator. Information is power and there is no question that we are ensconced in the Information Age.

The Futant path is a simplified one, living in a minimalistic way in concert with the teachings of Ningishzida-Thoth in the New Testament and the Emerald Tablets, both of which the teacher tells his children that he holds the keys to the kingdom of heaven. For those that are not familiar with the future mutant acronym (Futant), Timothy Leary coined the term in the 1960s to denote a human that had enhanced DNA, programmed to function differently than most, formulated to be an example of how the Anunnaki benevolent game masters desire mankind to play the game of life. According to Leary, 1.5 to 2% of the human population is of the Futant class. Here is a link on YouTube featuring Dr. Leary explaining the term [41]. The discussion about Leary begins at time marker 2 minutes and 45 seconds into the aggregated video. The whole upload is great viewing and educational.

A very important theory connecting energy and matter is proposed by Dr. Leary. His premise is that there are latent DNA sequences or circuits which are designed into our genes to elevate our consciousness. These stages coincide with the Hindu Chakra system and are imprinted at various developmental stages in our lives. I wonder which genetic engineer dreamt up that primitive worker feature. We can narrow it down to an Enkiite, either Enki himself or Ningishzida-Thoth who did the genetic upgrade so the primitive workers could procreate and meet the African gold mining labor requirements.

In the Leary-Wilson model, the first circuit is termed **Biosurvival Circuit** and is imprinted by the mother or mothering object and is subsequently conditioned by either nourishment or threat. The second latent DNA coding is the **Emotional Territorial Circuit.** This circuit is imprinted when the infant stands up, walks around, and begins to struggle for power in the family structure or hierarchy. The third circuit is the **Time Binding Semantic Circuit.** It is imprinted by human symbol systems and artifacts. This is what controls the local paradigm. The fourth circuit is the **Socio-Sexual Circuit.** It is imprinted by the first orgasm mating experience and also by tribal taboos. It processes sexual pleasure, definitions of right or wrong behavior, reproduction, parental rules, and the raising of young. The fifth circuit is the **Neuro-Semantic Circuit**. It is imprinted by ecstatic or spiritual experiences. The sixth circuit is the **Collective Neuro-Genetic Circuit** which contains our entire evolutionary script covering the past, present, and future. This circuit state was referred to by the philosopher Carl Jung as the collective unconsciousness. It is also affiliated with the distinct archetypes. The seventh circuit is the **Meta-Programming Circuit**. This is the realm of conscious reprogramming and re-imprinting of the other circuits. This is the level where personal development programs have their positive effects. Here, the individual consciously chooses to re-imprint the unconscious mind through the application of symbols and internal imagery. The final circuit described by the Leary-Wilson model is the **Non-Local Quantum Circuit**. Operations here occur trans personally, beyond the ego. This is the realm of out of body and near death experiences. DNA is therefore a universal intentional design, a computer programming language if you will.

Enki's Home in the Far Away: Eridu

According to the chronology of events which brought the Anunnaki to Earth, Enki first established Eridu circa 450,000 years ago. It appears to have many layers which indicates occupation of the city occurred in stages at different times. It is commonly found that later generations rebuild on the same foundations established by their ancestors. Eridu is named as the first city in which the concept of kingship was brought to Earth.

First King of Eridu

As was described in previous discussions, the first kingship was instituted in Eridu, having been lowered from Heaven-Nibiru, with Alulim ruling for 8 sars (shars) lasting or 28,800 years. See Figure 3 below. This unbelievable duration, in my first exposure, seemed as if it had to be a printing error. How could this be? This is not how long King Alulim lived, it is his length of rule! We do not know how long the being lived, perhaps he is still around somewhere watching the whole world simulator unfolding.

The Sumerian Kings list

Ruler	Epithet	Length of reign	Approx. dates	Comments
"After the kingship descended from heaven, the kingship was in Eridug. In Eridug, Alulim became king; he ruled for 28800 years."				
Alulim		8 sars (28,800 years)	Between 35th and 30th century BC	
Alaingar		10 sars (36,000 years)		
"Then Eridug fell and the kingship was taken to Bad-tibira."				
En-men-lu-ana		12 sars (43,200 years)		
En-men-gal-ana		8 sars (28,800 years)		
Dumuzid, the Shepherd	"the shepherd"	10 sars (36,000 years)		
"Then Bad-tibira fell and the kingship was taken to Larag."				
En-sipad-zid-ana		8 sars (28,800 years)		
"Then Larag fell and the kingship was taken to Zimbir."				
En-men-dur-ana		5 sars and 5 ners (21,000 years)		
"Then Zimbir fell and the kingship was taken to Shuruppag."				
Ubara-Tutu		5 sars and 1 ner (18,600 years)		
"Then the flood swept over."				

Figure 3: First Sumerian King

Given Alulim was the first king to rule on Earth, the following special introductory statement as to how the authority from heaven was given to set up the kingship figurehead on the seventh planet, Ki, came about.

Sumerian Kings List

"After the kingship descended from heaven, the kingship was in Eridug. In Eridug, Alulim became king: he ruled for 28,800 years".

This is a shockingly long time to rule a city, apart from the glaring question "**so how long could Alulim live if he was able to rule for that long?**"

Even more stunning is the 12 sars served by En-Men-Lu-Anna as king of the Sumerian city of Bad Tibira, totaling 43,200 years. This was the Anunnaki metallurgy processing headquarters. Wow!!!

This first lowering of the "authority of kingship" happened in Eridu, Enki's first city in Sumer. Assuming that it is true that they came to the Earth circa 445,000 years ago, let's add up the number of years that the first 8 rulers occupied the throne on behalf of the

Sumerians.

We see that they ruled as kings for 176,400 Earth years. Subtracting 176,400 years from the initial arrival date of 445,000 years when Enki arrived in the Persian Gulf, we have 268,600 years ago. Now back off another 600 years from the Genesis and Atrahasis accounts that corroborate that Noah's flood occurred exactly at this point in the Shurrupak King's rule. This is the time Enlil tolerated (Atrahasis Tablet 1 states 600 years) the primitive breeding program that facilitated meeting the labor requirements for the South African gold mining operation.

Again, this puts us at 268,000 years ago. Now, allocate some unspecified time for Enki and Ninhursag to fabricate the genetic chimera primitive worker on orders of the Anunnaki Council that was to became we humans. Let's be conservative and allocate a complete *shar* for the two lab rats to get the job done. This final time frame of 264,400 years ago is most likely how long that the Igigi were working in the mines. No wonder they wanted relief. Can you imagine working in those conditions for so long? For a slight perspective change, consider that the Igigi were also counting their time in *shars (sars)* wherein 1 year on Nibiru was equal to 3,600 Earth years which is equivalent to only 73 Niburian years. Still a long time counting in one's own years to work underground. Another point of interest from our first table of Sumerian Kings is the fact that the location changed 4 times after originating in Eridu. Then some catastrophe befell the city and kingship was moved to Bad Tibira. Again this occurred at Bad Tibira, Laraq, Zimbir, and finally Shurrupak (Shurruppag). A final point of interest is the fact that ruler ship ends after 8 kings and 176,400 years shown in first table of kings, ending with Noah's flood as denoted.

Revolving Sumerian Kingship and Destruction

The reason that the kingship fell and was moved so many times is not addressed by the list, other than stating it was defeated and moved elsewhere, over and over. By reading one king's account of how Ur's Second Dynasty fell in the Lamentations shown, left to us by none other than Nannar himself, we can extrapolate that other kingships were "defeated" causing a change in command and location. See Figure 4 below.

Recall the spirit of the slave taskmaster in the African mines is embodied in his father, Enlil. Here is the full but sad tale of the extent to which the wrathful commander holding the rank 50 and operating as Lord of the Command treated the primitive workers and his own family.

Second Dynasty of Uruk

Ruler	Epithet	Length of reign	Approx. dates	Comments
En-shag-kush-ana		60 years	ca. 25th century BC	said to have conquered parts of Sumer; then Eannatum of Lagash claims to have taken over Sumer, Kish, and all Mesopotamia.
Lugal-kinishe-dudu or Lugal-ure		120 years		contemporary with Entemena of Lagash
Argandea		7 years		

"Then Unug was defeated and the kingship was taken to Urim (Ur)."

Second Dynasty of Ur

Ruler	Epithet	Length of reign	Approx. dates	Comments
Nanni		120 years	ca. 25th century BC	
Mesh-ki-ang-Nanna II	*"the son of Nanni"*	48 years		
(?)		2 years		

"Then Urim was defeated and the kingship was taken to Adab."

Dynasty of Adab

Ruler	Epithet	Length of reign	Approx. dates	Comments
Lugal-Ane-mundu		90 years	ca. 25th century BC	said to have conquered all Mesopotamia from the Persian Gulf to the Zagros Mountains and Elam

Dynasty of Mari

Ruler	Epithet	Length of reign	Approx. dates	Comments
Anbu		30 years	ca. 25th century BC	
Anba	*"the son of Anbu"*	17 years		
Bazi	*"the leatherworker"*	30 years		
Zizi of Mari	*"the fuller"*	20 years		
Limer	*"the 'gudug' priest"*	30 years		
Sharrum-iter		9 years		

"Then Mari was defeated and the kingship was taken to Kish."

Figure 4: Nannar Sin, King of 2ⁿᵈ Dynasty of Ur

Note that Alulim is named as the first in a long line of liaison kings that were installed by the Anunnaki, which provided a middle management layer in the simulator. Figure 4 above depicts Nannar Sin's kingly 2ⁿᵈ Dynasty of Ur's listing, ending with the bland power transition statement that *"then Urim (Ur) was defeated and the kingship was taken to Adab"*. Makes one wonder what happened causing the kingship to move from city to city with little to no detail as to why this happened. This is especially curious after seeing the duration of the ruler ships prior to the flood.

The Sumerian Lamentation document which follows was apparently authored by Nannar or his spouse Ningal and gives us a clue to the unknown forces that caused the kingship merry-go-round issue which is evident in the Sumerian King's List. Considering the honorable relationship a son expects to have with his father, do the actions of the father reflect the same courtesy? You decide after reading the dreadful account for the destruction of the city of Ur.

Lamentations for the Destruction of Ur

Many lament texts have been found, each mourning the destruction of a different Sumerian city [13]. This one speaks for itself.

"The goddess of Ur, Ningal, tells how she suffered under her sense of coming doom."

When I was grieving for that day of storm, that day of storm, destined for me, laid upon me, heavy with tears, that day of storm, destined for me, laid upon me heavy with tears, on me, the queen.

Though I was trembling for that day of storm, that day of storm destined for me -- I could not flee before that day's fatality. And of a sudden I espied no happy days within my reign, no happy days within my reign.

Though I would tremble for that night, that night of cruel weeping destined for me, I could not flee before that night's fatality.

Dread of the storm's flood like destruction weighed on me, and of a sudden on my couch at night, upon my couch at night no dreams were granted me.

And of a sudden on my couch oblivion, upon my couch oblivion was not granted. Because (this) bitter anguish had been destined for my land -- as the cow to the (mired) calf -- even had I come to help it on the ground,

I could not have pulled my people back out of the mire. Because (this) bitter dolor had been destined for my city, even if I, birdlike, had stretched my wings, and, (like a bird), flown to my city, yet my city would have been destroyed on its foundation, yet Ur would have perished where it lay.

Because that day of storm had raised its hand, and even had I screamed out loud and cried; "Turn back, O day of storm, (turn) to (thy) desert," the breast of that storm would not have been lifted from me.

Then verily, to the assembly, where the crowd had not yet risen, while the Anunnaki, binding themselves (to uphold the decision), were still seated, I dragged my feet and I stretched out my arms, truly I shed my tears in front of An.

Truly I myself mourned in front of Enlil: "May my city not be destroyed!" I said indeed to them. "May Ur not be destroyed!" I said indeed to them. "And may its people not be killed!" I said indeed to them. But An never bent towards those words, and Enlil never with an, "It is pleasing, so be it!" did soothe my heart.

(Behold,) they gave instruction that the city be destroyed, (behold,) they gave instruction that Ur be destroyed, and as its destiny decreed that its inhabitants be killed.

Enlil called the storm. The people mourn. Winds of abundance he took from the land. The people mourn.

Good winds he took away from Sumer, the people mourn. Deputed evil winds. The people mourn. Entrusted them to Kingaluda, tender of storms.

He called the storm that annihilates the land. The people mourn. He called disastrous winds. The people mourn.

Enlil -- choosing Gibil as his helper -- called the (great) hurricane of heaven. The people mourn.

The (blinding) hurricane howling across the skies -- the people mourn -- the tempest unsubduable like breaks through levees, beats down upon, devours the city's ships, (all these) he gathered at the base of heaven. The people mourn.

(Great) fires he lit that heralded the storm. The people mourn. And lit on either flank of furious winds the searing heat of the desert.

Like flaming heat of noon this fire scorched.

The storm ordered by Enlil in hate, the storm which wears away the country, covered Ur like a cloth, veiled it like a linen sheet.

On that day did the storm leave the city; that city was a ruin. O father Nanna, that town was left a ruin. The people mourn.

On that day did the storm leave the country. The people mourn.

Its people ('s corpses), not potsherds, littered the approaches.

The walls were gaping; the high gates, the roads, were piled with dead.

In the wide streets, where feasting crowds (once) gathered,
jumbled they lay. In all the streets and roadways bodies lay. In
open fields that used to fill with dancers, the people lay in heaps.

The country's blood now filled its holes, like metal in a mold;
bodies dissolved -- like butter left in the sun.

(Nannar, god of the Moon and spouse of Ningal, appeals to his
father, Enlil)

O my father who engendered me! What has my city done to you?
Why have you turned away from it?

O Enlil! What has my city done to you? Why have you turned
away from it? The ship of first fruits no longer brings first fruits
to the engendering father, no longer goes in to Enlil in Nippur
with your bread and food portions!

....

O my father who engendered me! Fold again into your arms my
city from its loneliness!

O Enlil! Fold again my Ur into your arms from its loneliness!

Fold again my (temple) Ekishnugal into your arms from its
loneliness!

Let renown emerge for you in Ur! Let the people expand for you: let the ways of Sumer, which have been destroyed, be restored for you!

Enlil answered his son Suen (saying): "The heart of the wasted city is weeping, reeds (for flutes) of lament grow therein, its heart is weeping, reeds (for flutes) of lament grow therein, its people spend the day in weeping.

O noble Nanna, be thou (concerned) about yourself, what truck have you with tears?

There is no revoking a verdict, a decree of the assembly, a command of An and Enlil is not known ever to have been changed.

Ur was verily granted a kingship -- a lasting term it was not granted.

From days of yore when the country was first settled, to where it has now proceeded,

Who ever saw a term of office completed? Its kingship, its term of office, has been uprooted. It must worry (you) my Nanna, do you not worry! Leave your city!"

Wow, what a sorrowful lamentation spawned from son to

father over a devastating act of destruction. Some key points that are worthy of discussion from the Lamentation are now addressed. First, we firmly establish that Nannar-Suen (Sin) is the moon god in the city of Ur. His wife the Queen is the Anunnaki goddess Ningal. The following Sumerian King's List snippet captures the Second Dynasty of Ur where Nannar (Nanni) was enthroned when the Lamentation account was written. He ruled for 120 years before Enlil destroyed the entire city. Although, the table shows that Ur was ruled for another 48 years by Nannar's son, then two more years under an unknown ruler before kingship was transferred to the Sumer city of Adab.

Anu appears to have turned his head looking the other way while Enlil wrought the unstoppable destruction to Ur. Ningal was devastated and appears to have gone down with her symbolic ship, whereas Nannar survives by lifting off into the air in his Anunnaki flying craft to get away from what appears to be a nuclear assault on both flanks of the city at the same time. My point here is that given the number of Lamentation documents describing similar carnage by other Sumerian Kings, this may be the reason kingship moved from city to city so frequently. The final devastating statement Enlil makes to his son is a resounding expose on the nature of his destructive spirit;

(Enlil)

Ur was verily granted a kingship -- a lasting term it was not granted. "Who ever saw a term of office completed? Its kingship, its term of office, has been uprooted. It must worry (you) my Nanna, do you not worry! Leave your city!"

In the excerpt from the Lamentation above, Enlil provides a cursory explanation as to why the city of Ur was destroyed, even though his son Nannar was the king and his son! In other words, whatever Enlil does can be retracted by stating that the agreement he had was not forever, changing his mind. Then, to add insult to injury, Nannar's own father tells him not to fret over all the death and carnage he caused in Ur, just leave the city, act like nothing transpired. Where is the soul in this being so hell-bent on destruction, often times done seemingly without cause? Enlil further sates simply that the kingship is being uprooted. No mention is made about Ningal's safety or her go-forward plan as she is probably one of the victims. Yikes, what a god of wrath and vengeance!!! Could the vengeance part be real, unleashing his passive aggressive grudge against Nannar for leading the Igigi rebellion in the South African mines?

This seminal Sumerian historical document forced me to address my own belief system, a "Lamentation" explaining the end of a ruler ship, recorded for us today to reflect upon. The account is a devastating retelling of the destruction of Ur by its king and queen; Nannar-Suen and his consort Ningal.

Nannar is Enlil's son who appeared at the African mine rebellion scene where he took the leadership role as a fellow God, acted as a community organizer, and then led the armed miners in a rebellion to his father Enlil's fortress, surrounding him at night. Imagine the grudge that the high ranking commander Enlil probably held toward Nannar for leading the Igigi rebellion, which disrupted progress toward the gold mining efforts. The rebellion led by Alla(h)-Nannar-Suen(Sin) potentially embarrassed his father in front of his father Anu after leaving the African mines unattended. Enlil was rebuked by his father for his destructive offer to kill a miner to end the rebellion and get the productivity numbers back on the high end of the bell curve.

Consider the spirit of this being that left Africa operating as a tyrannical overseer, a brutal taskmaster, landing in the Sumerian Kingship headquarters at the time, Ur. According to the Sumerian King's List, Ur was the place where kingship was transferred from the previous city of Uruk, home of King Gilgamesh. See Figure 4 above.

This same spirit, represented symbolically with his Lord of the Air mascot, the Bald Eagle. Death from above, hoo rah!!! As a former chopper pilot in the US Army, I heard this kind of saber rattling from many fronts in my soldiering days. So, how do we transit from Mesopotamian cities where mass carnage ensued, to a connection of this spirit of the dark forces leading the New World Order rebellion? Just follow the symbols and they will lead you back to the causal source of it all.

Biblical Lifespans Questioned

I am often asked if I believe the lifespan durations listed in Genesis 5:25 are true. Some lived upwards of 1000 years at maximum, Methuselah lived the longest at 969 years old with Enoch spending only 365 years in the simulator at which time he walked with God and did not return. His special case is listed from the New International Version Bible.

My answer has been pretty consistent. When comparing the lives to those shown in the Sumerian King's list, the Genesis list pales in comparison, with just under one thousand years in Genesis 5:25.

A pattern of strange telling trigger my hackles to pay attention whenever it appears that a smear campaign or cover story is being proffered in place of the truth.

An incident involving Noah and his wine consumption curse on Ham's son Canaan following the flood is just such an event as detailed in this book. The teaser story here is that a lie was perpetuated regarding an important father-son relationship whereby Noah is portrayed to have more kids than he actually does. This ignoble act of falsifying a cover story in order that birthright and kingship supplantation could be achieved is a very fallen state indeed.

Genesis 5:21 (NIV)

When Enoch had lived 65 years, he became the father of Methuselah. And after he became the father of Methuselah, Enoch walked with God 300 years and had other sons and daughters. Altogether, Enoch lived 365 years. Enoch walked with God; then he was no more, because God took him away.

The remaining cast of well-known characters and their lifespans are shown in Table 4 for ease of reference.

Adam to Noah Name	Lifespan Years	Comment
Adam	930	
Seth	912	

Enosh	905	
Kenan	910	
Mahalael	895	
Jared	962	
Enoch	365	# days in year
Methuselah	969	Lived the longest
Lamech	777	Slot machine inventor?
Noah	950	Enki's son

Table 4: Adam to Noah Genealogy Table

Of all the Biblical patriarchs, only Enoch is said to have walked with God. I find it interesting that his story is told in *"The Lost Book of Enoch"* and conveniently left out of the Bible, except for his genealogy table cited here. An added mystery is that his age at death matched the number of days it takes for the Earth to revolve about the sun (with rounding error ignored), 365.

Figure 5: Eridu Zoom Level 1

Figure 5 above depicts the ancient city of Eridu using Google Earth. Notice the close proximity to the Persian Gulf where the Tigris and Euphrates Rivers empty their water laden sediment escaping the filtering root structure in the sea of reeds feeding the sea.

Figure 6: Eridu Zoom Level 2

The sand and silt depicted in Figure 6 almost completely disguises the fact that baked bricks from Enki's first city on Earth breach the drifting dunes, begging to be explored in depth. My mother, as an aspiring archeologist in her dreamy youth, always wanted to explore the Egyptian pyramids. It is my wish that this deep dive into ancient history, done in order to accomplish my mission to locate the entities of interest in my part of the simulator, partially fulfills her dream vicariously. Feel free to look at all the images that have been released of Eridu, the location of the Garden of Eden (ED.IN from the cuneiform tablet sources).

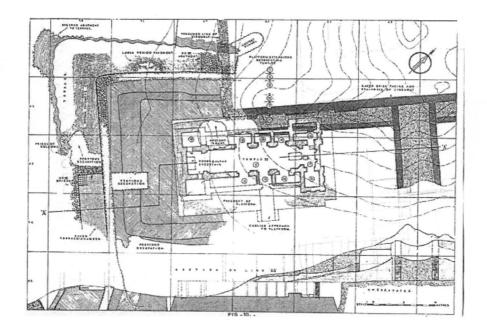

Figure 7: Eridu Temple Complex Sketch

The final image presented for the reader is that of Eridu's sacred district, the temple complex. Each Anunnaki-occupied Sumerian city had at its center a Ziggurat temple. Figure 7 shows how complex the building site is, along with stages of occupation. The final renaissance for Eridu happened around 3800 BCE.

Flower of Life Sacred Geometry

While researching the Anunnaki story was consuming most of my research efforts in the year 2004, I somehow stumbled onto the field of sacred geometry as well. Being an engineer, always looking to optimize, decode, and solve problems, I must have had a little extra bandwidth to pursue this space. The numerical mystery involving the Fibonacci sequence led me to consider the relationship between structures. In particular, my interest in alternative energy, even as a youngster, led me to consider various structures and shapes whose structure and function were significantly correlated. Given the fact that my son JJ had a genetic disorder, I was on the lookout for a key that could unlock the method by which DNA could be repaired.

From my exposure to structural integration (Rolf Method of Structural Integration www.rolfguild.org), and having used human energy field imaging and analysis software during the term of my private practice (Gravitybody Fitness and Structural Academy 2004-2011), I had come to the conclusion that structure and function were intertwined. The imaging room where clients were seen was equipped with full-spectrum lighting. All exterior light from the outside was blocked from incoming windows. The imaging system, relying on full-spectrum light sans shadows, consisted of an HD camera which fed a computer the video signal. The software would take a video that captures the interaction of photons with the energetic fields that surround the human body. A Before video segment was recorded (with open-minded inquisitive clients) in some cases along with an After video. This video data was fed into the polycontrast interference photography (PIP) software for analysis and display. I began to see a pattern in the color asymmetry on one side of the client's body during one of my imaging data analysis review sessions. Having worked with said client for some time, most issues relative to their structure were well known having been captured from four angles each session. Thus, both the client and the practitioner were hyper aware of the structural impediments at the time the energy body imaging experiments were performed.

Thus, there were eight photos per client per day that were captured. These images were taken at a known focal range with the client standing on a cross-hatch pattern located on the floor directly centered on the midline of a wall-hanging grid chart along with a plumb bob suspended from the ceiling about two feet directly in line with the camera and the center line of the chart. Thus, the plumb bob perfectly aligned with the chart center, the center of the camera lens, and the mid-sagittal line of the standing client. Camera images taken from all four before and after viewpoints recording the client's structural integration session were stored in the ClientView imaging database for rapid Before-After comparison between any session.

ClientView is an HTML web-based software program that which written by yours truly and updated significantly by my son Matthew (Senior at CalTech now) to establish a database to hold the client's before and after SI session images. The clients were always very excited to review the images in order to determine what level of change occurred during that day. This awareness of one's structure relative to the gravity field is not merely for postural vanity's sake. The visualization tool helped the client form an image of how they relate to gravity and to then pay attention to the areas discussed. This helps facilitate a better gravity distribution stance, stacking the seven segment body blocks like stacking river stones upon each other. When stacking objects, care must be taken to align the center of mass with the previous block below it. Note that altering any stone below another changes the stacking position for the ones above. This analogy is the same in the segmented human body, which I hypothetically modeled as an antenna relative to energy.

The Before-After imaging comparative review experience was most instructive for the clients who were able to create a mental image of their relationship to lines and planes in the body. The experience was enhanced and made more apparent by comparing the grid pattern behind along with the tell-no-lies diviner of verticality, the plumb bob in the front. The client is therefore segmented bilaterally from head to toe. This differential imaging system made structural changes more apparent by moving the Before-After images like a motion video frame, helping the eye detect the changes that sometimes were not as apparent in two static images, especially to the untrained eye. ClientView was a terrific tool to learn the next important issue that led me to an understanding of the sacred geometry field.

Some of the more advanced SI clients agreed to allow me to use the energy body recording and analysis software as part of the imaging service my company offered. This is the first time that I began to see a direct correlation between the human energy body and its related structure issues. The bottom line is that if there is a structural impediment in the body, there will be an affiliated energy disparity that is visible. The finding was so illuminating, verifying the verbal feedback that was often provided as clients would report significant shifts in the way they felt energetically following the typical 1.5 to 2 hour structural integration sessions.

I was reminded of the data I discovered in the field of Sacred Geometry, which had indicated the presence of the number phi, a ratio value derived from the Fibonacci Sequence which is a special case of the Golden Mean Spiral. For those who did not read my first book, the derivation of phi equaling the fractional rounded number 1.618 was detailed [3, Pgs. 187-188]. The ratio Phi shows up in nature and the human body design. I noted that the ratio for Earth/Venus solar orbital days also equals the number phi. Thus, many consider the number to be the design ratio chosen by the CREATOR OF ALL, in order that those who were looking to make mathematical sense of our creation would have a teaser to go on.

That said, the Egyptians recognized this number in the Flower of Life Symbol and the human body, where the measure of beauty for a female (males slightly differ) could be determined first and foremost by structural measurements. The Golden Mean ratio predicated that by measuring from the woman's head to the ground (let it be X) and the distance from the belly button to the ground (let it be Y), when divided X/Y should be 1.618. If not, then the segment that was too short could be identified and addressed to work for the perfect symmetry, which we consider beautiful. This symmetry stems from a geometric model that approximates the Golden Mean Spiral, a digital set of samples from the spiral if you will. This is the Fibonacci quantized sequence. The curve is easily derived using rectangles in place of the numbers. First we will list a short part of the Fibonacci sequence and relate it to the Golden Mean Spiral.

Fibonacci Sequence

1,1,2,3,5,8,13...

Using this short sequence from the continuous series, we can draw the rectangles with the same values from the numbers. See Figure 8 below which depicts the start of the Golden Mean Spiral drawn atop the discrete quantized points in the Fibonacci Series.

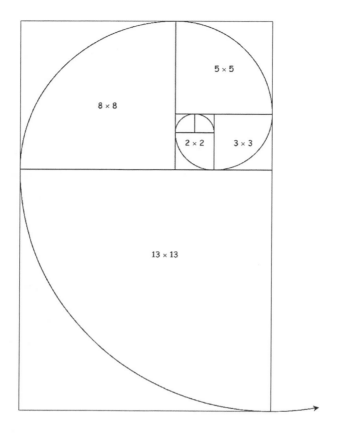

Figure 8: Golden Mean Spiral and Sacred Geometry

Taking the field of Sacred Geometry further into the body, Drunvalo Melchizedek decodes the meaning of the Flower of Life symbol, relating it to the three-part magical cycle of a tree which produces fruit and subsequently seeds that regenerate the tree. This circular process is represented by the Flower of Life Symbol seen in Figure 9 below. The cellular division process is shown to also follow the geometry specified by the vesica pisces petals in the flower design.

Figure 9: Flower of Life Symbol

When I was assimilating the Volumes 1 and 2 authored by Drunvalo [31-32], some practice was needed to recreate the symbol using a compass. The portions of the circle showing around the outer circumference of the perfectly inscribed circles was left so that one could see how the main circles are drawn. Once the pattern starts to take shape, the points to place the compass line up perfectly for the next full or partial circle. Give it a try and see what you learn. Without repeating the excellent work done by Drunvalo geometrically, just know that the symbol specifies the location of the chakras and the ten energy points listed in the Kabala as well. This symbol is considered the basis for the law of continuous creation as discussed in the seminal book "*Genesis of the COSMOS*" [24].

Slave Energy Transfer

The knowledge necessary to slay a being, conducting a rite thereby moving the released energy back into a chimera is beyond science fiction, unless we are looking at how the Anunnaki created their very first Avatar. This term implies that the body is merely a container host for the spirit energy that occupies it. Reversing the sequence is what we try to understand as death. This concept will be dealt with in depth throughout this book, so for those watching Reality TV Ghost chasing shows, hang on to your seats!!!

What a crazy concept to fathom, energy transfer between beings, as it unites the seemingly unconnected ideas of life, death, energy, matter, and the implications that we as humans are simply containers for energy-consciousness. The fact that Enki takes the spirit-energy of the slain god Llawela and puts it into the Adapa is beyond belief. Dr. Frankenstein attempted this feat in his classic horror tale in which he infuses plain old electricity into a cadaver with an augmented brain. Infusing energy and creating life from unintelligible lightning strikes is far different than capturing the soul essence at death and performing instant reincarnation on the spot, without a lawyer present.

This is reverse exorcism in a way. Instead of kicking out an evil spirit with a cross and a priest, the high priest Enki is coaxing the spirit of Llawela out of the already dead body into a new chimera body of Adapa, using rites and rituals to ensure success. "Let his drumbeat (heartbeat) be heard forever…" stated Enki in the Atrahasis account for the creation of man.

Fate Versus Destiny

Consider this from Enki's perspective for us primitive workers as a jumpstart versus new species. One of the issues I like to discuss is the difference between fate and destiny, a philosophical question bandied about by intellects through the ages. Are we destined to live the life we do? Or is there opportunity to choose each fork in the fated path the destiny we long to achieve in this life? This could add a phrase or possibly an entire passage to humanity's progressive and cumulative dialog, moving the conversation away from darkness and toward the utopian ideals we share. We each dream of a better life, possibly back in time to Atlantis or perhaps going all the way back in time, to the beginning encounters with the Anunnaki geneticist in the Garden of Eden in the mad scientist Enki's city of Eridu.

Enki even questioned his own authority and right to augment a foreign life form on a distant planet to do their assigned tasks getting the gold. If one has the intelligence to understand the mind of GOD, written in the seeds of life, then modifications with intentional design can be performed. The question for him, as it is for us today, is just because we can do some amazing task, like creating a nuclear weapon or cloning a sheep, does not mean we should do so. Enki justified the act of altering the targeted chimeric DNA donor, Neanderthal man, by telling himself that:

1. He was given the intelligence to know how to alter the DNA and had a circumstance that needed the labor force to replace rebelling miners. He does not seem to have given enough credence to the idea of opting for heavy tool fabrication for some reason, we are not told.

2. The idea of augmenting an already evolving species, cutting out potentially millions of years of evolutionary time, was not as difficult as the first item. It is a temporary enslavement with the beneficial tradeoff being intelligence and a longer lifespan of 120 years. The average life for Neanderthal donors was most certainly far less than 40 years on average. Anthropologist Rachel Caspari said that by examining Neanderthal dental records, her team established that 130,000 years ago, "no-one survived past 30" [37] years old. In the next chapter, the reader is taken back to Enki's domain of Africa with him playing the role of Mary Shelly's famous Dr. Frankenstein, animator of

material form, able to manifest material from light, a mere simulator sprite to be taught a lesson by the mad scientist.

CHAPTER 3: Enki's Igigi Replacements

Given the fact modern humans are the chimeric offspring of the Anunnaki and more primitive bipedal hominids corralled from the steps of the African plains, we now examine our energetic human antenna design. Readers with the courage to wade through this simple mathematics used in Chapter 6 of my first book, "*The Anunnaki of Nibiru*" [3], know that we ended up with an equation for human energy that was a function of wavelength, frequency, gravity, and weight. Now a deconstruction of material man into energy and matter is explored as it relates to Enki's amazing primitive worker design, us.

Composition of Man

Man is deemed to have a three-fold composition which is a subset of nine (9) total elements, as above, so below on Earth:

1. **Physical**-blood movement facilitates the heart beating. *Magnetism traveling through nerve ganglia and pathways is claimed to provide energy for cells and tissue. The Akasa flows through subtle channels in the body for a complete system*. The three-fold composition work in

unison allowing life in the body. The skeletal system is formed from the system where the *Akasa* subtle energy flows, like an antenna as I have posited. Mastering the elements allows the Secret of Life in the body (**ba**?) to be activated, enabling one to choose to relinquish the body only when the mission is accomplished on Earth! Based on the three energy body distinctions provided by Drunvalo (Chakra, Prana, Auric) these fall under Physical.

2. **Astral**-this energy component has three aspects

    a. **Mediator** between the above and below

    b. **Non-Spiritual.** Not sure how Spirit and the energy nature are differentiated. I oft use the term Spirit and energy interchangeably. The energy field that has the potential to use the Earth portal is the **ba**. The Mer-Ka-Ba star tetrahedron field has the key element cited for this access, the **ba** *SUN-soul key*. See Chapter 5 for a more detailed study of this Tablet.

    c. **Non-Physical.** Able to move above and below which is what we here on Earth term an out of body experience or OOBE.

3. **Mental**-The mind also has three natures:

    a. **Carrier of the Will of the Great One**

    b. **Arbiter of Cause**

GERALD CLARK

c. **Arbiter of Effect**

The Human Mer-Ka-Ba Field

Thoth provides us with the terms *ka* and *ba* from the Supplemental Emerald Tablets. Additionally, the allusion to the Flower of Life is discussed throughout the Tablets. This symbol was the connection for me discovering that Thoth was indeed the holder of the Keys of Wisdom, and that although I did not comprehend the significance of Drunvalo's work initially, in retrospective reflection, the pieces of the puzzle began to assemble. The focal point of a Flower of Life Sacred Geometry Workshop attended in 2004 was the seminar host-guided Mer-Ka-Ba meditation. The 17-breath Mer-Ka-Ba meditation, along with the instruction about male and female energy that were represented by the Star Tetrahedron geometric figure, was conducted in a group setting, located in a quaint private residence north of San Francisco, nestled in the redwood forest.

Caduceus Energy and the Chakras

The superposition composite signal created by the seven or more Chakras located along the central conductor (spine) hits the bottom pole (-) at the Ganglion of Impar at the tip of the Coccyx bone where the coiled snake representing the Kundalini energy lies dormant, ready to become activated. This may simply be another name for the *ba* field discussed later in the Emerald Tablets. An image of the Caduceus is shown in Figure 9A and 31 to connect the symbol to the description

(a)

Figure 9A: Caduceus Symbol of Enki and Thoth

Ascending entwined serpents (DNA changing energy of the Nadis) travels up the central pole (spine via spinal fluid conductor) as the rising snakes (Ida and Pingala Nadis and Double Helix of the DNA) travels ever upward toward the nob (pineal gland) atop the spine, subsequently releasing the wings of Hermes (lateral ventricles in the brain begin working correctly) as the spirit molecule (DMT) is produced targeting built-in brain receptors.

Electromagnetic signal transduction is achieved bi-directionally using DMT. Thus it is termed the Spirit Molecule.

The Pelvis forms a bowl at the base of the spine along with oddly shaped foramen (holes thru the bone) of the Ischium. Additionally, the Sacrum, when inspected from the posterior viewpoint, also exhibits strange foramen as well. What are these openings for? To let the electromagnetic spectrum enter a wave guide for some broadcast frequency to be received within the pelvic bowl? If so, if the electromagnetic impact on the black box device under test pelvises were conducted, we could determine where the signal poles (narrow band energy), zeros (cancelled energy), and how the resultant signal behaves. These measurements would also include the signal amplitude and phase response at various points near the foramen as discussed. Using this data, an electrical engineer, with a communications theory focus, could establish the scientific basis for the human antenna theory as described.

As for biological to electromagnetic signal transmission testing, a suggested approach to verify that humans are transmitting their brainwaves into the electromagnetic spectrum is to simply consider all the imaging systems used by Western medicine for disease diagnosis. These systems can measure the frequency profile for the entire body. We already mentioned our long-held technical ability to see our brain wave using the electroencephalogram (EEG). Additional New World Order military industrial complex techies have had the ability to read a license plate and brainwaves from satellite altitudes since 1964, as I disclosed on several radio programs, uploaded for your viewing and listening edification on my YouTube channel. This added ability to snoop on Enki's primitive worker meat-MODEM design shouldn't surprise anyone given Edward Snowden's disclosures which have gone viral regarding network and smartphone prying eyes (and ears too). As a matter of disclosure, I have worked on two very advanced programs involving the Predator drone, which will go unnamed. The last time was as a Senior Developer as part of the California Institute for Telecommunications and Information Technology (Calit2   http://www.calit2.net/index.php) team at UCSD, which has recently been renamed the Qualcomm Institute, following in the marketing footsteps the Padres had their baseball field renamed Qualcomm Stadium previous called Padre Stadium. Marketing!

Composition of Man Anunnaki Communications: Telepathy

Of particular interest is the possible translation from the brain's thoughts, electrical signals measurable using an electroencephalogram (EEG), to the electromagnetic spectrum (transmit). The reverse path (receive) is just as important in that if one were able to place data, like voice or binaural beats modulated onto a carrier wave whose frequency range fell within the known brain wave range for humans, then it would be possible to place images or thoughts into another's mind remotely, like a radio broadcast. I believe this is the basis for the phenomenon termed telepathy. If the brain is already creating an electrical signal, even though it is a small one, all electrical signals emanate into the electromagnetic field which extends indefinitely into space-time. Thus, if one were able to place a high gain receiver sensitive to the frequencies emitted from the human antenna, the concept might not seem so foreign. Specifically, my claims about the human body being designed in such a way that we have the ability to receive and transmit like a modulator-demodulator or the common acronym MODEM.

Hillbilly Lessons on Knowledge Gathering

An excellent organizational method to approach the information consists of 5 stages I call QS3R. Question, Survey, Read, Recite, Review.

1. **Question**: Try to have the questions that must be answered in mind before cracking the book. Create a void in your memory to fill with the answer.

2. **Survey**: Skim through the material, look at the pictures, and get an overview of what you are about to read.

3. **Read**: Read the material while being on the lookout for the answers to your questions.

4. **Recite**: Once you have the answers, record them as needed and recite until the short term memory has the data. This is later explained in the Rote stage of learning. We are still just memorizing here. This is not the end game, flushing at the next party when the exam is over. Read on.

5. **Review**: This is the activity that one does casually, remaining calm and relaxed on test day. The calm demeanor improves test scores. Feel the confidence entering the test knowing that you did your best with the time you had available (be a good steward of your precious time in the simulator) to dedicate to each subject. Spend more time on the difficult subjects for you as the ones you like will come easier to you.

Like a good seeking student, the ***Rote Memorization*** step is not the end of the learning process, only the beginning. These are the four cumulative stages of *learnin'* according to Gerald Clark:

1. ***Rote***: This is simply memorizing data for some period long enough to regurgitate it thanks to the idiots who set curriculum at the National Education Association (NEA).

Rote memorization is where most students remain while seeking a student loan to further dig themselves into a bad financial relationship to the enslaving government supporting bankers. Using silly acronym phrases can be helpful for very long lists. Flash cards can help too. Start early, depending on how much exposure your mind needs to memorize stuff. Everyone is different.

2. **Understanding**: I like to think of this phase as "standing under" a holographic display within a six degree of freedom cockpit simulator, seeking a bird's eye view of the information that just got jammed into my sensor. This fusion acquired short-term bi-directional associative memory pyramidal cells which weaves a complex neural network in the Cortex region in the final stage of our Mammalian brain evolution-genetic upgrade, the Cerebellum. Within our brain's outer layer, this fissured marvel contained within our protective helmeted cranium, resides a very thin cortical layer containing a complex neural network of connected brain cells (pyramidal cells being an example). I studied a specialized area of Artificial Intelligence while in graduate school working toward a doctoral degree in electrical engineering at the University of California at San Diego. My interest in this field arose from my research into Evolvable Hardware, which used an

AI Genetic Algorithm to solve the input to output mapping problem I was facing to make this inferential technical leap in the field. This is the physical location in the brain where one must submit the short term memory filled with memorized data from the **Rote** step, merely the first level on the road to higher knowledge. Unfortunately this is where public sponsored schools are failing the young Heroes on their archetypal journey back home to the LIGHT. Let this neural network have exposure to the short-term memory, seeking Understanding. This is where the seeker may encounter Divine intervention leading eventually to true wisdom. See Figure 10 for a neural network representing brain cells processing the synaptic threshold function updating the weights at the inputs to each brain neuron node, learning by exposure to large data sets, just like the human brain. Predictions and pattern recognition are popular uses for these brain-mimicking software programs.

GERALD CLARK

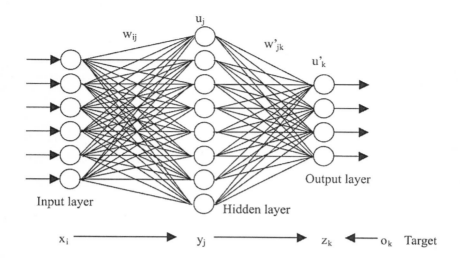

Figure 10: Neural Network Flow Chart

It is interesting to me that UCSD emblem features the Trident (Enki) along with the five-pointed star in the feminine position (Isis) and a waving banner that states Let There Be Light!. What an interesting synchronicity for me to find this symbolism from my Alma Mater just now.

Figure 11: UCSD Emblem and Logo

Thanks Enki and Isis. Sorry I was asleep when I could have found what I was looking for right before my eyes. I spent over 7 years working as staff and student on the campus.

3. **Application**: Once you have read a book, you must apply the lessons that you got from step 2, the **Understanding** that rang true with you, and I mean right away. We are all familiar with the purge phenomenon that occurs after cramming for a test, filling our minds with endless details, completing the exam, then quickly flushing the memory banks to make room for the next temporary informational onslaught and the process repeats itself, often for life. The time it takes for data to get purged from your short term memory is the time you have to do the **Application** part of

learning. Do what the term states, apply the lesson to your simulation state and see which fork in the road leads you to the LIGHT of WISDOM.

4. **Correlation**: This is the highest hillbilly level of learning. This is where life lessons logged into your long-term memory belong. Success is imminent as we see the lessons learned, our golden nuggets of acquired TRUTH in the prior three being wired together, the closer we get to our sought-after destiny. Become a dot connector operating at the **Correlation** level whenever possible, recording your lessons and neural mappings with the rest of the game players, especially the innocent victims playing the barely survivable game here on Earth. Here on the *Seventh Planet, Mercury is Rising*, many of those dots being connected are destructive, affecting real game players who are often targeted due to their meekness. Instead, may they inherit the new Earth!!!

The *Mer-Ka-Ba* field is claimed to extend into all dimensions. Thus, would it be possible that once one activates this field that eight additional copies of *you* are suddenly synchronized on their independent paths back to the Light, whereas before they may have been off course? This would be prior to the synchronizing energetic activation event. Think of oneself as the sponsor that facilitates and occasionally intervenes in your brethren's journey, empowering their path to overcome darkness, just when there seemed to be no way out.

This seventeen breath technique is an auditory and visualization meditation activating the star tetrahedron field that extends approximately 55 feet away from your body. I believe that activating the *Mer-Ka-Ba* energy field, after practicing the technique for many years, is a fundamental exercise that should not be overlooked by the serious seeker. I highly suggest using a guided meditation with the text printed out nearby. Alternatively, try one of the many YouTube videos offered online and see what reality you can potentially access using this technique.

The Human Energy Equation – Warning: Technical Information Below!

As an engineer and scientist, having an equation that mathematically represents the desired measurement is a given. Nerds like questions that have difficult, and sometimes unobtainable solutions. The equation that is depicted below is still shown intentionally as EQ5A. This is the variable I remember the formula by. I derived this equation beginning from what we know about energy, so far as we know and can verify.

I will briefly reconstruct the thinking that led to a measurable value, given the instrumentation we have to gather the data.

$$E_{max} = \frac{W}{g}\left(\Sigma_{i=1}^{i=7}\left(\lambda_i \nu_i\right)\right)^2 \quad \text{[EQ5A]}$$

Without going through any symbolic variable substitutions visually, which often turns off the non-scientific reader, the equation will be described using natural language instead. For those who desire to see the derivation, please see [3, Chapter 6].

The maximum human energy that we should be able to measure is shown on the left hand side of the equation as E_{max}. This human energy is a function of some constants (W, g) and some variables (lambda, nu, and the count variable lower case i).

Wavelength and frequency, *lambda* and *nu* respectively, are related to the speed of light equaling *lambda* times *nu*. This is assuming that the speed of light is always constant, possibly just an assumption by modern physics? The other relationship we need to establish is that weight is equal to the mass times gravity. We desire to find the mass term, so we will divide the gravity by the weight and use it as a variable in the equation. Finally, we want the wavelength and frequency of each Chakra summed up and squared as shown. Once the interior of the equation is summed from integer i=1..7, then we multiply that squared sum times the ratio of weight by gravity. Whew, that is why most mathematicians and scientists do not use natural language to describe equations, rather choosing to use Greek symbols like lambda, nu, and the summation sign. Using natural language to describe an equation requires more space and still one cannot see the relationships between variables. At least I can't do it as well. Anyway, I hope between the derivation in the first book and the natural language description in this book, one can appreciate how important functioning Chakras are to the resulting energy. Additionally, the importance of integrating oneself with the gravity field cannot be overemphasized as we now know that the state of our body structure relative to the gravity field has a significant impact on the resultant energy as well. Since gravity is in the denominator of EQ5A, the better one becomes in finding the vertical Rolf line, the less affect that gravity's field has on one's mass (the maximum value for variable E_{max}, as gravity approaches zero in EQ5A is infinite. *Our conclusion is that if you want to experience the maximum effective energy on a particular planet like Earth, one must integrate one's structure (skeleton and tissues) with the gravity field.* The minimum energy is zero if the denominator variable gravity is allowed to grow toward infinity. Even we hillbillies know that when you divide a fixed number by an ever increasing bottom number, the resultant energy E_{max} will decrease toward zero. Nap time.

The last interesting point to note is that if you sum up seven pairs of wavelengths and frequencies as shown composing the Chakra nodes, this is a seven times higher energy result than only operating at the root Chakra where the count variable (i) is set to one (1). Under this condition, we are looking at a much simplified version of EQ5A that is effectively the same as the one Einstein left us. This states that energy equals the mass times the speed of light squared, and in his famous sentence which has contributed to our composite human dialog.   Here we only get to sum up one wavelength and frequency pair which we established earlier is always equal to the speed of light. Our conclusion should be that under the same circumstances (weight and gravity constants), when the Chakras begin functioning as they should, following the Kundalini potential energy threshold catalytic release event, each added ganglia that is fully filled with LIGHT, although at different wavelengths or colors, adds to the final resultant E_{max} by a scalar factor of the speed of light squared. This is something to work for if one desires this heightened life state, which in my experience, is the point to truly take responsibility for our relationship to the CREATOR OF ALL manufactured force we call gravity. Doing so will change your life, energy, and consciousness at an increasing sequence of quantized states that correlate with your Chakras.

Drunvalo's Take on Human Energy Body

Drunvalo Melchizedek describes the human energy as fields existing in layers around the body. This coincides with my experience using Resonant Field Imaging devices and software to capture the Chakra frequency converting it to a wavelength for viewing on a computer. The various energy fields Drunvalo discusses are the Chakra, Auric, and Pranic fields [32 or 33, Pg. 343].

He further states that the Mer-Ka-Ba is a geometric field of light created by our consciousness, claiming that only 0.1 percent of the human populace has activated this field. If this is true, then they are living the illusion of *ka* as Thoth states. Drunvalo is optimistic that with the coming transit through the Galactic Center that more will activate their Mer-Ka-Ba fields due to the external energy triggering event that is resident in the dark rift high energy belt. My premise is that adding energy to the human antenna changes the state of the meat MODEM, producing inaudible static, and some discernible chatter on the line. If you are seeking you will most likely be finding at this special time of the Galaxy's processional wobble cycle, a Great Year indeed!

Emerald Tablet Model of Human Energy

We are provided a slightly different model in *Supplemental Emerald Tablet XV: Secret of Secrets*, where a new label is used to describe a subtle energy the human bio field, Akasa, which uses the skeletal system as the conductor.

Tuning in an OOBE, Thoth and Monroe

I find this one so interesting because if my human antenna model has any legs, then the rib cage makes a perfect set of fins for tuning in a receiver frequency. Alternatively they can be used while transmitting a pulsating signal (dipole) up and down our central conductor (spine) holding the ribs. This oscillating energy is described in the Emerald Tablets and in more detail by Robert Monroe, who studied and taught Out-of-body experiences (OOBE). Based on my experience and research, the brain wave state that allows us to be awake yet very trancelike is the Alpha region, suggesting approximately 7.8 Hertz (initially) as the desired target. This frequency makes sense to me as it is just below waking consciousness (the veil) and approximates the Schumann resonant frequency generated by the sun's radiation striking a metal containing sphere, i.e. the Seventh Planet AKA Earth.

Findings from my personal OOBE experiences and training indicate that once the borderland dream state is achieved with the mind fully awake, a train-like roar begins to sound in one's head. Adding a white noise generator or a fan at the right oscillation frequency can help in tuning into the Alpha waves which we attribute to Thoth's communication frequency.

Robert Monroe discusses the actual process of tuning in the vibrations [30, Pg. 213]. My experience is that doing the process when feeling refreshed after an earlier short nap really helps prevent just falling asleep. Here is an abbreviated process. I will let the reader support Robert Monroe by getting his book, *Journeys Out Of The Body*, and starting on Chapter 16, Preliminary Exercises [30, Pgs. 203-211].

1. Lie down in a relaxed state with head facing north aligned along a north-south axis.

2. Remove all jewelry.

3. Remain covered and warmer than normal sleeping temperature.

4. Adjust limbs not to impede circulation and remove tight clothes.

5. Darken the room almost completely keeping an LED or some other visual point of reference easily seen.

6. Allocate uninterrupted time block to mitigate distractions.

7. Achieve state of relaxation using whatever method desired, keeping the mouth half open. Using a visualization technique, focus on the image until the borderland state is achieved. Loosen your visual focus and allow your mind to slow down even more bringing your brain waves to the Alpha region toward 7.8 Hertz.

8. When in the borderland state, the body is asleep and the mind is awake. This is the state from which one begins tuning in the brain wave frequency that produces the sound of a train in your head. Mentally repeat to yourself "I will consciously perceive and remember all that I encounter during this session". Relax past the jerky state of frequency sweeping down the brainwave scale from

Beta toward Alpha range, near 7.8 Hertz. You should hear the train coming en route.

9. Now amplify the hissing sound by visualizing it oscillating along the body's long axis where it should smooth out on its own within 10 seconds. I believe this is the process of tuning in a brain wave frequency that allows one to disassociate one's energy body from the physical, possibly the Schumann Resonance Frequency. Robert offers his thought that the carrier wave tuned in is at a higher frequency, nearly 27 Hz. Unless he has measurements to show otherwise, this initial frequency falls within the brain wave region of 0.5 to 20 Hertz. Robert's number is outside our EEG range, thus my premise that is more in the Alpha range. The 27 Hertz signal could be a carrier wave sub-modulated or a harmonic thereof falling within the brain wave region for humans.

10. Once you get the vibe oscillating, move your visual focal point (eyes still closed) to coincide with a spot about 6 feet away and 90 degrees up above the head toward the ceiling, in line with the north-south body axis. Mentally reach for this spot, willing your energy body to climb. My experience is that visualizing sitting up and focusing on the ceiling above the head works to separate one's energy with a mental reaching toward the spot, although I am not sure

why. What also seems to work is to visualize sitting up to get to the spot on the ceiling as well. If still vibrating and successful, one will get the sensation of suddenly falling but in the upward direction, which also has an associated dizzying sensation. Instead of thinking of sitting up to exit the body, another technique is rolling out sideways. This one is more mentally challenging to try as one worries about rolling off the bed until getting used to the fact that the body is immobilized during an OOBE just as it is during rapid eye movement (REM) sleep. It is thought that the brain produces a chemical that immobilizes the REM or OOBE participant so that they do not act out the motion felt in the altered state of being, potentially causing self-injury. Once you achieve this feeling of dizziness, your astral body will arrive in the local room, possibly viewing your physical body motionless in bed from a floating position above. From this state, travel occurs immediately to a person, place or thing desired. This is where you learn about the power of your intention and thoughts, e.g., what you think manifests, so plan on eventually visiting the Duat Earth portal, having memorized the key phrases detailed in Chapter 5, Supplemental Tablet XV. These phrases can be used to initiate the OOBE as Thoth suggests, as an alternative to the Robert Monroe method discussed in abbreviation here. Enjoy your alternative reality, but don't forget to plan a six hour trip to Arulu and be sure to keep a journal!

The details provided in *Journeys Out of the Body* [30, Pg. 203] are sufficient to follow for just about anyone willing, even a 17-year-old teenage hillbilly from Arkansas, which was when I first read the book by recommendation from a high school teacher. Once we hear the train-like noise in our ears, it is time to sweep the signal up and down the body thinking of ourselves like an antenna with both a positive and negative poles (head and tailbone respectively) at some unspecified frequency from Thoth, but at 27 Hertz from Monroe.

CHAPTER 4: Adapa Goes to Heaven

What motive did Ea-Enki have in sending Adapa, his first successful primitive worker design, to meet Anu on Nibiru-Heaven? The reason was most likely to avert bad press on Nibiru, to inform Anu of the being's design constraints in order to mitigate his potential concern over the methods and "tools" which were being used to achieve the mining tasks in Africa. According to the story, Enki inscribes a tablet and gives it to Ningishzida (the messenger). The most sensitive knowledge was that of "heaven and earth", which the higher level Anunnaki guarded closely as witnessed by the internal power struggles over the ME planetary colonizing tablets, known as the Tablets of Destiny.

An interesting story is depicted in the Sumerian account. A funny vignette in which Adapa is supposedly fishing when a storm blew in, sinking his boat [2, Pgs. 182-187]. In his anger, apparently Adapa "cursed the South Wind" garnering the attention of Anu, based on Nibiru (heaven) in the account. Adapa is taken to Heaven, AKA Nibiru, where Anu resides. According to the records, Dumuzi was a son of Enki as was Ningishzida. The name Gizzida is used for Ningishzida, much like the name Elil was used in lieu of Enlil in the Atrahasis, written in a similar repetitive Sumerian style. The *Myth of Adapa* is a Mesopotamian story that could be seen as symbolic of the Fall of Man. Longevity constraints, specifically 120 years cited in the Bible and elsewhere in the Sumerian accounts, were placed on Adapa by Ea and he intended to explain to Anu why human beings were designated to be mortal. The god of wisdom, Ea, creates the first man, Adapa, and endows him with great intelligence and wisdom but not with eternal life. When immortality is offered Adapa by the great god Anu, Ea counseled Adapa into refusing the gift, indicating it caused death not eternal life. Anu detects this anomalous behavior from Adapa and asks for an explanation.

Ea and Gizzida, also known as Enki and Ningishzida, are two of the main characters in the story. Enki groomed seven antediluvian sages who were responsible for bringing civilizing traits to mankind. Adapa was the first sage or priest to serve Enki at his temple in Eridu. Earth Station One, which was located at the head of the Persian Gulf, also known as Eridu, was close to the Euphrates River and a short jaunt to Ur of the Chaldees.

Yet another name for Adapa was Uan which, when converted to Greek by Berossus, became Oannes. What follows is the account recorded in the book the Myths from Mesopotamia. This version does not contain the detail which describes the special mission for Adapa, as discussed in the book Divine Encounters [36] in which Anu sends the Adapa back to Earth and decreed that he would start a line of priests who will be adept at curing diseases [36, Pgs. 50-54].

The ADAPA Tale

(Several lines missing)

Thoughtfulness [ ]

His word command like the word of [Anu]

He (Ea) made broad understanding perfect in him

(Adapa), to disclose the design of the land.

To him he gave wisdom, but did not give eternal life.

At that time, in those years, he was a sage, son of Eridu.

Ea created him as a protecting spirit (?) among mankind.

A sage-nobody rejects his word-

Clever, extra-wise, he was one of the Anunnaki,

Holy, pure of hands, the pašīšu-priest who always tends the rites.

He does baking with the bakers,

Does the baking with the bakers of Eridu,

He does the food and water of Eridu every day,

Sets up the offerings table with his pure hands,

Without him no offering table is cleared away.

He takes the boat out and does the fishing for Eridu.

At that time Adapa, the son of Eridu,

When he had got the [leader (?)] Ea out of bed,

Used to 'feed' the bolt of Eridu every day.

At the holy quay Kar-usakar he embarked in a sailing boat

And without a rudder his boat would drift,

124

Without a steering-pole he would take his boat out

[   ] into the broad sea.

(Gap of uncertain length)

[   ]

South Wind [   ]

Send him (?) to live in the fishes' home.

'South Wind, though you send your brothers

Against me, however many there are,

I shall still break your wing!'

No sooner had he uttered these words

Than South Wind's wing was broken;

For seven days South Wind did not blow towards the land.

Anu called out to his vizier Ilabrat,

'Why hasn't South Wind blown toward the land for seven days?'

His vizier Ilabrat answered him,

'My lord, Adapa the son of Ea has broken South Wind's wing.'

When Anu heard this word,

He cried '(Heaven) help (him)!', rose up from his

Throne.

'[Send for him to] be brought here!'

Ea, aware of heaven's ways, touched him

And [   ]

made him wear his hair unkempt,

[Clothed him in] mourning garb,

Gave him instructions,

'Adapa, you are to go before king Anu.

You will go up to heaven,

And when you go up to heaven,

When you approach the Gate of Anu,

Dumuzi and Gizzida will be standing in the Gate of Anu,

Will see you, will keep asking you questions,

"Young man, on whose behalf do you look like this?

On whose behalf do you wear mourning garb?"

(You must answer)

"Two gods have vanished from our country,

And that is why I am behaving like this."

(They will ask)

"Who are the two gods that have vanished from the country?"

(You must answer)

"They are Dumuzi and Gizzida."

They will look at each other and laugh a lot,

Will speak a word in your favour to Anu,

Will present you to Anu in a good mood.

When you stand before Anu,

They will hold out for you the bread of death, so you must not eat.

They will hold out for you the water of death, so you must not drink.

They will hold out a garment for you: so put it on.

They will hold out oil for you: so anoint yourself.

You must not neglect the instructions I have given you:

Keep to the words that I have told you.'

The envoy of Anu arrived.

'Send to me Adapa,

Who broke South Wind's wing.'

He made him take the way of heaven

And he (Adapa) went up to heaven.

When he came up to heaven,

When he approached the Gate of Anu,

Dumuzi and Gizzida were standing in the Gate of Anu.

They saw Adapa and cried '(Heaven) help (him)!

Young man, on whose behalf do you look like this?

Adapa, on whose behalf do you wear mourning garb?'

'Two gods have vanished from the country,

And that is why I am wearing mourning garb.'

'Who are the two gods who have vanished from the country?'

'Dumuzi and Gizzida.'

They looked at each other, and laughed a lot.

When Adapa drew near to the presence of King Anu,

Anu saw him and shouted,

'Come here, Adapa! Why did you break South Wind's wing?'

Adapa answered Anu,

'My lord, I was catching fish in the middle of the sea

For the house of my lord (Ea).

But he inflated (?) the sea into a storm (?).

And South Wind blew and sank me!

I was forced to take up residence in the fishes' home.

In my fury I cursed South Wind.'

Dumuzi and Gizzida responded from beside him,

Spoke a word in his favour to Anu.

His heart was appeased, he grew quiet.

'Why did Ea disclose to wretched mankind

The ways of heaven and earth,

Give them a heavy heart?

It was he who did it!

What can we do for him?

Fetch him the bread of (eternal) life and let him eat!.'

They fetched him the bread of (eternal) life, but he would not eat.

They fetched him the water of (eternal) life, but he would not drink.

They fetched him a garment, and he put it on himself.

They fetched him oil, and he anointed himself.

Anu watched him and laughed at him.

'Come, Adapa, why didn't you eat? Why didn't you drink?

Didn't you want to be immortal? Alas for downtrodden people!'

'(But) Ea my lord told me: "You mustn't eat!

You mustn't drink!"

Take him and send him back to earth.'

(Gap of unknown length to end of story)

A piece of text known as Fragment D may give an alternative ending, and it is followed by an incantation against disease, invoking Adapa.

According to Sitchin, Dumuzi is held back on Nibiru for a shar on Anu's orders. Why? Potentially to study the earth's environmental effects on a fellow Niburian in order to assess the potential biological impact to the Anunnaki physique. These concerns may have been genetic, structural, and related to both the gravity and radiation exposure potentially absorbed the workers and staff assigned by Anu himself.

The sought after genetic seeds warehoused on Nibiru were being sent back with Dumuzi, by order of Anu. Added food sources provided from heaven were welcome indeed. Could the genetic material have been requested by the scientists Enki or Ningishzida to augment the food supply available on Ki-Earth? Or was it a humanitarian aid shipment by the king of Nibiru, a gracious gesture showing his support for difficult and dangerous task given the colonizing pioneers on a remote planet? The account does not specify. In any event, many pioneering ancient astronauts from Nibiru languished in the Fertile Crescent approximately 12,000 years ago. Without primitive workers, having been wiped out in the ice-age ending flood cataclysm on Enlil's orders, anxiously awaited Dumuzi's return to Ki. Some genetic gems that were received by the stranded but recovering Anunnaki near Mount Ararat, Turkey were genetic seeds that included the essence of ewes and cattle as well as a variety of edible flora like seed grains to make bread.

Next we will dive into the real meat of the book, the Emerald Tablets in the next chapter.

CHAPTER 5: The Emerald Tablets of Thoth

The Emerald Tablets are organized in seven rubrics or paragraphs. The word Rubric is derived from the Latin word *rubeo*, meaning the color red, most likely because it was the color of orichalcum composing the pillars of Atlantis. This organizational method was so designated red as it referenced the color used to highlight the first letter or the beginning of a paragraph.

The first rubric asks us to come to a higher awareness and to be open to deeper truths. The Doctrine of Correspondences describes a vertical relationship between matter and spirit, termed the second rubric. It is the portal in which Alchemists of the past claim to have lifted the veil into alternative dimensional realities. As compared to the vertical axis, the horizontal axis describes the relationship between matter objects, kind of like billiard balls sans spirit. The third rubric pertains to the nature of the "One Thing" implying the First Matter or Universal Life Force. The first two sentences of the rubric portray the Four Elements as Fire, Water, Air and Earth respectively. Alchemical correlations with the Four Elements are: calcinations, dissolution, separation, and conjunction. The fourth rubric is the most mystical part of the Emerald Tablet and seems to be telling us how to enter the spiritual realm defined as the Above. [1, Pg. 9]. Fermentation, distillation, and coagulation are the last alchemy operations for a total of seven. The fifth rubric discusses the results of the last rubric, whose result is a pure "Quintessence".

Figure 12: Emerald Tablets of Thoth

A summarized meta-perspective is given in the sixth rubric. It suggests that a universal pattern exists that leads one to total transformation in a multidimensional reality (simulator). This specific pattern is reported to be endemic in the laws of evolution of matter and the guiding force seen in nature.

The final rubric also identified the author of the tablet as "Thrice Greatest Hermes". Hermes was the name given to the Greek God, also known as (AKA) The Egyptian God of Wisdom, Thoth. While in Egypt, Thoth was credited with introducing writing, mathematics, and music to the primitive workers. Known as Mercury to the Romans, he purportedly was deemed "Thrice Greatest" given the fact that he had conquered obscure knowledge about accessing all three levels of reality: the physical plane, the mental plane, and the spiritual plane. This could also be representative of the number of incarnations he experienced up to that time, but according to the details within the tablets, he is immortal and his soul can occupy human bodies through the ages!!!

Thoth built the Giza Pyramid complex, circa 10,500 BC during the age of Leo. The Sphinx has a lion's body related to the Zodiacal sign, and the face of Ningishzida according to the Emerald Tablets. The deluge mentioned in the Sumerian King's List, Atrahasis-Noah's Biblical flood story, occurred after the first nine rulers had served the Anunnaki as kings for 176,000 years. This brings us to the timeframe of one of the many "Great Flood" events discussed by the Egyptian priest from Sais who divulged Greece's history to Solon. Following the destructive flood, an Era the Egyptians called ZEP TEPI, "The First Times", an occult group of Anunnaki gods made an attempt to restructure civilization for the survivors by providing the basics of civilization, as seen slightly earlier in the Mesopotamian culture of Sumer. Thoth and the Osirian mysteries occupied the Egyptian peoples, while Quetzalcoatl, Viracocha and Kulkulcan reigned in advanced civilizations in the Yucatan. These survivors and ancient alien pioneers were considered the pre-diluvian heroes of old. Names such as Enoch, Methuselah, and Noah mentioned in Genesis come to mind. Efforts to locate ancient buried mysteries continues to this day.

Ground penetrating radar has significantly improved the chances of finding fossil fuels reservoirs like natural gas and oil beneath the ground. This technology has also been applied to locating and mapping underground structures among archeologists in recent years. The SIRA radar system was used in Egypt circa 1978 to map an underground complex beneath the Egyptian pyramids. The Egyptian president, Anwar Sadat, facilitated thirty years of secret excavations using the ground penetrating radar systems. A key figure and scientist, Dr. Jim Hurtak, previewed some film footage he gathered using the radar derived data. "Chambers of the Deep" based on the Giza project, revealed the discovery of a vast megalithic metropolis, 15,000 years old, reaching several levels below the Giza plateau. A legendary "City of the Gods" was revealed laying underground with massive chambers and enormous statues. The city spans an area as large as the Nile Valley complete with submerged waterways [7]. The technology used to create the in-situ city is impressive, asserting that the surface Giza Pyramid and the Sphinx are insignificant above-ground reference points.

Given the recent radar findings below the surface in Egypt, it is interesting to compare what Thoth said in this writings about the structures in the Emerald Tablets. Perhaps the account he gave indicating the location of the Halls of Amenti coincide with Dr. Hurtak's secretive underground discoveries, previewed in the film "Chambers of the Deep", which he claims will be released to the populace at the end of the century. I read this statement of future intent to disclose such an important discovery with disdain. Why wait to the end of the century Dr. Hurtak to inform the public?

The technology discovered in the "City of the Gods" far exceeds the industrial machinery we modern folks are familiar with. Arthur C. Clark stated that "any technology beyond our own would seem like magic to us." Dr. Hurtak's findings indicate links to the Atlantean civilization claiming unequivocal evidence indicating that all languages, cultures and religions can be accredited to this "Parent Civilization".

Reference is made to a "language of light" and discusses the priest-scientist Enoch, existing in a previous time cycle. According to Dr. Hurtak's findings, Enoch was associated with building the Great Pyramid Complex and establishing an ascension strategy involving genetics and light energy interacting with matter. Enoch is a notorious figure from Genesis and the Biblical Canon. As the father of Methuselah and grandfather of Noah, Enoch was credited as the original architect of Zion, a city he built and dedicated to Enlil-Yahweh, as well as being credited with introducing language and the calendar to humanity in Sumer, Egypt, and the Yucatan. Recall from the Bible that Enoch is taken into the skies by the Anunnaki to teach him the secrets of the earth and heaven. Additionally, he lives 365 years, according to Genesis 5:23, after which time he is taken to be with the Gods. His discussions in the Lost Book of Enoch about his illuminating physics lessons in space are epic. Additionally, the birth account of Noah provided by Enoch in his Lost Book, further emphasizes Enoch's ethereal role counseling Lamech and his family as to the true nature of the baby and his mission relative to man. As fitting for a messenger, Enoch brings back weights and measures from the gods in heaven to the primitive workers as a civilizing gesture.

Known to the Egyptians as Thoth, "Lord of Magic and Time", Ningishzida or Gizzida to the Sumerians, Enoch was considered to hold the keys to the secrets of immortality. Thoth promises to return at the end of time "with the keys to the gates of the sacred land" according to the Emerald Tablets. Could this return coincide with that of Quetzalcoatl promised at the Winter Solstice, 2012? Is this return timing somewhat suspicious given the plans seen by the Illuminati concerning their attempts to roll out the New World Order, now all over the headlines and on the internet? The year 2012 came and went, just like the millennial Y2K scare over digital data memory allocation issues with concerns the date would not roll over correctly bringing the digital devices to an error state. The fearful cried wolf but it was a non-event. Was it a psychological operation to experiment with societal fear levels? If, as I have stated in my first book, Thoth could and did incarnate in many cultures, including the incarnation of Jesus-Yehoshua, he can be seen as casting a line to the suppressed primitive workers. The goal Thoth had in mind was continuing the teachings he headed up in the Mystery schools in Egypt.

As pointed out in John 1:12, to all who received him (Thoth-Ningishzida-Jesus) in the frequency dispensing dying rising god ritual, to them he gave power (energy as a frequency dispensation to the receptor nerve ganglion of Impar located in the human Sacrum at the tip of the Coccyx bone) with the ability to become (transform) the sons of God. This is the first key to ascension, recognizing who Ningishzida-Jesus really was and how the process of getting out of the simulator works. Let's now take a look at the actual Emerald Tablets of Thoth as translated by Dr. Doreal in 1930 [10].

Preface to the original: Emerald Tablets

According to the document, the tablets date back 36,000 years BC and are accredited to Thoth the Atlantean Priest-King who returned to Egypt to establish civilization following the destruction of Atlantis. He was credited with building the Giza Pyramids wherein he preserved his ancient wisdom and knowledge for future generations of humanity.

His reign is recorded as lasting from 50,000 BC to 36,000 BC during which he imparted his civilizing ways upon the barbarians he encountered upon his return from Atlantis. Thoth is supposedly an immortal being, having overcome death's sting. Upon his departure from Egypt, Thoth erected the Great Pyramid over the entrance to the Great Halls of Amenti. High priests and appointed guardians of his hidden knowledge were appointed to guard the knowledge vault. The descendants of these guardians eventually became pyramid priests who deified Thoth as the God of Wisdom, the one whose records illuminated those in the age of darkness after he departed. Legends arose relating the Halls of Amenti to the "underworld" where the soul passed after death for judgment, AKA the Biblical Hell.

It is claimed that in later ages that the "ego" of Thoth could be transferred into the bodies of men as described in the tablets. Recall the Atrahasis account where Enki chose a god to sacrifice, transferring his energy (soul) into the Adapa during the genetic trials. Is this a similar trick that Ningishzida-Thoth was taught by his father Enki? Each tablet, including the supplements will be analyzed and summary lessons *gleaned and correlated with the ascension focus of this book, finding our way out of the holographic simulator prison we find ourselves in.*

The writer Doreal, claimed to have connections with the Great White Lodge affiliated with the Egyptian priesthood. His position appears to be significant, signing as the Supreme Voice of the Brotherhood. He claims that he was instructed to recover and return the Emerald Tablets and deposit them at the Great Pyramid in Egypt. He was given permission to publish a part of the tablets.

Incredibly, the material composition of the tablets is purportedly emerald green and manufactured through an alchemical process rendering the historical stone impervious to ionization or destruction, resistant to all elements and substances. Accordingly, the atomic structure is permanent, with molecular bonds impervious to breaking. The engraved characters are the Ancient Atlantean language which responds to *"attuned thought waves, releasing the associated mental vibration in the mind of the reader"* [10].

GERALD CLARK

The wisdom contained in the tablets is the foundation of the ancient mysteries. For the one who reads with open eyes and mind, his wisdom shall be increased a hundred fold.

The history of the tablets translated in the following pages is strange and beyond the belief of modern scientists. Their antiquity is stupendous, dating back some 36,000 years B.C. The writer is Thoth, an Atlantean Priest-King, who founded a colony in ancient Egypt after the sinking of the mother country.

He was the builder of the Great Pyramid of Giza, erroneously attributed to Cheops. In it he incorporated his knowledge of the ancient wisdom and also securely secreted records and instruments of ancient Atlantis.

For some 16,000 years, he ruled the ancient race of Egypt, from approximately 52,000 B.C. to 36,000 B.C. During that time, the ancient barbarous race among which he and his followers had settled had been raised to a high degree of civilization.

Thoth was an immortal, that is, he had conquered death, passing only when he willed and even then not through death. His vast wisdom made him ruler over the various Atlantean colonies, including the ones in South and Central America.

As noted, when the time came for him to leave Egypt, he erected the Great Pyramid over the entrance to the Great Halls of

Amenti, placed in it his records, and appointed guards for his secrets from among the highest of his people.

Also, as stated, in later times, the descendants of these guards became the pyramid priests, by which Thoth was deified as the God of Wisdom, The Recorder, by those in the age of darkness which followed his passing. *In legend, the Halls of Amenti became the underworld, the Halls of the gods, where the soul passed after death for judgment.*

During later ages, the ego of Thoth passed into the bodies of men in the manner described in the tablets. As such, he incarnated three times, in his last being known as Hermes, the Thrice-Born.

In this incarnation, he left the writings known to modern occultists as the Emerald Tablets, a later and far lesser exposure of the ancient mysteries.

The tablets translated in this work are ten which were left in the Great Pyramid in the custody of the pyramid priests. The ten are divided into thirteen parts for the sake of convenience.

The last two are so great and far-reaching in their import that at present it is forbidden to release them to the world at large. However, in those contained herein are secrets which will prove of inestimable value to the serious student.

They should be read, not once, but a hundred times for only thus can the true meaning be revealed. A casual reading will give glimpses of beauty, but more intensive study will open avenues of wisdom to the seeker.

But now a word as to how these mighty secrets came to be revealed to modern man after being hidden so long.

Some thirteen hundred years B.C., Egypt, the ancient Khem, was in turmoil and many delegations of priests were sent to other parts of the world.

Among these were some of the pyramid priests who carried with them the Emerald Tablets as a talisman by which they could exercise authority over the less advanced priest-craft of races descended from other Atlantean colonies.

The tablets were understood from legend to give the bearer authority from Thoth.

One particular group of priests bearing the tablets immigrated to South America where they found a flourishing race, the Mayas, who remembered much of the ancient wisdom.

The priests settled and remained among the Mayan people. In the tenth century, the Mayas had thoroughly claimed the Yucatan, and the tablets were placed beneath the altar of one of the great temples of the Sun God.

Following the conquest of the Mayas by the Spaniards, these cities were abandoned and the treasures of the temples forgotten.

It should be understood that the Great Pyramid of Egypt has been and still is a temple of initiation into the mysteries. Jesus, Solomon, Apollonius and others were initiated there.

The writer, Doreal, (who has a connection with the **Great White Lodge** which also works through the pyramid priesthood) was instructed to recover and return to the Great Pyramid the ancient tablets.

This, after adventures which need not be detailed here, was accomplished. Before returning them, he was given permission to translate and retain a copy of the wisdom engraved on the tablets.

This was done in 1925 and only now has permission been given for part to be published. It is expected that many will scoff. Yet the true student will read between the lines and gain wisdom.

If the light is in you, the light which is engraved in these tablets will respond.

Now, a reminder again about the material aspect of the tablets.

They consist of twelve tablets of emerald green, formed from a substance created through alchemical transmutation.

They are imperishable, resistant to all elements and substances. In effect, the atomic and cellular structure is fixed, no change ever taking place.

In this respect, they violate the material law of ionization.

Upon them are engraved characters in the ancient Atlantean language: characters which respond to attuned thought waves, releasing the associated mental vibration in the mind of the reader.

The tablets are fastened together with hoops of golden-colored alloy suspended from a rod of the same material. So much for the material appearance.

The wisdom contained therein is the foundation of the ancient mysteries. And for the one who reads with open eyes and mind, his wisdom shall be increased a hundred-fold.

Read. Believe or not, but read. And the vibration found therein will awaken a response in your soul.

In the following pages, I will reveal some of the mysteries which as yet have only been touched upon lightly either by myself or other teachers or students of truth.

Man's search for understanding of the laws which regulate his life has been unending, yet always just hidden beyond the veil. This veil shields the higher planes from material man's vision the truth that has always existed, ready to be assimilated by those who enlarge their vision by turning inward, not outward, in their search.

In the silence of material senses lies the key to the unveiling of wisdom. He who talks does not know; he who knows does not talk.

The highest knowledge is unutterable, for it exists as an entity in lanes which transcend all material words or symbols.

All symbols are but keys to doors leading to truths, and many times the door is not opened because the key seems so great that the things which are beyond it are not visible.

If we can understand that all keys, all material symbols are manifestations, and are but extensions of a great law and truth, we will begin to develop the vision which will enable us to penetrate beyond the veil.

All things in all universes move according to law, and the law which regulates the movement of the planets is no more immutable than the law which regulates the material expressions of man.

One of the greatest of all Cosmic Laws is that which is responsible for the formation of man as a material being.

The great aim of the mystery schools of all ages has been to reveal the workings of the Law which connect Man the Material and Man the Spiritual.

The connecting link between the Material Man and the Spiritual Man is the Intellectual Man, for the mind partakes of both the material and immaterial qualities.

The aspirant for higher knowledge must develop the intellectual side of his nature and so strengthen his will which is able to concentrate all powers of his being on and in the plane he desires.

The great search for light, life and love only begins on the material plane. Carried to its ultimate, its final goal is complete oneness with the universal consciousness. The foundation in the material is the first step; then comes the higher goal of spiritual attainment.

In the following pages, I will give an interpretation of the Emerald Tablets and their secret, hidden and esoteric meanings.

Concealed in the words of Thoth are many meanings that do not appear on the surface.

Light of knowledge brought to bear upon the Tablets will open many new fields for thought.

"Read and be wise" but only if the light of your own consciousness awakens the deep-seated understanding which is an inherent quality of the soul.

Introduction to the Original Interpretation

Doreal provides a meta-analysis in his introductory interpretation and explanation of the sacred texts. He makes an interesting statement as to the "veil" which has been imposed on mankind's search for meaning. Victor Frankl wrote a seminal book called *"Man's Search for Meaning"* in which he explored the idea of ultimate freedom which he taught could even be found behind the bars of a prisoner of war camp, the event that inspired him to write the book. This need to know our primary questions is seminal. Who are we, how did we get here, and where are we headed as a species. These questions strike at the heart of the quest for life's meaning. According to Doreal:

"Man's search for understanding of the laws which regulate his life has been unending, yet always just beyond the veil which shields the higher plane from material man's vision, the truth has existed, ready to be assimilated by those who enlarge their vision by turning inward, not outward, in their search." [10, page 4]

As discussed in Chapter 3, it should be clear that we are

electrical beings and this composes the holographic veil between the material and spiritual world alluded to by Doreal. *This enslavement is the basis for the supposition that we are segregated from the frequencies which represent higher consciousness, and not just within the visual spectrum either.* This is an electromagnetic issue which manifests in the design of the sensors that we humans are equipped with as meat-MODEMS. Our direct environmental sensors are but a few whose functions include seeing, hearing, touching, tasting, and smelling. Recall as an example that our vision is quite limited, only spanning 400-700 nanometers in wavelength. For those who prefer it in a frequency, 400 nanometers is $7.5x10^{14}$ Hz and 700 nanometers is equivalent to $4.285x10^{14}$ Hz.

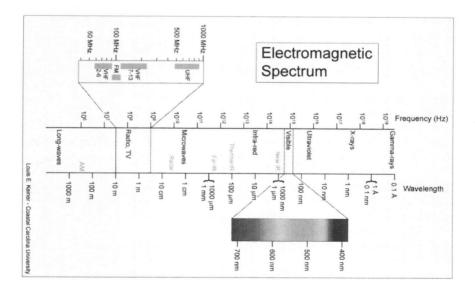

Figure 13: Electromagnetic Visual Spectrum Limitation

As one can plainly see, the visible spectrum for humans is quite narrow. Imagine that we could see into the near infrared or the ultraviolet light range which sandwiches the rainbow color spectrum we perceive. Perhaps we would find out that we are not alone. In this case, the physical visual veil spoken of by Doreal can be understood scientifically. Thus, searching for meaning in the transient material world is discouraged, whereas an internal search for the areas where energy meets matter is where the quest must be focused. So, for those of you headed to the military surplus store to acquire some night vision or infrared binoculars, consider the advice from Doreal. Go within yourself, optimizing the Chakra wavelengths where the energy vortices within the body animate our physical matter.

We hear poorly as a species, limited in frequency from approximately 10 hertz to 20 kilo Hertz. Consider that even dogs hear more effectively than humans and most predatory birds and cats have not only night vision but better range and sensitivity to light. Perhaps if we evolve as a species, or get another genetic upgrade, we could utilize solar radiation via our pineal glands again to regulate our skin color and energy absorption like an iguana. Nature's creatures are far better equipped than the Anunnaki primitive workers are, combat equipped with useful sensors for the electromagnetic spectrum interface to the holographic veiled simulator.

"All symbols are but keys to doors leading to truths, and many times the door is not opened because the key seems too great that the things which are beyond it are not visible. If we can understand that all keys, all material symbols are manifestations, and are but extensions for a great law and truth, we will begin to develop the vision which will enable us to penetrate beyond the veil." [10, page 4]

As far as Doreal's statement about material man's vision and an inward focus, this is reminiscent of the teachings of Jesus in the New Testament as well as Buddhism and other spiritual disciplines from around the globe. As a reminder, controversy arose in the religious community regarding the interpretation of the phrase "The Kingdom of Heaven is Within". This is where energy meets matter, in our physical bodies. The first statement about the physical eye sensitivity range has been discussed by me many times as the quintessential example of our sensor limitation: a visual clamp down by the Anunnaki. We see what they want us to see in the simulator, most control mechanisms are hidden from the populace. If we could visually sense a larger spectrum, what might we discover? Consider the benefit of thermal sights. The military uses this capability projected onto a heads up display or CRT allowing operations in complete darkness, coupled with a pilot night vision system using a noble gas, electricity, and light amplification techniques that allow us to operate like a predatory owl, minus the depth perception one would expect as a binocular viewing telemetric meat-MODEM.

"The great search for light, life and love only begins on the material plane. Carried to its ultimate, its final goal is complete oneness with the universal consciousness. The foundation in the material is the first step; then comes the higher goal of spiritual attainment." [10, page 4]

In my spiritual path, a relational generalization has emerged as I connect the dots regarding this statement. We begin as children establishing a sensory understanding of the objective-physical world. Eventually, if paying attention, our relationship to objects can be categorized as intelligent or not. Generally speaking, where there is order among the objects with which one is given stewardship, then an intelligence is operational. The opposite is also true, in that where there is disorder there is little or no intelligence applied to the material involved in the scenario of one's imagining. No relationship (symmetry) is sought to order one's material world since there is no understanding of the nature of beauty and structure, which I theorize creates function and energy. Thus, functionally the human body is a bi-directional communication vessel that is meant to utilize energy from the environment to augment our feelings of beauty. Compare and contrast the energy and feel of a room that is intentionally

GERALD CLARK

arranged by a trained decorator, optimizing functionality and symmetry, Feng Shui, if you will, with a disheveled dump that has no material order. Beauty is structural symmetry and this applies to inanimate objects as well, optimizing the energetic feel we perceive with our senses. Sensing the difference between the two states is designed to move us toward the truth that we are , indeed, electrical beings.

Once one establishes an intelligent relationship to the material object world, the next relational generalization can then be applied to non-static objects, other beings and animals. This is also a "horizontal" relationship involving stewardship toward other sentient beings in the simulator. Recall in Genesis the Anunnaki declared that mankind would be fruitful and multiply having dominion over the animal kingdom as stewards. Recognizing that all are enslaved in the simulator, a sense of compassion can be fostered for the downtrodden and through a loving heart overcome the judgmental labels we attach to the unwanted in an attempt to make ourselves feel more empowered and in control. This is an illusion. *If you did it not to the least of these you did it not to me is a statement Jesus made and really sticks with me.*

Finally, once the horizontal relationships are experienced, both animate and inanimate, this lesson can be seen in the context of a sequence leading to a higher goal, energy optimization in our

154

bodies, where higher consciousness resides. When we can overcome judgment and begin to empower others along their spiritual paths, we are then ready to work more closely on the vertical relationship with our creators, the Anunnaki. This is where the internal focus leads to a perception of the intelligence broadcast on a different mental frequency. Intelligence is the bridge for the material brain to the electromagnetic spectrum wherein controllers of the layered holographic veil reign supreme. One must be dedicated to the acquisition of knowledge, often hidden in symbolism in plain sight. Concealed in Thoth's written gift to humanity are esoteric meanings. *"Read and be wise" but only if the light of your own consciousness awakens the deep-seated understanding which is an inherent quality of the soul."* [10, page 4].

Tablet I: The History of Thoth, the Atlantean

"The first rubric asks us to come to a higher awareness and to be open to deeper truths."

Thoth introduces himself as an Atlantean master of mysteries and magician, a mighty king and keeper of the records. He states emphatically that he lives from generation to generation sometimes taking a hiatus in the Halls of Amenti. His goal was to preserve his Great Atlantis wisdom for the guidance of those that are to come after his departure from Egypt-Khem, and during his absence. Thoth, having three incarnations, originated in his current manifestation in a material body in the great city of Keor on the island of Undal. He does not divulge how long ago it was, but indicates it was a time far in the past. His father, Thotme, is referenced as the greatest among the children of men, keeper of the great temple. As we know, the Atlanteans were headed by Poseidon-Enki in his island kingdom described by Plato in the Critias. Thus, as was the case in Sumer, Ningishzida-Thoth is clearly Enki's son. This is yet another AKA name for Ea-Nudimud-Enki. Enki-Thotme, dwelling in the great temple of Atlantis, who had the mission of playing liaison between the "Children of Light" and the races of men inhabiting the ten islands.

Thoth's incarnation is distinguished from mankind's, stating that he began as a mighty one of Atlantis living from aeon to aeon, renewing his life in the Halls of Amenti. The source of his Amenti-spawned immortality is given as coming from the river of life that flows eternally onward [10, page 5]. Recall the water of eternal life that Anu offered to the Adapa during his visit to Heaven-Nibiru. Could this be a colloidal solution of monoatomic gold, also known as Starfire Gold? As discussed in my first book, the Anunnaki elite were clearly partaking of a conical bread cake formed from the white power found beneath a stone in the floor of Hathor's Temple on Mount Sinai. The next line brings into question just how many times Thoth has incarnated versus renewing his current incarnation.

A hundred times ten have I descended the dark way that led into light, and as many times have I ascended from the darkness into the light, my strength and power renewed.

Thoth indicates that his renewal process in the Amenti longevity chamber is overdue and that he will be going there soon. His initial audience is disclosed as those in the land of Khem or Egypt, as we now know it. A prophecy is given that in some unknown future time Thoth will rise again, mighty and potent, requiring an accounting of those left behind under the tutelage of the priesthood left to guard the Emerald Tablets. They are warned to keep his doctrine pure and avoid falsely betraying the Emerald

Tablet lessons, or suffer a curse that will befall them.

A brief discussion regarding the fall of Atlantis is presented. Gradually the state of consciousness was eroded in the Kingdoms of Atlantis, being replaced with the spawn of a lower star or state of being. At the end of Plato's historical accounting regarding Atlantis, it becomes clear that the high moral character which was once the aspiration of all island inhabitants versus material gain, came to a cataclysmic end. The reason for the fallen state was attributed to the intermixing of genetic material, leading to a loss of connection to the higher state of consciousness prolific among the more pure-bred citizens. Plato's account ends with Zeus being inserted into a judgmental counsel position which, from what we know of Enlil-Zeus, nothing good could come. Additionally, Thoth indicates other trouble was afoot, claiming that the dweller of Agwanti was summoned and subsequently changed the "flower of life" frequency or intensity or both. Drunvalo Melchizedek wrote two books in a series titled "The Ancient Secret of the Flower of Life" [32-33] in which he describes an energetic grid around the Earth whose origins and structure derive from this ancient symbol. Interestingly enough, I learned how to draw this symbol using only a compass. It was used as artwork on one of the didgeridoos I fabricated out of a Yucca cactus in San Diego, California. See Figure 14 below.

Figure 14: Flower of Life Symbol

Now we proceed to the actual tablet text.

I, THOTH, the Atlantean, master of mysteries,

keeper of records, mighty king, magician,

living from generation to generation,

being about to pass into the halls of Amenti,

set down for the guidance of

those that are to come after,

these records of the mighty wisdom of Great Atlantis.

In the great city of KEOR on the island of UNDAL,

in a time far past, I began this incarnation.

Not as the little men of the present age did

the mighty ones of Atlantis live and die,

but rather from aeon to aeon did they renew

their life in the Halls of Amenti where the river of life
flows eternally onward.

A hundred times ten
have I descended the dark way that led into light,
and as many times have I ascended from the
darkness into the light my strength and power renewed.

Now for a time I descend,
and the men of KHEM (Khem is alchemy in ancient Egypt)
shall know me no more.

But in a time yet unborn will I rise again,
mighty and potent, requiring an accounting
of those left behind me.

Then beware, O men of KHEM,
if ye have falsely betrayed my teaching,
for I shall cast ye down from your high estate
into the darkness of the caves from whence ye came.

Betray not my secrets
to the men of the North
or the men of the South
lest my curse fall upon ye.

Remember and heed my words,
for surely will I return again
and require of thee that which ye guard.
Aye, even from beyond time and
from beyond death will I return,
rewarding or punishing
as ye have requited your trust.

Great were my people in the ancient days,
great beyond the conception of the
little people now around me;
knowing the wisdom of old,
seeking far within the heart of infinity
knowledge that belonged to Earth's youth.

Wise were we with the wisdom
of the Children of Light who dwelt among us.
Strong were we with the power drawn
from the eternal fire.

And of all these, greatest among the
children of men was my father, THOTME,
keeper of the great temple,
link between the Children of Light
who dwelt within the temple and the
races of men who inhabited the ten islands.

Mouthpiece, after the Three,
of the Dweller of UNAL,
speaking to the Kings
with the voice that must be obeyed.

Grew I there from a child into manhood,
being taught by my father the elder mysteries,
until in time there grew within the fire of wisdom,
until it burst into a consuming flame.

Naught desired I but the attainment of wisdom.
Until on a great day the command came from the
Dweller of the Temple that I be brought before him.
Few there were among the children of men
who had looked upon that mighty face and lived,
for not as the sons of men are the
Children of Light when they are not incarnate
in a physical body.

Chosen was I from the sons of men,
taught by the Dweller so that his
purposes might be fulfilled,
purposes yet unborn in the womb of time.

Long ages I dwelt in the Temple,
learning ever and yet ever more wisdom,

until I, too, approached the light emitted
from the great fire.

Taught me he, the path to Amenti,
the underworld where the great king sits
upon his throne of might.

Deep I bowed in homage before the Lords of Life
and the Lords of Death,
receiving as my gift the Key of Life.

Free was I of the Halls of Amenti,
bound not by death to the circle of life.
Far to the stars I journeyed until
space and time became as naught.

Then having drunk deep of the cup of wisdom,
I looked into the hearts of men and there found I
greater mysteries and was glad.
For only in the Search for Truth could my Soul
be stilled and the flame within be quenched.

Down through the ages I lived,
seeing those around me taste of the cup
of death and return again in the light of life.

Gradually from the Kingdoms of Atlantis passed waves
of consciousness that had been one with me,
only to be replaced by spawn of a lower star.

In obedience to the law,
the word of the Master grew into flower.
Downward into the darkness turned the
thoughts of the Atlanteans,
Until at last in this wrath arose from his AGWANTI,
the Dweller, (this word has no English equivalent;
it means a state of detachment)
speaking The Word, calling the power.

Deep in Earth's heart, the sons of Amenti heard,
and hearing, directing the changing of the flower of fire
that burns eternally, changing and shifting, using the LOGOS,
until that great fire changed its direction.

Over the world then broke the great waters,
drowning and sinking,
changing Earth's balance
until only the Temple of Light was left
standing on the great mountain on UNDAL
still rising out of the water;
some there were who were living,
saved from the rush of the fountains.

Called to me then the Master, saying:

Gather ye together my people.

Take them by the arts ye have learned of far across the waters,

until ye reach the land of the hairy barbarians,

dwelling in caves of the desert.

Follow there the plan that ye know of.

Gathered I then my people and

entered the great ship of the Master.

Upward we rose into the morning.

Dark beneath us lay the Temple.

Suddenly over it rose the waters.

Vanished from Earth,

until the time appointed,

was the great Temple.

Fast we fled toward the sun of the morning,

until beneath us lay the land of the children of KHEM.

Raging, they came with cudgels and spears,

lifted in anger seeking to slay and utterly destroy the Sons of

Atlantis.

Then raised I my staff and directed a ray of vibration,

striking them still in their tracks as fragments

of stone of the mountain.

Then spoke I to them in words calm and peaceful,
telling them of the might of Atlantis,
saying we were children of the Sun and its messengers.
Cowed I them by my display of magic-science,
until at my feet they groveled, when I released them.

Long dwelt we in the land of KHEM,
long and yet long again.
Until obeying the commands of the Master,
who while sleeping yet lives eternally,
I sent from me the Sons of Atlantis,
sent them in many directions,
that from the womb of time wisdom
might rise again in her children.

Long time dwelt I in the land of KHEM,
doing great works by the wisdom within me.
Upward grew into the light of knowledge
the children of KHEM,
watered by the rains of my wisdom.

Blasted I then a path to Amenti so
that I might retain my powers,
living from age to age a Sun of Atlantis,
keeping the wisdom, preserving the records.

Great grew the sons of KHEM,
conquering the people around them,
growing slowly upwards in Soul force.

Now for a time I go from among them into
the dark halls of Amenti,
deep in the halls of the Earth,
before the Lords of the powers,
face to face once again with the Dweller.

Raised I high over the entrance, a doorway, a gateway
leading down to Amenti.

Few there would be with courage to dare it,
few pass the portal to dark Amenti.
Raised over the passage, I, a mighty pyramid,
using the power that overcomes Earth force (gravity).
Deep and yet deeper place I a force-house or chamber;
from it carved I a circular passage
reaching almost to the great summit.

There in the apex, set I the crystal,
sending the ray into the "Time-Space,"
drawing the force from out of the ether,
concentrating upon the gateway to Amenti.

Other chambers I built and left vacant to all seeming,
yet hidden within them are the keys to Amenti.
He who in courage would dare the dark realms,
let him be purified first by long fasting.

Lie in the sarcophagus of stone in my chamber.
Then reveal I to him the great mysteries.
Soon shall he follow to where I shall meet him,
even in the darkness of Earth shall I meet him, I,
Thoth, Lord of Wisdom, meet him and hold him
and dwell with him always.

Builded I the Great Pyramid,
patterned after the pyramid of Earth force,
burning eternally so that it, too,
might remain through the ages.

In it, I builded my knowledge of "Magic-Science"
so that I might be here when again I return from Amenti,
Aye, while I sleep in the Halls of Amenti,
my Soul roaming free will incarnate,
dwell among men in this form or another. (Hermes, thrice-born.)

Emissary on Earth am I of the Dweller,
fulfilling his commands so many might be lifted.
Now return I to the halls of Amenti,

leaving behind me some of my wisdom.
Preserve ye and keep ye the command of the Dweller:
Lift ever upwards your eyes toward the light.

Surely in time, ye are one with the Master,
surely by right ye are one with the Master,
surely by right yet are one with the ALL.

Now, I depart from ye.
Know my commandments,
keep them and be them,
and I will be with you,
helping and guiding you into the Light.

Now before me opens the portal.
Go I down in the darkness of night.

Tablet II: The Halls of Amenti

According to Thoth, mankind was observed to be enslaved and an intervention plan was hatched causing thirty-two of the Anunnaki benevolent overseers to intercede on our behalf. According to the Tablet, their higher dimensional energy was used to manifest in a container body here on Earth, plotting to free the enslaved primitive workers caught up the toils of the holographic simulator.

During their mission, it appears that significant guarded underground structures were carved deep within the Earth, established as their residences away from the primitive workers. Within the underground chamber Thoth indicates that he place a frequency emanating (crystal) to drive back the one installed by the dark ones. This is the basis for the flower of life symbol written about by Drunvalo Melchezidek, whose emitted rays bathed the thirty-two Children of Light living therein. The energy appears to renew their manifested bodies. How interesting! Additionally, the Masters living underground have the ability to astral project out of their bodies to have encounters with mankind. Specifically, they can occupy the primitive worker containers in order to teach and guide them in their evolutionary spiritual paths.

It is claimed that those who grow out of darkness are the ones they seek to help, guiding them by wisdom and knowledge to become a Master of Life able to dwell with the infinite helping agents in their radiant underground rejuvenation hall. An additional seven Lords sharing their mission, hailing from the Space-Time above, are described seated within the flower of life radiating device in the same hall. A final cast of nine additional beings are also present to assist in Thoth's mission. He affiliates them with planetary cycles, probably similar to the Satya Yuga and Kali Yuga time tracking mechanisms. The lead agent owns the ninth cycle appointed over cycle Account Managers Three, Four, Five, and Six, Seven and Eight. These entities, a total of seven, coincide with the human quantized consciousness levels described as Chakras. They are the consciousness cops that judge and weigh the spiritual readiness of the seeker before permitting progression to the next nerve ganglia or Chakra.

Thoth expounds on his ascendency path to meet the Master at which time he specifies the work he wants to do as an infinite being able to come and go as he pleases, freed from the Halls of Amenti, renewing his life force in the flower of life renewal chamber at will. "Let me be a teacher of men" leading them to the light. I am thankful for his decision not to abandon the primitive workers who have toiled and suffered greatly in darkness.

Deep in Earth's heart lie the Halls of Amenti,
far 'neath the islands of sunken Atlantis,
Halls of the Dead and halls of the living,
bathed in the fire of the infinite ALL.

Far in a past time, lost in the space time,
the Children of Light looked down on the world.
Seeing the children of men in their bondage,
bound by the force that came from beyond.
Knew they that only by freedom from bondage
could man ever rise from the Earth to the Sun.

Down they descended and created bodies,
taking the semblance of men as their own.
The Masters of everything said after their forming:

"We are they who were formed from the space-dust,
partaking of life from the infinite ALL;
living in the world as children of men,
like and yet unlike the children of men."

Then for a dwelling place, far 'neath the earth crust,
blasted great spaces they by their power,
spaces apart from the children of men.

Surrounded them by forces and power,

shielded from harm they the Halls of the Dead.

Side by side then, placed they other spaces,

filled them with Life and with Light from above.

Builded they then the Halls of Amenti,

that they might dwell eternally there,

living with life to eternity's end.

Thirty and two were there of the children,

sons of Lights who had come among men,

seeking to free from the bondage of darkness

those who were bound by the force from beyond.

Deep in the Halls of Life grew a flower, flaming,

expanding, driving backward the night.

Placed in the center, a ray of great potence, Life

giving, Light giving, filling with power all who came near it.

Placed they around it thrones, two and thirty,

places for each of the Children of Light,

placed so that they were bathed in the radiance,

filled with the Life from the eternal Light.

There time after time placed they their first created bodies

so that they might by filled with the Spirit of Life.

One hundred years out of each thousand must the

Life-giving Light flame forth on their bodies.
Quickening, awakening the Spirit of Life.

There in the circle from aeon to aeon,
sit the Great Masters,
living a life not known among men.
There in the Halls of Life they lie sleeping;
free flows their Soul through the bodies of men.

Time after time, while their bodies lie sleeping,
incarnate they in the bodies of men.
Teaching and guiding onward and upward,
out of the darkness into the light.

There in the Hall of Life, filled with their wisdom,
known not to the races of man, living forever 'neath the cold fire
of life, sit the Children of Light.
Times there are when they awaken,
come from the depths to be lights among men,
infinite they among finite men.

He who by progress has grown from the darkness,
lifted himself from the night into light,
free is he made of the Halls of Amenti,
free of the Flower of Light and of Life.

Guided he then, by wisdom and knowledge,
passes from men, to the Master of Life.

There he may dwell as one with the Masters,
free from the bonds of the darkness of night.
Seated within the flower of radiance sit seven
Lords from the Space-Times above us,
helping and guiding through infinite Wisdom,
the pathway through time of the children of men.

Mighty and strange, they,
veiled with their power,
silent, all-knowing,
drawing the Life force,
different yet one with the
children of men.
Aye, different, and yet One
with the Children of Light.

Custodians and watchers of the force of man's bondage,
ready to loose when the light has been reached.
First and most mighty,
sits the Veiled Presence, Lord of Lords,
the infinite Nine, over the other from each
the Lords of the Cycles;

Three, Four, Five, and Six, Seven, Eight,
each with his mission, each with his powers,
guiding, directing the destiny of man.
There sit they, mighty and potent,
free of all time and space.

Not of this world they,
yet akin to it,
Elder Brothers they,
of the children of men.
Judging and weighing,
they with their wisdom,
watching the progress
of Light among men.

There before them was I led by the Dweller,
watched him blend with ONE from above.

Then from HE came forth a voice saying:
"Great art thou, Thoth, among children of men.
Free henceforth of the Halls of Amenti,
Master of Life among children of men.
Taste not of death except as thou will it,
drink thou of Life to Eternity's end,
Henceforth forever is Life,

thine for the taking.
Henceforth is Death at the call of thy hand.

Dwell here or leave here when thou desireth,
free is Amenti to the son of man.
Take thou up Life in what form thou desireth,
Child of the Light that has grown among men.
Choose thou thy work, for all should must labor,
never be free from the pathway of Light.

One step thou has gained on the long pathway upward,
infinite now is the mountain of Light.
Each step thou taketh but heightens the mountain;
all of thy progress but lengthens the goal.

Approach ye ever the infinite Wisdom,
ever before thee recedes the goal.
Free are ye made now of the Halls of Amenti
to walk hand in hand with the Lords of the world,
one in one purpose, working together,
bring of Light to the children of men."

Then from his throne came one of the Masters,
taking my hand and leading me onward,
through all the Halls of the deep hidden land.

Led he me through the Halls of Amenti,
showing the mysteries that are known not to man.

Through the dark passage, downward he led me,
into the Hall where site the dark Death.
Vast as space lay the great Hall before me,
walled by darkness but yet filled with Light.

Before me arose a great throne of darkness,
veiled on it sat a figure of night.
Darker than darkness sat the great figure,
dark with a darkness not of the night.
Before it then paused the Master, speaking

The Word that brings about Life, saying;
"Oh, master of darkness,
guide of the way from Life unto Life,
before thee I bring a Sun of the morning.
Touch him not ever with the power of night.
Call not his flame to the darkness of night.
Know him, and see him,
one of our brothers,
lifted from darkness into the Light.
Release thou his flame from its bondage,
free let it flame through the darkness of night."

Raised then the hand of the figure,
forth came a flame that grew clear and bright.
Rolled back swiftly the curtain of darkness,
unveiled the Hall from the darkness of night.

Then grew in the great space before me,
flame after flame, from the veil of the night.
Uncounted millions leaped they before me,
some flaming forth as flowers of fire.

Others there were that shed a dim radiance,
flowing but faintly from out of the night.

Some there were that faded swiftly;
others that grew from a small spark of light.
Each surrounded by its dim veil of darkness,
yet flaming with light that could never be quenched.
Coming and going like fireflies in springtime,
filled they with space with Light and with Life.

Then spoke a voice, mighty and solemn, saying:
"These are lights that are souls among men,
growing and fading, existing forever,
changing yet living, through death into life.
When they have bloomed into flower,
reached the zenith of growth in their life,

swiftly then send I my veil of darkness,
shrouding and changing to new forms of life.

Steadily upward throughout the ages, growing,
expanding into yet another flame,
lighting the darkness with yet greater power,
quenched yet unquenched by the veil of the night.

So grows the soul of man ever upward,
quenched yet unquenched by the darkness of night.

I, Death, come, and yet I remain not,
for life eternal exists in the ALL;
only an obstacle, I in the pathway,
quick to be conquered by the infinite light.

Awaken, O flame that burns ever inward,
flame forth and conquer the veil of the night."

Then in the midst of the flames
in the darkness grew there one that
drove forth the night, flaming, expanding,
ever brighter, until at last was nothing but Light.

Then spoke my guide, the voice of the master:
See your own soul as it grows in the light,
free now forever from the Lord of the night.

Forward he led me through many great spaces
filled with the mysteries of the Children of Light;
mysteries that man may never yet know of until
he, too, is a Sun of the Light.

Backward then HE led me into the Light
of the hall of the Light.
Knelt I then before the great Masters,
Lords of ALL from the cycles above.

Spoke HE then with words of great power saying:

Thou hast been made free of the Halls of Amenti.
Choose thou thy work among the children of men.

Then spoke I:
O, great master,
let me be a teacher of men,
leading then onward and upward until they,
too, are lights among men;
freed from the veil of the night that surrounds them,
flaming with light that shall shine among men.

Spoke to me then the voice:
Go, as yet will. So be it decreed.
Master are ye of your destiny,
free to take or reject at will.

Take ye the power, take ye the wisdom.
Shine as a light among the children of men.

Upward then, led me the Dweller.
Dwelt I again among children of men,
teaching and showing some of my wisdom;
Sun of the Light, a fire among men.

Now again I tread the path downward,
seeking the light in the darkness of night.
Hold ye and keep ye, preserve my record,
guide shall it be to the children of men.

Tablet III: The Key of Wisdom

Thoth points out the importance of wisdom, equating it with power and for humans to avoid the ego trap of being prideful, remaining open to knowledge irrespective of the source. We are counseled to follow our hearts living an extraordinary life of Love, abiding by the law and to stand up and speak out against evil. Greatness among men is characterized by possessing knowledge and gentleness and sharing it with the broad community.

A clue to start the path to freedom is to distinguish by study the difference between matter and energy. The energetic key to immortality is specified similar to our physics concept of the law of conservation of energy. Energy is neither created nor destroyed, it merely changes state which is true for us electrical meat- MODEMs which they designed as well. We are analogized to having a star in our body that can be spawned to a bright flame leading to the understanding that we are eternal energy derived from the infinite One. Matter is designated as a transient mirage; continuity and change are the wheels in perpetual motion.

The seven seated in the flower of life chamber mentioned in the previous tablet, the masters of the cycles, are listed along with their specific functional roles. The numbers assigned to the beings appear to coincide with a total of nine galactic or planetary cycles, only seven of which are present ranging from 3-9 versus 1-7. I believe these beings are affiliated with the Mayan underworld frequencies, of which there were nine. Therefore, the numbers could represent the Mayan 3rd Sun cycle to the 9th Sun cycle. This would imply our Chakra frequencies are controlled by them similar to what I disclosed in The Anunnaki of Nibiru with the added affiliation that the Hindu Gods were functionally controlling the same quantized energy levels for their flock. Could the seven masters of the Space-Time cycles have an AKA name as a Hindu deity, probably so? Let us continue.

I, Thoth, the Atlantean,
give of my wisdom,
give of my knowledge,
give of my power.
Freely I give to the children of men.
Give that they, too, might have wisdom
to shine through the world from the veil of the night.

Wisdom is power and power is wisdom,
one with each other, perfecting the whole.

Be thou not proud, O man, in thy wisdom.
Discourse with the ignorant as well as the wise.
If one comes to thee full of knowledge,
listen and heed, for wisdom is all.

Keep thou not silent when evil is spoken for Truth
like the sunlight shines above all.
He who over-steppeth the Law shall be punished,
for only through Law comes the freedom of men.
Cause thou not fear for fear is a bondage,
a fetter that binds the darkness to men.

Follow thine heart during thy lifetime.
Do thou more than is commanded of thee.
When thou hast gained riches,
follow thou thine heart,
for all these are of no avail if
thine heart be weary.
Diminish thou not the time of
following thine heart.
It is abhorred of the soul.

They that are guided go not astray,
but they that are lost cannot find a straight path.
If thou go among men, make for thyself,
Love, the beginning and end of the heart.

If one cometh unto thee for council,
let him speak freely,
that the thing for which he hath
come to thee may be done.

If he hesitates to open his heart to thee,
it is because thou, the judge, doeth the wrong.

Repeat thou not extravagant speech,
neither listen thou to it,
for it is the utterance of one
not in equilibrium.
Speak thou not of it,
so that he before thee may know wisdom.

Silence is of great profit.
An abundance of speech profiteth nothing.
Exalt not thine heart above the children of men,
lest it be brought lower than the dust.

If thou be great among men,
be honored for knowledge and gentleness.
If thou seeketh to know the nature of a friend,
ask not his companion,
but pass a time alone with him.
Debate with him,
testing his heart by his words and his bearing.

That which goeth into the store-house must come forth,
and the things that are thine must be shared with a friend.

Knowledge is regarded by the fool as ignorance,
and the things that are profitable are to him hurtful.
He liveth in death.
It is therefore his food.

The wise man lets his heart overflow
but keeps silent his mouth.
O man, list to the voice of wisdom;
list to the voice of light.

Mysteries there are in the Cosmos
that unveiled fill the world with their light.
Let he who would be free from the bonds of darkness
first divine the material from the immaterial,
the fire from the earth;
for know ye that as earth descends to earth,
so also fire ascends unto
fire and becomes one with fire.
He who knows the fire that is within
himself shall ascend unto the eternal fire
and dwell in it eternally.

Fire, the inner fire,
is the most potent of all force,
for it overcometh all things and
penetrates to all things of the Earth.

Man supports himself only on that which resists.
So Earth must resist man else he existeth not.

All eyes do not see with the same vision,
for to one an object appears of
one form and color
and to a different eye of another.
So also the infinite fire,
changing from color to color,
is never the same from day to day.

Thus, speak I, THOTH, of my wisdom,
for a man is a fire burning bright
through the night;
never is quenched in the veil of the darkness,
never is quenched by the veil of the night.

Into men's hearts, I looked by my wisdom,
found them not free from the bondage of strife.
Free from the toils, thy fire, O my brother,
lest it be buried in the shadow of night!

Hark ye, O man, and list to this wisdom:
where do name and form cease?
Only in consciousness, invisible,
an infinite force of radiance bright.

The forms that ye create by brightening
thy vision are truly effects that follow thy cause.

Man is a star bound to a body,
until in the end,
he is freed through his strife.
Only by struggle and toiling thy
utmost shall the star within thee
bloom out in new life.
He who knows the commencement of all things,
free is his star from the realm of night.

Remember, O man, that all which exists
is only another form of that which exists not.
Everything that has being is passing into yet other
being and thou thyself are not an exception.

Consider the Law, for all is Law.
Seek not that which is not of the Law,
for such exists only in the illusions of the senses.
Wisdom cometh to all her children
even as they cometh unto wisdom.

All through the ages,
the light has been hidden.
Awake, O man, and be wise.

Deep in the mysteries of life have I traveled,
seeking and searching for that which is hidden.

List ye, O man, and be wise.
Far 'neath the earth crust,
in the Halls of Amenti,
mysteries I saw that are hidden from men.

Oft have I journeyed the deep hidden passage,
looked on the Light that is Life among men.
There 'neath the flowers of Life ever living,
searched I the hearts and the secrets of men.
Found I that man is but living in darkness,
light of the great fire is hidden within.

Before the Lords of hidden Amenti
learned I the wisdom I give unto men.

Masters are they of the great Secret Wisdom,
brought from the future of infinity's end.
Seven are they, the Lords of Amenti,
overlords they of the Children of Morning,
Suns of the Cycles, Masters of Wisdom.

Formed are not they as the children of men?
THREE, FOUR, FIVE AND SIX, SEVEN,
EIGHT, NINE are the titles of the Masters of men.

Far from the future, formless yet forming,
came they as teachers for the children of men.
Live they forever, yet not of the living,
bound not to life and yet free from death.

Rule they forever with infinite wisdom,
bound yet not bound to the dark Halls of Death.
Life they have in them, yet life that is not life,
free from all are the Lords of the ALL.

Forth from them came forth the Logos,
instruments they of the power o'er all.
Vast is their countenance,
yet hidden in smallness,
formed by a forming, known yet unknown.

THREE holds the key of all hidden magic,
creator he of the halls of the Dead;
sending forth power, shrouding with darkness,
binding the souls of the children of men;
sending the darkness, binding the soul force;
director of negative to the children of men.

FOUR is he who looses the power.
Lord, he, of Life to the children of men.

Light is his body, flame is his countenance;
freer of souls to the children of men.

FIVE is the master, the Lord of all magic -
Key to The Word that resounds among men.

SIX is the Lord of Light, the hidden pathway,
path of the souls of the children of men.

SEVEN is he who is Lord of the vastness,
master of Space and the key of the Times.

EIGHT is he who orders the progress;
weighs and balances the journey of men.

NINE is the father, vast he of countenance,
forming and changing from out of the formless.

Meditate on the symbols I give thee.
Keys are they, though hidden from men.

Reach ever upward, O Soul of the morning.
Turn thy thoughts upward to Light and to Life.
Find in the keys of the numbers I bring thee,
light on the pathway from life unto life.

Seek ye with wisdom.
Turn thy thoughts inward.
Close not thy mind to the flower of Light.

Place in thy body a thought-formed picture.
Think of the numbers that lead thee to Life.

Clear is the pathway to he who has wisdom.
Open the door to the Kingdom of Light.

Pour forth thy flame as a Sun of the morning.
Shut out the darkness and live in the day.

Take thee, O man! As part of thy being,
the Seven who are but are not as they seem.
Opened, O man! Have I my wisdom.
Follow the path in the way I have led.

Masters of Wisdom,
SUN of the MORNING LIGHT and LIFE
to the children of men.

Tablet IV: The Space Born

Thoth the immortal describes his childhood on Atlantis and his disposition toward gaining cosmic knowledge. He uses the term SUN and SUN of the Morning as a self-referential terms. This analogy to the New Testament Jesus sounds familiar, and predates the Isaiah 14:12 King James Version (KJV) and New International Versions (NIV) by thousands of years. In the Bible reference we find the KJV calling out the fallen destructive being Lucifer whose name gets replaced with Son of the morning star. I believe this was done to hide Enlil's other namesake and to overshadow Thoth's role and symbolism who also calling himself *the star of the morning*.

The argument that modern translations use to deny the deity of Christ is based on connecting several dots. First, In Isaiah 14:12 in the KJV we read:

"How art thou fallen from heaven, O Lucifer, son of the morning? How art thou cut down to the ground, which didst weaken the nations?"

Modern translations—except for the New KJV—have something like *"day star"* or "morning star" instead of the name *"Lucifer"*. The KJV advocates claim that Isaiah 14:12 must be a prophecy about the devil falling from heaven based on Luke 10:18

where Jesus tells his disciples, *"I saw Satan fall like lightning from heaven."* In Rev 9:1 we read, *"I saw a star fallen from heaven to earth, and he was given the key to the shaft of the bottomless pit"* (ESV). These New Testament passages seem to be alluding to Isaiah 14:12, connecting the fall of the one mentioned there with the fall of Satan [23].

Back to Thoth as a child, it appears that he began experimenting as a child having out of the body experiences (OOBEs) exploring what Robert Monroe in his book *Journeys Out of the Body* [30] discusses as Locales 1-3. During his OOBE travels, he discovers the mathematical order in the Cosmos, the "As Above" portion discovery that later gets connected to Earth inhabitants experiencing the same order from the phrase "So Below." This means the same laws governing planetary circuits also energetically govern mankind's physical body. This is a focus on the energy that animates all matter, planets and their peoples. A generalization is noted by Thoth that all the beings on various planets, some more successful than others, are struggling toward the same evolution of consciousness goals we humans embrace on Earth. He discusses meeting some more evolved beings, highly scientific, who fashioned their own space traveling vessel, creating fabulous cities out of thin air and manifesting life in all its varied forms at will using a mere image in their minds to make it so!

Thoth reminds us that we too are children of the Infinite Cosmic Light and our heritage is to return to the Source. He specifies that the pathway involves achieving wisdom and being open to the flower of life and its ability to extend our consciousness, a broadcast frequency if you will. We are instructed to meditate silently and fast as necessary to free ourselves of desires. Then he provides the borderland sleep state formula that Robert Monroe uses to leave his body in an OOBE triggered by vibrations. A prayer is suggested for the attainment of wisdom. This is a good idea to manifest your intentions before leaving the body. Also declaring that only benevolent beings are sought helps reduce the fear factor for those trying the OOBE for the first time.

List ye, O man, to the voice of wisdom,
list to the voice of THOTH, the Atlantean.

Freely I give to thee of my wisdom,
gathered from the time and space of this cycle;
master of mysteries, SUN of the morning,
living forever, a child of the LIGHT,
shining with brightness, star of the morning,

THOTH the teacher of men, is of ALL.
Long time ago, I in my childhood,

lay 'neath the stars on long-buried ATLANTIS,
dreaming of mysteries far above men.

Then in my heart grew there a great longing to
conquer the pathway that led to the stars.
Year after year, I sought after wisdom,
seeking new knowledge, following the way,
until at last my SOUL, in great travail,
broke from its bondage and bounded away.

Free was I from the bondage of earth-men.
Free from the body, I flashed through the night.
Unlocked at last for me was the star-space.
Free was I from the bondage of night.
Now to the end of space sought I wisdom,
far beyond knowledge of finite man.

Far into space, my SOUL traveled freely
into infinity's circle of light.
Strange, beyond knowledge, were some of the planets,
great and gigantic, beyond dreams of men.

Yet found I Law, in all of its beauty, working
through and among them as here among men.

Flashed forth my soul through infinity's beauty,
far through space
I flew with my thoughts.

Rested I there on a planet of beauty.
Strains of harmony filled all the air.

Shapes there were, moving in Order,
great and majestic as stars in the night;
mounting in harmony, ordered equilibrium,
symbols of the Cosmic, like unto Law.

Many the stars I passed in my journey,
many the races of men on their worlds;
some reaching high as stars of the morning,
some falling low in the blackness of night.

Each and all of them struggling upward,
gaining the heights and plumbing the depths,
moving at times in realms of brightness,
living through darkness, gaining the Light.

Know, O man, that Light is thine heritage.
Know that darkness is only a veil.
Sealed in thine heart is brightness eternal,
waiting the moment of freedom to conquer,
waiting to rend the veil of the night.

Some I found who had conquered the ether.
Free of space were they while yet they were men.
Using the force that is the foundation of ALL things,
far in space constructed they a planet,
drawn by the force that flows through the ALL;
condensing, coalescing the ether into forms,
that grew as they willed.

Outstripping in science, they, all of the races,
mighty in wisdom, sons of the stars.
Long time I paused, watching their wisdom.
Saw them create from out of the ether cities
gigantic of rose and gold.
Formed forth from the primal element,
base of all matter, the ether far flung.

Far in the past, they had conquered the ether,
freed themselves from the bondage of toil;
formed in their mind only a picture and swiftly
created, it grew.

Forth then, my soul sped, throughout the Cosmos,
seeing ever, new things and old;
learning that man is truly space-born,
a Sun of the Sun,
a child of the stars.

Know ye, O man, whatever form ye inhabit,
surely it is one with the stars.

Thy bodies are nothing but planets revolving
around their central suns.

When ye have gained the light of all wisdom,
free shall ye be to shine in the ether --
one of the Suns that light outer darkness --
one of the space-born grown into Light.

Just as the stars in time lose their brilliance,
light passing from them in to the great source,
so, O man, the soul passes onward,
leaving behind the darkness of night.

Formed forth ye, from the primal ether,
filled with the brilliance that
flows from the source,
bound by the ether coalesced around,
yet ever it flames until at last it is free.

Lift up your flame from out of the darkness,
fly from the night and ye shall be free.

Traveled I through the space-time,
knowing my soul at last was set free,

knowing that now might I pursue wisdom.

Until at last, I passed to a plane,

hidden from knowledge,

known not to wisdom,

extension beyond all that we know.

Now, O man, when I had this knowing,

happy my soul grew,

for now I was free.

Listen, ye space-born,

list to my wisdom:

know ye not that ye, too, will be free.

List ye again, O man, to my wisdom,

that hearing, ye too, might live and be free.

Not of the earth are ye -- earthy,

but child of the Infinite Cosmic Light.

Know ye not, O man, of your heritage?

Know ye not ye are truly the Light?

Sun of the Great Sun, when ye gain wisdom,

truly aware of your kinship with Light.

Now, to ye, I give knowledge,

freedom to walk in the path I have trod,

showing ye truly how by my striving,
I trod the path that leads to the stars.

Hark ye, O man, and know of thy bondage,
know how to free thyself from the toils.
Out of the darkness shall ye rise upward,
one with the Light and one with the stars.

Follow ye ever the path of wisdom.
Only by this can ye rise from below.
Ever man's destiny leads him onward
into the Curves of Infinity's ALL.

Know ye, O man, that all space is ordered.
Only by Order are ye One with the ALL.
Order and Balance are the Law of the Cosmos.
Follow and ye shall be One with the ALL.

He who would follow the pathway of wisdom,
open must be he to the flower of life,
extending his consciousness out of the darkness,
flowing through time and space in the ALL.

Deep in the silence,
first ye must linger until at last ye
are free from desire,
free from the longing to speak in the silence.

Conquer by silence, the bondage of words.
Abstaining from eating until we have conquered
desire for food, that is bondage of soul.

Then lie ye down in the darkness.
Close ye your eyes from the rays of the Light.
Centre thy soul-force in the place of thine consciousness,
shaking it free from the bonds of the night.

Place in thy mind-place the image thou desireth.
Picture the place thou desireth to see.
Vibrate back and forth with thy power.
Loosen the soul from out of its night.
Fiercely must thou shake with all of thy power
until at last thy soul shall be free.

Mighty beyond words is the flame of the Cosmic,
hanging in planes, unknown to man;
mighty and balanced, moving in Order,
music of harmonies, far beyond man.

Speaking with music, singing with color,
flame from the beginning of Eternity's ALL.
Spark of the flame art thou, O my children,
burning with color and living with music.
List to the voice and thou shalt be free.

Consciousness free is fused with the Cosmic,
One with the Order and Law of the ALL.
Knew ye not man, that out of the darkness,
Light shall flame forth, a symbol of ALL.

Pray ye this prayer for attaining of wisdom.
Pray for the coming of Light to the ALL.

Mighty SPIRIT of LIGHT that shines through the
Cosmos, draw my flame closer in harmony to thee.
Lift up my fire from out of the darkness,
magnet of fire that is One with the ALL.
Lift up my soul, thou mighty and potent.
Child of the Light, turn not away.
Draw me in power to melt in thy furnace;
One with all things and all things
in One, fire of the life-strain and
One with the Brain.

When ye have freed thy soul from its bondage,
know that for ye the darkness is gone.
Ever through space ye may seek wisdom,
bound not be fetters forged in the flesh.

Onward and upward into the morning, free flash,
O Soul, to the realms of Light. Move thou in Order,

move thou in Harmony, freely shalt move
with the Children of Light.

Seek ye and know ye, my KEY of Wisdom.
Thus, O man, ye shall surely be free.

Tablet V: The Dweller of UNAL

Thoth introduces us to a past Atlantean King of nations and master of wisdom SUNTAL, the Master of UNAL. He was able to occupy bodies as one among men. Thoth meets a Master named HORLET endowed with the KEY of WISDOM. HORLET chose three disciples who took fifteen years to train and graduate where they occupied the Island of Undal as Light Bearers and teachers. Thoth was summoned by one of the three HORLET disciples which elevated his knowledge base tremendously. HORLET could manifest buildings and object with his mind using the power of YTOLAN. The DWELLER of Undal assigns Thoth to be their preserver of wisdom through the ages of darkness, kind of like what we have experienced throughout the entire last Zodiacal house of Pisces.

While dwelling in the Temple, exploring all avenues to higher wisdom, he encounters some bad seed Atlanteans summoning dark forces that would lead to opening forbidden gateways to Earth's destruction. The DWELLER finds out about the ploy, summons his three disciples, and intervenes by visiting the Seven Lords in the Halls of Amenti commanding a change to the Earth's balance-orbit. This event caused a watery death for the remaining Atlanteans, whose destructive power is commemorated throughout history. Only the island of UNAL survived the flood spawned by halting or slowing the angular momentum of the Earth. Some Light bearers were saved to be used later. Thoth was then given the mission to take the sacred wisdom and leave UNDAL, going forth as a teacher of men. How noble is that? He is ordered to gather the sons of Atlantis and their precious records and then departs in a space craft headed for the land of KHEM (Egypt). He describes hiding his spaceship in the Earth below the Sphinx, placing the sacred records below the Pyramids, and raising the children of KHEM to the LIGHT. A prophecy is given by Thoth in which the craft will be used in a future time to easily smite some invaders from the deep. He also gives us an Indiana Jones scavenger hunt task to take the KEY of the SEVEN to open the hidden records chamber. Based on some data disclosed later in this book, we know that the records from Atlantis were derived from Enki's twin pillars at his Poseidon Temple. Eventually the wisdom from Thoth's father Poseidon, carved on the twin Atlantean pillars for all to see, made its way to the actual Emerald Tablets which you, the fine reader, are assimilating now on your way to the LIGHT. He hid them in the Pyramid of Giza as stated. This connects to the Doreal claim to have been allowed to make a copy of the Tablets before returning them to their rightful place, chosen by Thoth the author.

Oft dream I of buried Atlantis,
lost in the ages that have passed into night.
Aeon on aeon thou existed in beauty,
a light shining through the darkness of night.

Mighty in power, ruling the earth-born,
Lord of the Earth in Atlantis' day.

King of the nations, master of wisdom,
LIGHT through SUNTAL,
Keeper of the way,
dwelt in his TEMPLE,
the MASTER of UNAL,
LIGHT of the Earth in Atlantis' day.

Master, HE, from a cycle beyond us,
living in bodies as one among men.

Not as the earth-born,
HE from beyond us,
SUN of a cycle, advanced beyond men.

Know ye, O man, that HORLET the Master,
was never one with the children of men.

Far in the past time when Atlantis first grew as a power,
appeared there one with the KEY of WISDOM,
showing the way of LIGHT to all.

Showed he to all men the path of attainment,
way of the Light that flows among men.
Mastering darkness, leading the MAN-SOUL,
upward to heights that were One with the Light.

Divided the Kingdoms, HE into sections.

Ten were they, ruled by children of men.

Upon another, built HE a TEMPLE,
built but not by the children of men.

Out of the ETHER called HE its substance,
moulded and formed by the power of YTOLAN
into the forms HE built with His mind.

Mile upon mile it covered the island,
space upon space it grew in its might.

Black, yet not black, but dark like the space-time,
deep in its heart the ESSENCE of LIGHT.

Swiftly the TEMPLE grew into being,
moulded and shaped by the WORD of the DWELLER,
called from the formless into a form.

Builded HE then, within it, great chambers,
filled them with forms called forth from the ETHER,
filled them with wisdom called forth by His mind.

Formless was HE within his TEMPLE,
yet was HE formed in the image of men.

Dwelling among them yet not of them,
strange and far different
was HE from the children of men.

Chose HE then from among the people,
THREE who became his gateway.

Choose HE the THREE from the Highest
to become his links with Atlantis.

Messengers they, who carried his council,
to the kings of the children of men.

Brought HE forth others and taught them wisdom;
teachers, they, to the children of men.

*Placed HE them on the island of UNDAL to stand as
teachers of LIGHT to men.*

*Each of those who were thus chosen,
taught must he be for years five and ten.*

*Only thus could he have understanding to bring
LIGHT to the children of men.*

*Thus there came into being the Temple, a dwelling place
for the Master of men.*

*I, THOTH, have ever sought wisdom,
searching in darkness and searching in Light.*

*Long in my youth I traveled the pathway,
seeking ever new knowledge to gain.*

*Until after much striving, one of the THREE,
to me brought the LIGHT.*

*Brought HE to me the commands of the DWELLER,
called me from the darkness into the LIGHT.
Brought HE me, before the DWELLER,
deep in the Temple before the great FIRE.*

There on the great throne, beheld I,
the DWELLER, clothed with the LIGHT
and flashing with fire.
Down I knelt before that great wisdom,
feeling the LIGHT flowing through me in waves.

Heard I then the voice of the DWELLER:
"O darkness, come into the Light.

Long have ye sought the pathway to LIGHT.

Each soul on earth that loosens its fetters,
shall soon be made free from the bondage of night.

Forth from the darkness have ye arisen,
closer approached the Light of your goal.

Here ye shall dwell as one of my children,
keeper of records gathered by wisdom,
instrument thou of the LIGHT from beyond.

Ready by thou made to do what is needed,
preserver of wisdom through the ages of darkness,
that shall come fast on the children of men.

Live thee here and drink of all wisdom.

Secrets and mysteries unto thee shall unveil."

Then answered I, the MASTER OF CYCLES, saying:
"O Light, that descended to men,
give thou to me of thy wisdom that
I might be a teacher of men.
Give thou of thy LIGHT that I may be free."

Spoke then to me again, the MASTER:
"Age after age shall ye live through
your wisdom, Aye, when o'er Atlantis the ocean waves roll,
holding the Light, though hidden in darkness, ready to come
when e'er thou shalt call.

Go thee now and learn greater wisdom. Grow thou through
LIGHT to Infinity's ALL."

Long then dwelt I in the Temple of the DWELLER until at last I
was One with the LIGHT.

Followed I then the path to the star planes, followed I then the
pathway to LIGHT.

Deep into Earth's heart I followed the pathway, learning the
secrets, below as above; learning the pathway to the HALLS of
AMENTI; learning the LAW that balances the world.

To Earth's hidden chambers pierced I by my wisdom, deep through the Earth's crust, into the pathway, hidden for ages from the children of men.

Unveiled before me, ever more wisdom until I reached a new knowledge: found that all is part of an ALL, great and yet greater than all that we know.

Searched I Infinity's heart through all the ages.

Deep and yet deeper, more mysteries I found.

Now, as I look back through the ages, know I that wisdom is boundless, ever grown greater throughout the ages, One with Infinity's greater than all.

Light there was in ancient ATLANTIS.
Yet, darkness, too, was hidden in all.

Fell from the Light into the darkness,
some who had risen to heights among men.

Proud they became because of their knowledge,
proud were they of their place among men.
Deep delved they into the forbidden,
opened the gateway that led to below.

Sought they to gain ever more knowledge but
seeking to bring it up from below.

He who descends below must have balance,
else he is bound by lack of our Light.

Opened, they then,
by their knowledge,
pathways forbidden to man.

But, in His Temple, all-seeing, the DWELLER,
lay in his AGWANTI, while through Atlantis,
His soul roamed free.

Saw HE the Atlanteans, by their magic,
opening the gateway that would
bring to Earth a great woe.

Fast fled His soul then, back to His body.
Up HE arose from His AGWANTI.
Called HE the Three mighty messengers.
Gave the commands that shattered the world.
Deep 'neath Earth's crust to the HALLS of AMENTI,
swiftly descended the DWELLER.
Called HE then on the powers the Seven Lords wielded;
changed the Earth's balance.

Down sank Atlantis beneath the dark waves.

Shattered the gateway that had been opened;

shattered the doorway that led down below.

All of the islands were shattered except UNAL,

and part of the island of the sons of the DWELLER.

Preserved HE them to be the teachers,

Lights on the path for those to come after,

Lights for the lesser children of men.

Called HE then, I THOTH, before him,

gave me commands for all I should do, saying;

"Take thou, O THOTH, all of your wisdom.

Take all your records, Take all your magic.

Go thou forth as a teacher of men.

Go thou forth reserving the records

until in time LIGHT grows among men.

LIGHT shalt thou be all through the ages,

hidden yet found by enlightened men.

Over all Earth, give WE ye power,

free thou to give or take it away.

Gather thou now the sons of Atlantis.

Take them and flee to the people of the rock caves.

Fly to the land of the Children of KHEM."

Then gathered I the sons of Atlantis.
Into the spaceship I brought all my records,
brought the records of sunken Atlantis.
Gathered I all of my powers,
instruments many of mighty magic.

Up then we rose on wings of the morning.
High we arose above the Temple,
leaving behind the Three and DWELLER,
deep in the HALLS 'neath the Temple,
closing the pathway to the LORDS of the Cycles.

Yet ever to him who has knowing,
open shall be the path to AMENTI.
Fast fled we then on the wings of the morning,
fled to the land of the children of KHEM.
There by my power,
I conquered and ruled them.

Raised I to LIGHT,
the children of KHEM.
Deep 'neath the rocks,
I buried my spaceship,
waiting the time when man might be free.

Over the spaceship,
erected a marker in the form
of a lion yet like unto man.
There 'neath the image rests yet my spaceship,
forth to be brought when need shall arise.

Know ye, O man, that far in the future,
invaders shall come from out of the deep.
Then awake, ye who have wisdom.
Bring forth my ship and conquer with ease.
Deep 'neath the image lies my secret.
Search and find in the pyramid I built.

Each to the other is the Keystone;
each the gateway that leads into LIFE.
Follow the KEY I leave behind me.
Seek and the doorway to LIFE shall be thine.
Seek thou in my pyramid,
deep in the passage that ends in a wall.

Use thou the KEY of the SEVEN,
and open to thee the pathway will fall.
Now unto thee I have given my wisdom.
Now unto thee I have given my way.

Follow the pathway.

Solve thou my secrets.

Unto thee I have shown the way.

Tablet VI: The Key of Magic

This tablet begins by setting the historical background for the emergence of the darkness and warfare with the light, occurring in the first days of man. The battle is depicted as age old and crosses all cultures appearing in various forms. Thoth indicates that when they arrived on Earth the age old light-dark battle was already in motion. Dark or black magic is blamed for the darkness that envelopes man's soul. Dark Force Secret Societies were formed to operate stealthily, enslaving with darkness and blinding the soul. They are accused by Thoth of negatively affecting mankind's dream state and putting destructive thoughts into his mind. We are warned to test the spirit of being that is encountered to avoid ensnarement by the Dark Brothers, posing as children of LIGHT.

We are further counselled not to take the easy path, following the group. Walk your own path, striving for wisdom and seeking always the light. The road is not easy to light or wisdom, but is the right path ultimately conquering the darkness. Don't ever give up the quest for light and truth, for the LIGHT BROTHERS are also secretly with us, battling the hidden dark forces. Good news, light always wins, have no fear! We are given guidance to be responsible for our thoughts, examining them before the negative ones become our own. If we feel darkness sneaking in, we are told to use a vibratory frequency oscillating in the full body to rid the evil. Next, one of my favorite methods to rid oneself of darkness is to perform the standing ritual whose focus is on the ascended masters seated within the flower of life chamber discussed earlier, where seven masters of the cycles from above are summoned to free one from darkness and fill one with light. We are given their names to use directly. I believe these seven beings are each assigned to a different Chakra, probably the same Gods reference by Hindu teachings who control the energy center operation and activation. We are told the process can be used to intervene for someone else in trouble as well. I have done this one so many times it is memorized for immediate use.

Hark ye, O man, to the wisdom of magic.
Hark the knowledge of powers forgotten.
Long ago in the days of the first man,
warfare began between darkness and light.
Men then as now,
were filled with both darkness and light;
and while in some darkness held sway,
in other light filled the soul.

Aye, age old in this warfare,
the eternal struggle between darkness and light.

Fiercely is it fought all through the ages,
using strange powers hidden to man.

Adepts have there been filled with the blackness,
struggling always against the light;
but others there are who, filled with brightness,
have ever conquered the darkness of night.
Where e'er ye may be in all ages and plane,
surely, ye shall know of the battle with night.
Long ages ago,
The SUNS of the Morning
descending, found the world filled with night,
there in that past, began the struggle,
the age old Battle Darkness & Light.

Many in the time were so filled with darkness
that only feebly flamed the light from the night.

Some they were, masters of darkness, who sought
to fill all with their darkness:
Sought to draw others into their night.
Fiercely withstood they, the masters of brightness:
fiercely fought they from the darkness of night
Sought ever to tighten the fetters,
the chains that bind men to the darkness of night.
Used they always the dark magic,

brought into men by the power of darkness.
magic that enshrouded man's soul with darkness.

Banded together as in order,
BROTHERS OF DARKNESS,
they through the ages,
antagonist they to the children of men.
Walked they always secret and hidden,
found, yet not found by the children of men.

Forever, they walked and worked in darkness,
hiding from the light in the darkness of night.
Silently, secretly use they their power,
enslaving and binding the soul of men.

Unseen they come, and unseen they go.
Man, in his ignorance calls THEM from below.

Dark is the way of the DARK BROTHERS travel,
dark of the darkness not of the night,
traveling o'er Earth
they walk through man's dreams.
Power they have gained
from the darkness around them
to call other dwellers from out of their plane,

in ways that are dark and unseen by man.
Into man's mind-space reach the DARK BROTHERS.

Around it, they close the veil of their night.
There through its lifetime
that soul dwells in bondage,
bound by the fetters of the VEIL of the night.
Mighty are they in the forbidden knowledge
forbidden because it is one with the night.

Hark ye O old man and list to my warning:
be ye free from the bondage of night.
Surrender not your soul to the BROTHERS OF DARKNESS.
Keep thy face ever turned towards the Light.
Know ye not, O man, that your sorrow,
only has come through the Veil of the night.
Aye man, heed ye my warning:
strive ever upward,
turn your soul toward the LIGHT.
The BROTHERS OF DARKNESS seek for their brothers
those who traveled the pathway of LIGHT.
For well know they that those who have traveled
far towards the Sun in their pathway of LIGHT
have great and yet greater power
to bind with darkness the children of LIGHT.

List ye, O man, to he who comes to you.
But weigh in the balance if his words be of LIGHT.
For many there are who walk in DARK BRIGHTNESS
and yet are not the children of LIGHT.

Easy it is to follow their pathway,
easy to follow the path that they lead.
But yet O man, heed ye my warning:
Light comes only to him who strives.
Hard is the pathway that leads to the WISDOM,
hard is the pathway that leads to the LIGHT.
Many shall ye find, the stones in your pathway:
many the mountains to climb toward the LIGHT.

Yet know ye, O man, to him that o'ercometh,
free will he be of the pathway of Light.
For ye know, O man,
in the END light must conquer
and darkness and night be banished from Light.

Listen, O man, and heed ye this wisdom;
even as darkness, so is the LIGHT.

When darkness is banished and all Veils are rended,
out there shall flash from the darkness, the LIGHT.

Even as exist among men the DARK BROTHERS,
so there exists the BROTHERS OF LIGHT.
Antagonists they of the BROTHERS OF DARKNESS,
seeking to free men from the night.
Powers have they, mighty and potent.
Knowing the LAW, the planets obey.
Work they ever in harmony and order,
freeing the man-soul from its bondage of night.

Secret and hidden, walk they also.
Known not are they to the children of men.
Ever have THEY fought the DARK BROTHERS,
conquered and conquering time without end.
Yet always LIGHT shall in the end be master,
driving away the darkness of night.

Aye, man, know ye this knowing:
always beside thee walk the Children of Light.

Masters they of the SUN power,
ever unseen yet the guardians of men.
Open to all is their pathway,
open to he who will walk in the LIGHT.
Free are THEY of DARK AMENTI,
free of the HALLS, where LIFE reigns supreme.

SUNS are they and LORDS of the morning,
Children of Light to shine among men.
Like man are they and yet are unlike,
Never divided were they in the past.

ONE have they been in ONENESS eternal,
throughout all space since the beginning of time.
Up did they come in Oneness with the ALL ONE,
up from the first-space, formed and unformed.

Given to man have they secrets
that shall guard and protect him from all harm.
He who would travel the path of the master,
free must he be from the bondage of night.
Conquer must he the formless and shapeless,
conquer must he the phantom of fear.

Knowing, must he gain of all of the secrets,
travel the pathway that leads through the darkness,
yet ever before him keep the light of his goal.
Obstacles great shall he meet in the pathway,
yet press on to the LIGHT of the SUN.

Hear ye, O Man, the SUN is the symbol
of the LIGHT that shines at the end of thy road.
Now to thee give I the secrets:

now to meet the dark power,

meet and conquer the fear from the night.

Only by knowing can ye conquer,

Only be knowing can ye have LIGHT.

Now I give unto thee the knowledge,

known to the MASTERS,

the knowing that conquers all the dark fears.

Use this, the wisdom I give thee.

MASTER thou shalt be of THE BROTHERS OF NIGHT.

When unto thee comes a feeling,

drawing thee nearer to the darker gate,

examine thine heart and find if the feeling

thou hast has come from within.

If thou shalt find the darkness thine own thoughts,

banish them forth from the place in thy mind.

Send through thy body a wave of vibration,

irregular first and regular second,

repeating time after time until free.

Start the WAVE FORCE in thy BRAIN CENTER.

Direct it in waves from thine head to thy foot.

But if thou findest thine heart is not darkened,

be sure that a force is directed to thee.

Only by knowing can thou overcome it.

Only by wisdom can thou hope to be free.

Knowledge brings wisdom and wisdom is power.

Attain and ye shall have power o'er all.

Seek ye first a place bound by darkness.

Place ye a circle around about thee.

Stand erect in the midst of the circle.

Use thou this formula, and you shalt be free.

Raise thou thine hands to the dark space above thee. Close thou

thine eyes and draw in the LIGHT.

Call to the SPIRIT OF LIGHT through the Space-Time,

using these words and thou shalt be free:

"Fill thou my body, O SPIRIT OF LIFE,

fill thou my body with SPIRIT OF LIGHT.

Come from the FLOWER

that shines through the darkness.

Come from the HALLS where the Seven Lords rule.

Name them by name, I, the Seven:

THREE, FOUR, FIVE,

and SIX, SEVEN, EIGHT--NINE.

By their names I call them to aid me,

free me and save me from the darkness of night:

UNTANAS, QUERTAS, CHIETAL,
and GOYANA, HUERTAL, SEMVETA--ARDAL.
By their names I implore thee,
free me from darkness
and fill me with LIGHT

Know ye, O man, that when ye have done this,
ye shall be free from the fetters that bind ye,
cast off the bondage of the brothers of night.

See ye not that the names have the power
to free by vibration the fetters that bind?
Use them at need to free thou thine brother
so that he, too, may come forth from the night.

Thou, O man, art thy brother's helper.
Let him not lie in the bondage of night.

Now unto thee, give I my magic.
Take it and dwell on the pathway of LIGHT.

LIGHT unto thee, LIFE unto thee,
SUN may thou be on the cycle above.

Tablet VII: The Seven Lords

Thoth encourages seeking light through our dark life paths, and indicates that all is created based on ORDER and light which emanates from the eternal source, the INFINITE BRAIN. We are told that even INFINITY itself shall change far in the space-time. The seven cycle masters seated in the Halls of Amenti within the Flower of Life are able to communicate telepathically and make themselves available to Thoth for free visitations at will. They are from beyond the SPACE-TIME where all is formless, the Great Void, each having their duty in controlling certain forces or most likely the signal amplitude, phase, and frequency of the composite energy allowed at each Chakra.   Supporting evidence for the Holographic reality is offered: *"For know ye that which is formed truly is formless, having form only to our eyes."* A false perception, the illusion of transient matter. We also get confirmation that the seven masters of the cycles (THREE through NINE) are affiliated with some repeating timing event, a cycle, most likely the duration of a Mayan Sun or the Great Year precessional timing of 25,920 years. It would make sense to me that the seven Chakra police would be on high alert when the primitive worker energy started to raise the being higher using latent circuits described by Dr. Timothy Leary. The catalyst being the energy from GCR, Great Calendar Year. The Great Year most likely activates the reprinting

231

circuit [see Ch. 2, Futants Anyone] creating a newly reprogrammed being ready to operate energetically in the 4th dimension. The Chakra raising shift is caused by passing through the Milky Way Galaxy center or what the Mayans termed the *dark rift*. One must be tested by the seven cycle masters to occupy the full energy detailed by me using in EQ5A, the maximum human energy equation [3, Pg. 86].

We are told that in a future age, not created yet, we will all merge back into ONE together. We are advised by the number NINE, the master of the seven cycle Lords, to learn the Space-Time cycles, so we too can be free. This implies, to me, knowing about ascension windows, like the Great Year at which time we can ascend if we so choose. An added profound tip is provided by the ninth cycle rule and chieftain: An increase in consciousness is possible when TWO have become ONE...the barrier has lifted, and has proceeded to grow from form to formless, an energy shift. This could have to do with the composite energy available from two twin archetypal flames creating a higher frequency and amplitude signal in the Chakras. Thoth ends the tablet providing a short prayer to be used to facilitate intervention from the One LIGHT, ALL with ONE.

Hark ye O man, and list to my Voice.

Open thy mind-space and drink of my wisdom.

Dark is the pathway of LIFE that ye travel.

Many the pitfalls that lie in thy way.

Seek ye ever to gain greater wisdom.

Attain and it shall be light on thy way.

Open thy SOUL, O man, to the Cosmic

and let it flow in as one with thy SOUL.

LIGHT is eternal and darkness is fleeting.

Seek ye ever, O man, for the LIGHT.

Know ye that ever as Light fills thy being,

darkness for thee shall soon disappear.

Open thy souls to the BROTHERS OF BRIGHTNESS.

Let them enter and fill thee with LIGHT.

Lift up thine eyes to the LIGHT of the Cosmos.

Keep thou ever thy face to the goal.

Only by gaining the light of all wisdom,

art thou one with the Infinite goal.

Seek ye ever the Oneness eternal.

Seek ever the Light into One.

Hear ye, O man, list to my Voice

singing the song of Light and of Life.

throughout all space, Light is prevalent,
encompassing ALL with its banners it flames.
Seek ye forever in the veil of the darkness,
somewhere ye shall surely find Light.
Hidden and buried, lost to man's knowledge,
deep in the finite the Infinite exists.
Lost, but existing,
flowing through all things,
living in ALL is the INFINITE BRAIN.

In all space, there is only ONE wisdom.
Though seeming decided, it is ONE in the ONE.
All that exists comes forth from the LIGHT,
and the LIGHT comes forth from the ALL.

Everything created is based upon ORDER:
LAW rules the space where the INFINITE dwells.
Forth from equilibrium came the great cycles,
moving in harmony toward Infinity's end.

Know ye, O man, that far in the space-time,
INFINITY itself shall pass into change.
Hear ye and list to the Voice of Wisdom:
Know that ALL is of ALL evermore.
Know that through time thou may pursue wisdom
and find ever more light on the way.

Know that through time thou may pursue wisdom
and find ever more light on the way.
Aye, thou shall find that ever receding,
thy goal shall elude thee from day unto day.

Long time ago, in the HALLS OF AMENTI,
I, Thoth, stood before the LORDS of the cycles.
Mighty, THEY in their aspects of power;
mighty, THEY in the wisdom unveiled.

Led by the Dweller, first did I see them.
But afterwards free was I of their presence,
free to enter their conclave at will.
Oft did I journey down the dark pathway
unto the HALL where the LIGHT ever glows.

Learned I of the Masters of cycles,
wisdom brought from the cycles above.
Manifest THEY in this cycle
as guides of man to the knowledge of ALL.
Seven are they, mighty in power,
speaking these words through me to men.
Time after time, stood I before them
listening to words that came not with sound.

Once said THEY unto me:
O man, wouldst thou gain wisdom?
Seek for it in the heart of the flame.
Wouldst thou gain knowledge of power?
Seek ye it in the heart of the flame.
Wouldst be one with the heart of the flame?
Seek then within thine own hidden flame.

Many the times spoke THEY to me,
teaching me wisdom not of the world;
showing me ever new paths to brightness;
teaching me wisdom brought from above.
Giving knowledge of operation,
learning of LAW, the order of ALL.

Spoke to me again, the Seven, saying:
From far beyond time are WE, come, O man,
Traveled WE from beyond SPACE-TIME,
aye, from the place of Infinity's end.
When ye and all of thy brethren were formless,
formed forth were WE from the order of ALL.
Not as men are WE,
though once WE, too, were as men.
Out of the Great Void were WE formed forth
in order by LAW.

For know ye that which is formed

truly is formless, having form only to thine eyes.

And again, unto me spoke the Seven, saying:

Child of the LIGHT, O THOTH, art thou,

free to travel the bright path upward

until at last ALL ONES become ONE

Forth were WE formed after our order:

THREE, FOUR, FIVE, SIX, SEVEN, EIGHT--NINE.

Know ye that these are the numbers of cycles

that WE descend from unto man.

Each having here a duty to fulfill;

each having here a force to control.

Yet are we ONE with the SOUL of our cycle.

Yet are WE, too, seeking a goal.

Far beyond man's conception,

Infinity extends into a greater than ALL.

There, in a time that is yet not a time,

we shall ALL become ONE

with a greater than ALL.

Time and space are moving in circles.

Know ye their law, and ye too, shall be free.

Aye, free shall ye be to move through the cycles--

pass the guardians that dwell at the door.

Then to me spoke HE of NINE saying:
Aeons and aeons have I existed,
knowing not LIFE and tasting not death.
For know ye. O man, that far in the future,
life and death shall be one with the ALL.

Each so perfected by balancing the other
that neither exists in the Oneness of ALL.
In men of this cycle, the life force is rampant,
but life in its growth becomes one with them ALL.

Here, I manifest in this your cycle,
but yet am I there in your future of time.
Yet to me, time exists not,
for in my world time exists not,
for formless are WE.
Life have WE not but yet have existence,
fuller and greater and freer than thee.

Man is a flame bound to a mountain,
but WE in our cycle shall ever be free.
Know ye, O man, that when ye have progressed
into the cycle that lengthens above,
life itself will pass to the darkness
and only the essence of Soul shall remain.

Then to me spoke the LORD of the EIGHT saying:
All that ye know is but part of little.
Not as yet have ye touched on the Great.
Far out in space where LIGHT beings supreme,
came I into the LIGHT.
Formed was I also but not as ye are.

Body of Light was my formless form formed.
Know I not LIFE and know I not DEATH,
yet master am I of all that exists.
Seek ye to find the path through the barriers.
Travel the road that leads to the LIGHT.

Spoke again to me the NINE saying:
Seek ye to find the path to beyond.
Not impossible is it to grow
to a consciousness above.
For when TWO have become ONE
and ONE has become the ALL,
know ye the barrier has lifted,
and ye are made free of the road.
Grow thou from form to the formless.
Free may thou be of the road.

Thus, through ages I listened,
learning the way to the ALL.

Now Lift I my thoughts to the ALL-THING.
List ye and hear when it calls.

O LIGHT, all pervading,
One with ALL and ALL with ONE,
flow thou to me through the channel.
Enter thou so that I may be free.
Make me One with the ALL-SOUL,
shining from the blackness of night.
Free let me be of all space-time,
free from the Veil of the night.
I, a child of LIGHT, command:
Free from the darkness to be.

Formless am I to the Light-Soul,
formless yet shining with light.
Know I the bonds of the darkness
must shatter and fall before light.

Now give I this wisdom.
Free may ye be, O man,
living in light and in brightness.
Turn not thy face from the Light.
Thy soul dwells in realms of brightness.
Ye are a child of the Light.

Turn thy thoughts inward not outward.
Find thou the Light-Soul within.
Know that thou art the MASTER.
All else is brought from within.
Grow thou to realms of brightness.
Hold thou thy thought on the Light.
Know thou art one with the Cosmos,
a flame and a Child of the Light.

Now to thee gave I warning:
Let not the thought turn away.
Know that the brightness
flows through thy body for aye.
Turn not to the DARK-BROTHERS
that come from the BROTHERS OF BLACK.
But keep thine eyes ever lifted,
thy soul in tune with the Light.

Take ye this wisdom and heed it.
List to my Voice and obey.
Follow the pathway to brightness,
and thou shall be ONE with the way.

Tablet VIII: The Key of Mysteries

Thoth informs us that he takes on different bodies during incarnations with mankind. We are told that man is in the process of changing to forms that are not of this world, approaching the formless or energetic spirit state to a place on the cycle above (a cycle above 3rd dimension is 4th dimension?). We are told that we have to lose our bodies (become formless) to merge with the LIGHT. Thoth instructs us to speak without words seeking light and wisdom (thoughts are telepathic via the electromagnetic spectrum) directed toward those underground benevolent cycle masters dwelling in their blue-light lit temple.

A past re-telling of the dark forces that mankind summoned from Ancient Atlantis arrived in this cycle, formless and unable to be seen by earth-men. Must reside outside of the meager 300 nanometer visible range (400-700 nm) our eyes can see in the simulator. They needed bodies (blood) to take on a physical form, mankind's to be exact. Now you know why blood sacrifices (think of the Catholic Mass and Bohemian Grove Cremation of Care ritual involving sacrifice) bring in dark forces as told herein. We are told that they were serpent-headed when their "glamour" was lifted but otherwise appear as men among men. This is frightening. Thoth states that certain sounds made them visible using his magic.

High places of authority were sought out by the dark body snatchers to rule over mankind. Light forces smack down the reptilian dark forces, but they return at a later time to repeat the battle against the Light.

We are advised about energetic boundaries around the Earth that are guarded by the HOUNDS of the Barrier. Do not transgress this hard limit. If they get your scent, escaping back into the body during an OOBE is discouraged as the HOUNDS will follow your astral body back to the physical. He advises moving in circles back to the body for protection, with a follow on ritual involving circles again. Better not to approach the outer boundary whose HOUNDS seek to consume the soul. The HOUNDS can only move in linear fashion, thus moving is a circle can be used to lose them. Scary.

When leaving the OOBE back to the body, Thoth instructs us to use the cross and the circle combined. The final prodding is to open one's mouth and speak the WORD to get free. Not sure what the WORD implies, perhaps just speaking anything in words once entering the body following an OOBE activates the mind and disconnects the astral thread that the HOUNDS use to pursue the trespasser? I recall waking up during an OOBE when I was 17, unable to move or speak. Once I could move and speak, the paralyzing brain chemical that keeps one from acting out the OOBE takes a few moments to wear off if one suddenly comes back to the body while conscious.

Unto thee, O man,
have I given my knowledge.
Unto thee have I given of Light.
Hear ye now and receive my wisdom
brought from space planes above and beyond.

Not as man am I
for free have I become of dimensions and planes.
In each, take I on a new body.
In each, I change in my form.
Know I now that the formless is all there is of form.

Great is the wisdom of the Seven.
Mighty are THEY from beyond.
Manifest THEY through their power,
filled by force from beyond.

Hear ye these words of wisdom.
Hear ye and make them thine own.
Find in them the formless.
Mystery is but hidden knowledge.
Know and ye shall unveil.
Find the deep buried wisdom
and be master of darkness and Light.

Deep are the mysteries around thee,

hidden the secrets of Old.

Search through the KEYS of my WISDOM.

Surely shall ye find the way.

The gateway to power is secret,

but he who attains shall receive.

Look to the LIGHT! O my brother.

Open and ye shall receive.

Press on through the valley of darkness.

Overcome the dweller of night.

Keep ever thine eyes of the LIGHT-PLANE,

and thou shalt be One with the LIGHT.

Man is in process of changing

to forms that are not of this world.

Grows he in time to the formless,

a plane on the cycle above.

Know ye, ye must become formless before ye are with the

LIGHT,

List ye, O man, to my voice,

telling of pathways to Light,

showing the way of attainment

when ye shall be One with the Light.

Search ye the mysteries of Earth's heart.
Learn of the LAW that exists,
holding the stars in their balance
by the force of the primordial mist.
Seek ye the flame of the EARTH'S LIFE.
Bathe in the glare of its flame.
Follow the three-cornered pathway
until thou, too, art a flame.

Speak thou in words without voice
to those who dwell down below.
Enter the blue-litten temple
and bathe in the fire of all life.

Know, O man, thou art complex,
a being of earth and of fire.
Let thy flame shine out brightly.
Be thou only the fire.

Wisdom is hidden in darkness.
When lit by the flame of the Soul,
find thou the wisdom and be LIGHT-BORN,
a Sun of the Light without form.
Seek thee ever more wisdom.
Find it in the heart of the flame.
Know that only by striving

and Light pour into thy brain.
Now have I spoken with wisdom.
List to my Voice and obey.
Tear open the Veils of the darkness.
Shine a LIGHT on the WAY.

Speak I of Ancient Atlantis,
speak of the days
of the Kingdom of Shadows,
speak of the coming
of the children of shadows.
Out of the great deep were they called
by the wisdom of earth-men,
called for the purpose of gaining great power.

Far in the past before Atlantis existed,
men there were who delved into darkness,
using dark magic, calling up beings
from the great deep below us.
Forth came they into this cycle.
Formless were they of another vibration,
existing unseen by the children of earth-men.
Only through blood could they have formed being.
Only through man could they live in the world.

In ages past were they conquered by Masters,
driven below to the place whence they came.
But some there were who remained,
hidden in spaces and planes unknown to man.
Lived they in Atlantis as shadows,
but at times they appeared among men.
Aye, when the blood was offered,
for they came to dwell among men.

In the form of man they amongst us,
but only to sight were they as are men.
Serpent-headed when the glamour was lifted
but appearing to man as men among men.
Crept they into the Councils,
taking forms that were like unto men.
Slaying by their arts
the chiefs of the kingdoms,
taking their form and ruling o'er man.
Only by magic could they be discovered.
Only by sound could their faces be seen.
Sought they from the Kingdom of shadows
to destroy man and rule in his place.

But, know ye, the Masters were mighty in magic,
able to lift the Veil from the face of the serpent,
able to send him back to his place.

Came they to man and taught him the secret,
the WORD that only a man can pronounce.
Swift then they lifted the Veil from the serpent
and cast him forth from the place among men.

Yet, beware, the serpent still liveth
in a place that is open at times to the world.
Unseen they walk among thee
in places where the rites have been said.
Again as time passes onward
shall they take the semblance of men.

Called may they be by the master
who knows the white or the black,
but only the white master may control
and bind them while in the flesh.

Seek not the kingdom of shadows,
for evil will surely appear.
For only the master of brightness
shall conquer the shadow of fear.

Know ye, O my brother,
that fear is an obstacle great.
Be master of all in the brightness,
the shadow will soon disappear.

GERALD CLARK

Hear ye and heed my wisdom,
the voice of LIGHT is clear.
Seek not the valley of shadow,
and LIGHT will only appear.

List ye, O man,
to the depth of my wisdom.
Speak I of knowledge hidden from man.
Far have I been
on my journey through SPACE-TIME,
even to the end of space of this cycle.
Aye, glimpsed the HOUNDS of the Barrier,
lying in wait for he who would pass them.
In that space where time exists not,
faintly I sensed the guardians of cycles.
Move they only through angles.
Free are they not of the curved dimensions.

Strange and terrible
are the HOUNDS of the Barrier.
Follow thy consciousness to the limits of space.
Think not to escape by entering your body,
for follow they fast the Soul through angles.
Only the circle will give ye protection,
save from the claws
of the DWELLERS IN ANGLES.

Once, in a time past,

I approached the great Barrier,

and saw on the shores where time exists not,

the formless forms

of the HOUNDS of the barrier.

Aye, hiding in the midst beyond time I found them;

and THEY, scenting me afar off,

raised themselves and gave the great bell cry

that could be heard from cycle to cycle

and moved through space toward my soul.

Fled I then fast before them,

back from time's unthinkable end.

But ever after me pursued they,

moving in strange angles not known to man.

Aye, on the gray shores of TIME-SPACE'S end

found I the HOUNDS of the Barrier,

ravening for the Soul

who attempts the beyond.

Fled I through circles back to my body.

Fled, and fast after me they followed.

Aye, after me the devourers followed,

seeking through angles to devour my Soul.

GERALD CLARK

Aye, know ye man,

that the Soul who dares the Barrier

may be held in bondage

by the HOUNDS from beyond time,

held till this cycle is completed

and left behind

when the consciousness leaves.

Entered I my body.

Created the circles that know not angles,

created the form

that from my form was formed.

Made my body into a circle

and lost the pursuers in the circles of time.

But, even yet, when free from my body,

cautious ever must I be

not to move through angles,

else my soul may never be free.

Know ye, the HOUNDS of the Barrier

move only through angles

and never through curves of space.

Only by moving through curves

can ye escape them,

for in angles they will pursue thee.

O man, heed ye my warning;

Seek not to break open
the gate to beyond.
Few there are
who have succeeded in passing the Barrier
to the greater LIGHT that shines beyond.
For know ye, ever the dwellers,
seek such Souls to hold in their thrall.

Listen, O man, and heed ye my warning;
seek ye to move not in angles but curves,
And if while free from thy body,
though hearest the sound like the bay of a hound
ringing clear and bell-like through thy being,
flee back to thy body through circles,
penetrate not the midst mist before.

When thou hath entered the form thou hast dwelt in,
use thou the cross and the circle combined.
Open thy mouth and use thou thy Voice.
Utter the WORD and thou shalt be free.
Only the one who of LIGHT has the fullest
can hope to pass by the guards of the way.
And then must he move
through strange curves and angles
that are formed in direction not know to man.

List ye, O man, and heed ye my warning:
attempt not to pass the guards on the way.
Rather should ye seek to gain of thine own Light
and make thyself ready to pass on the way.

LIGHT is thine ultimate end, O my brother.
Seek and find ever the Light on the way.

Tablet IX: The Key of Freedom of Space

Thoth reminds us as a species that *"ye are the ultimate of all things"* but have forgotten our heritage, forced into bondage with our soul fettered by the chains of darkness. We are told we are only a spirit, the body is nothing but a shell to be cast off, and the Soul is ALL. Thoth states that all that exists is only an aspect of greater things and that space is not boundless, but rather partitioned by angles and curves. A holographic simulator it would seem, having transient matter for decoration. He instructs that we are connected by an energetic web to other space brethren.

We are told that there are nine dimensions or cycles of space and the same number of levels of consciousness controlled by the nine lords of the cycles, seven of which were highlighted (THREE through NINE, the chieftain). The access to the nine worlds within worlds inside us (33, Pgs. 314-324 posited) most likely allude to the wavelength/frequency of each nerve ganglia or Chakra. Most traditions only account for seven but others show up to thirteen. Only the one who is seeking may ever hope to get free! The flame is the source of all things, containing all things in potentiality. The WORD is the source of all existence. Thoth asks the LORD OF THE NINE to divulge the secret of the WORD, answering through ORDER, ye shall find the way. Is this an allusion to sacred geometry or law and order? We are instructed that the WORD came from Chaos and LIGHT came from FIRE. To get order, balance thy life, quell all the chaos of emotions (meditate) and there will be order in LIFE. Establishing order out of chaos brings forth the WORD of the SOURCE transforming the Soul force into an eternal flame.

List ye, O man, hear ye my voice,
teaching of Wisdom and Light in this cycle;
teaching ye how to banish the darkness,
teaching ye how to bring Light in thy life.

Seek ye, O man, to find the great pathway
that leads to eternal LIFE as a SUN.
Draw ye away from the veil of the darkness.
Seek to become a Light in the world.
Make of thyself a vessel for Light,
a focus for the Sun of this space.

Lift thou thine eyes to the Cosmos.
Lift thou thine eyes to the Light.
Speak in the words of the Dweller,
the chant that calls down the Light.
Sing thou the song of freedom.
Sing thou the song of the Soul.
Create the high vibration

that will make thee One with the Whole.
Blend all thyself with the Cosmos.
Grow into ONE with the Light.
Be thou a channel of order,
a pathway of LAW to the world.

Thy LIGHT, O man, is the great LIGHT,
shining through the shadow of flesh.
Free must thou rise from the darkness
before thou art One with the LIGHT.

Shadows of darkness surround thee.
Life fills thee with its flow.
But know, O man, thou must arise
and forth thy body go
far to the planes that surround thee
and yet are One with thee, too.

Look all around thee, O man.
See thine own light reflected.
Aye, even in the darkness around thee,
thine own Light pours forth through the veil.

Seek thou for wisdom always.
Let not thine body betray.
Keep in the path of the Light wave.

Shun thou the darkened way.
Know thee that wisdom is lasting.
Existing since the ALL-SOUL began,
creating harmony from by the
Law that exists in the WAY.

List ye, o man, to the teachings of wisdom.
List to the voice that speaks of the past-time.
Aye, I shall tell thee knowledge forgotten,
tell ye of wisdom hidden in past-time,
lost in the midst of darkness around me.

Know ye, man,
ye are the ultimate of all things.
Only the knowledge of this is forgotten,
lost when man was cast into bondage,
bound and fettered
by the chains of the darkness.

Long, long ago, I cast off my body.
Wandered I free
through the vastness of ether,
circled the angles
that hold man in bondage.
Know ye, O man, ye are only a spirit.
The body is nothing.

The Soul is ALL.
Let not your body be a fetter.
Cast off the darkness and travel in Light.
Cast off your body, O man, and be free,
truly a Light that is ONE with the Light.

When ye are free from the fetters of darkness
and travel in space as the SUN of the LIGHT,
then ye shall know that space is not boundless
but truly bounded by angles and curves.
Know ye, O man, that all that exists
is only an aspect of greater things yet to come.
Matter is fluid and flows like a stream,
constantly changing from one thing to another.

All through the ages has knowledge existed;
never been changed, though buried in darkness;
never been lost, though forgotten by man.

Know ye that throughout the space
that ye dwell in
are others as great as your own,
interlaced through the heart of your matter
yet separate in space of their own.

Once in a time long forgotten,
I THOTH, opened the doorway,
penetrated into other spaces
and learned of the secrets concealed.
Deep in the essence of matter
are many mysteries concealed.

Nine are the interlocked dimensions,
and Nine are the cycles of space.
Nine are the diffusions of consciousness,
and Nine are the worlds within worlds.
Aye, Nine are the Lords of the cycles
that come from above and below.

Space is filled with concealed ones,
for space is divided by time.
Seek ye the key to the time-space,
and ye shall unlock the gate.
Know ye that throughout the time-space
consciousness surely exists.
Though from our knowledge it is hidden,
yet still forever exists.

The key to worlds within thee
are found only within.

For man is the gateway of mystery
and the key that is One with the One.

Seek ye within the circle.
Use the WORD I shall give.
Open the gateway within thee,
and surely thou, too, shall live.
Man, ye think that ye liveth,
but know it is life within death.
For as sure as ye are bound to your body,
for you no life exists.
Only the Soul is space-free,
has life that is really a life.
All else is only a bondage,
a fetter from which to be free.

Think not that man is earth-born,
though come from the earth he may be.
Man is light-born spirit.
But, without knowing, he can never be free.
Darkness surrounds the light-born.
Darkness fetters the Soul.
Only the one who is seeking
may ever hope to be free.

Shadows around thee are falling
darkness fills all the space
Shine forth, O LIGHT of the man-soul.
Fill thou the darkness of space.

Ye are son of the GREAT LIGHT
Remember and ye shall be free.
Stay not thou in the shadows.
Spring forth from the darkness of night
Light, let thy Soul be, O SUN-BORN,
fill with glory of Light,
Freed from the bonds of the darkness,
a Soul that is One with the Light.

Thou art the key to all wisdom.
Within thee is all time and space.
Live not in bondage to darkness.
Free thou, thy Light-form from night.

Great Light that fills all the Cosmos,
flow thou fully to man.
Make of his body a light-torch
that shall never be quenched among men.

Long in the past, sought I wisdom,
knowledge not known to man.

Far to the past, I traveled
into the space where time began.
Sought I ever new knowledge
to add to the wisdom I knew.
Yet only, I found, did the future
hold the key to the wisdom I thought.

Down, to the HOLES of AMENTI
I journeyed, the greater knowledge to seek.
Ask of thee, LORDS of the CYCLES,
thy way to the wisdom I sought.
Asked the LORDS this question:
Where is the source of ALL?
Answered, in tones that were mighty,
the voice of the LORD of the NINE:
Free thou thy soul from thy body
and come forth with me to the LIGHT.

Forth I came from my body,
a glittering flame in the night.
Stood I before the LORD,
bathed in the fire of LIFE.
Seized was I then by a force,
great beyond knowledge of man.
Cast was I to the Abyss
through spaces unknown to man.

Saw I the moldings of Order
from the chaos and angles of night.
Saw I the LIGHT, spring from Order
and heard the voice of the Light.
Saw I the flame of the Abyss,
casting forth Order and Light.
Saw Order spring out of chaos.
Saw Light giving forth Life.

Then heard I the voice.
Hear thou and understand.
The flame is the source of all things,
containing all things in potentiality.
The Order that sent forth light
is the WORD and from the WORD,
COME LIFE and the existence of all.

And again spoke the voice saying:
THE LIFE in thee is the WORD.
Find thou the LIFE within thee
and have powers to use of the WORD.

Long I watched the Light-flame,
pouring forth from the Essence of Fire,
realizing that LIFE but Order
and that man is one with the fire.

Back I came to my body
stood again with the Nine,
listened to the voice of the Cycles,
vibrate with powers they spoke:
Know ye, O Thoth, that LIFE
is but the WORD of the FIRE.
The LIFE forth ye seek before thee
is but the WORD in the World as a fire.
Seek ye the path to the WORD and Powers
shall surely be thine.

Then asked I of the Nine:
O Lord, show me the path.
Give the path to the wisdom.
Show me the way to the WORD.
Answered, me then,
the LORD OF THE NINE:
Through ORDER, ye shall find the way.
Saw ye that the WORD came from Chaos?
Saw ye not that LIGHT came from FIRE?

Look in thy life for this order.
Balance and order thy life.
Quell all the Chaos of the emotions
and thou shalt have order in LIFE.
ORDER brought forth from Chaos

will bring thee the WORD of the SOURCE,
will thee the power of CYCLES,
and make of thy Soul a force that
freewill extend through the ages,
a perfect SUN from the Source.

Listened I to the voice
and deep thanked the words in my heart.
Forever have I sought for order
that I might draw on the WORD.
Know ye that he who attains it
must ever in ORDER be for use
of the WORD though this order
has never and can never be.

Take ye these words, O man.
As part of thy life, let them be.
Seek thee to conquer this order
and One with the WORD thou shalt be.

Put forth thy effort in gaining LIGHT
on the pathway of Life.
Seek to be One with the SUN/state.
Seek to be solely the LIGHT.
Hold thou thy thought on the Oneness
of Light with the body of man.

Know that all is Order from Chaos
born into light.

Tablet X: The Key of Time

A subtle but interesting masculine personification is made for space. Thought, law, harmony, and order are attributed to the infinite brain. Freedom from the simulator is available by understanding the concept of TIME. We are reminded that once a phenomenon is understood, the mystery is no more. Understanding lifts the veil of the unknown. Thoth asks the DWELLER the question, what is time? He is told that prior to the creation of time, only a VOID existed: timeless, spaceless, nothingness. Thoth is told that a purposeful thought vibration was used to fill the VOID. Next the DWELLER is asked if the thought that entered the void was eternal. He is told that the LAW of TIME had to be created so that a purposeful creative thought sent into the VOID would also be eternal. It seems the Creator of All is eternal as are It's thoughts. The time law was needed to have the intended infrastructure established in order that the infinite brain's creative thought could exist. Thus the law of space pre-existed the law of TIME which is manufactured as a thought construct, probably based on large galactic wobbles.

TIME is fixed and unchanging, being a force that distinguishes events. We are told that that we move through time as our consciousness changes focus from one event to the other. Thought is responsible for the creation of time and we are all from ONE source even though events are distinguished, even by long periods or ages. Thoth gives a geometric discussion about how TIME exists in space, moving through strange angles during his OOBEs. It seems that the motion and path (linear, circular) one adopts during the OOBE, can be intended such that the bounds of TIME are circumvented. Time travel if you will. It appears that by traversing the path of the legs of a right triangle, the OOBE participant can leave the eternal construct, a thought construct TIME, piggybacking on the fabric of space behind. Thoth performs this right angle turn to the right after leaving his body, on a time journey back to man's creation event stating nothing is new. This may imply the concept the Egyptians embraced concerning the science of continuous creation [24]. We are told light is life and nothing can exist without it, being a constituent component of all formed matter. There are properties of light which science is just now starting to figure out as demonstrated in the field of Quantum Encryption Keying where the polarization state of paired photons is used to effect non-local transmission of a highly secure photonic key.

During a visit to the HALLS OF AMENTI, Thoth discloses that he was privy to an event involving the seven cycle masters who appear to be using sound vibration to open a portal circumventing the LAW OF TIME construct created by the Creator of All. The group appears to be singing or chanting a "song of the cycle" which opens the possibilities of time travel. How do events stay distinguished in this space dimension one might query? Once time is overcome, events are essentially in a sequenced Queue that can be accessed by a time traveler, moving his body through space and focusing the consciousness onto a particular event in the queue. This seems to cause time travel to that event by affiliating the traveler's thought to the desired event. My understanding is that in order for the INFINITE BRAIN to establish the LAW OF TIME, a velocity constant, the speed of light is used. Einstein agreed. Thus, the events can be ordered in the sequenced queue (construct) using cyclical cosmic wobbles seen in galaxies and solar systems. The Great Year is such a wobble cycle, lasting 25,920 Earth years. Thoth states that words have the power to open the portal that bypasses the Creator of All's LAW OF TIME. We are given the word ZIN-URU which we are told has power in its sound. Putting the pieces together, this word could have been the "song that opens the cycles" that Thoth overheard from the masters of the seven cycles in the Halls of Amenti. Thus, just saying the word may have little effect versus chanting in a special way. For instance, how long does one linger on each of the syllables? Is there a frequency sweep performed using the voice as is done when chanting the OM mantra?

Another fascinating part about this power word given to us is that the name shows up on the pre-history of Nibiru genealogy

THE 7th PLANET MERCURY RISING

table where ZIN.URU is the half-sister who is married to EN.URU, the youngest son of AN and ANTU who are the earliest progenitors in our prehistory of the Nibiru family tree. EN.URU is therefore ANU's grandfather and ZIN.URU is ANU's grandmother. Is this why the word has power? Invoking an ancestor's name that can open the portal to the space-time enabling time travel? I find it interesting that it is a female name. See Figure 15 below.

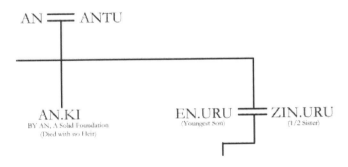

Figure 15: ZIN.URU Genealogy Tree

Next we are illuminated about the existence of a multi-dimensional reality, worlds within worlds. Now consider that if the LAW of TIME were suddenly removed or shut off in a mind experiment, that the events that were separated by a cosmic cycles would all become accessible to the pioneering time traveler. The secret to accessing events that are no longer separated by TIME is that they exist in the same space, separated by perceptional sensitivity tuning in the frequency of the desired dimension. This distinction ability has a direct measurable limitation. The minimum separation between events is established by a photon waveform spacing. In other words, how close can we stack wavelengths in a medium and still be able to distinguish one from the other? During my work at Lightpointe Communications, Incorporated, we worked with optical fibers and laser transceivers which exposed me to the theoretical and practical concept that we understand as photons. Placing an optical signal (wave) into a small glass wire the size of a human hair and smaller is the petri dish, so to speak. Telecommunications companies like Quest Communications invested heavily in fiber access for long haul regional interconnectivity. How many wavelengths, each carrying 2.5 Gbps bi-directionally can a single mode fiber, supporting carrier waves in the infrared spectrum at 1500 nanometers, can be stacked? Think of small spikes of energy vertically stacked side by side. How close can one signal be and not interfere with the adjacent light signal? This can be thought of as a measurement resolution issue or a physics problem. Light can cross paths with other light sources and they do not interfere. Shine two flashlight beams across one another and you will see there is not interference. This is true independent of the wavelength. So back to the question, how close can the independent wavelengths of light be separated and stuffed into an optical fiber, a dense waveform distributed multimodal (DWDM)? This problem was being funded and commercialized by Optical Micro Machines, a company based in San Diego, California. Small electro-optically controlled mirrors were being used to multiplex optical data carrier signals onto and off of a single mode optical fiber cable. Thus, the MUX-DEMUX problem dealing with optical wavelengths, parallel light dimensions if you will, was being addressed to create a very fat pipe (more wavelengths = more carrying capacity per fiber). The increased bandwidth focus was being done in anticipation of bandwidth hogging videos (MPEG-4) being accessed by internet users, opting to watch alternative independent news from a *vlogger* versus tuning into antiquated governments sponsored propaganda on TV. Figure 16 below depicts a dense waveform division multiplexing (DWDM) system indicating the C-Band telecommunications fiber optical carrier wave choice being 1550 nanometers.

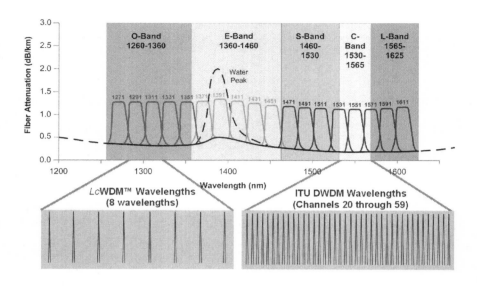

Figure 16: DWDM Multi-Wavelength System

The small vertical spikes at the bottom of the picture demonstrate the spacing options, dense waveforms and simpler systems like a single carrier. The advantage of a multi-carrier DWDM system is the data carrying capacity linearly increases with each added wavelength. Data carrying capacities are assigned to optical networks, OC-48 indicating bidirectional optical carriers supporting 2.5 gigabits per second (Gbps), bi-directionally for a total of 5 Gbps per carrier. Compare that with what you get on your crappy cable modem at home, perhaps a megabit per second throughput can be achieved in the middle of the night when no one else is on the network, except in India. My premise is that the spacing between the optical carriers, to the extent that it is not a measurement issue, establishes the spacing limits for the nine dimensions discussed by Thoth. These are the nine parallel realities that are accessible by frequency/wavelength as the two parameters are simply related by the speed of light.

My understanding is that the dimensional stacked events are co-existent, partitioned like musical notes. Let one of the parallel universes or events be E_0, the lowest or fundamental dimension that will be used initially. Now let's squeeze another event, E_1 in next to E_0 at the desired spacing, not to exceed the minimal value established by the photonic limits of interference. Repeat the process until we have a total of nine events occupying the same space, with some nominal but measurable distinctive spacing wavelength and there you have a nine dimension parallel event construct. Figure 17 shows the 13 segments of the chromatic scale and its affiliated musical notes. The overtones or octaves can be thought of as stacked spike as we did with photons in a DWDM system, but use acoustic vibration frequencies as our references instead of wavelengths better suited to measure light. Frequency numbers are very large when derived from dividing the wavelength into the speed of light and are usually given a term for ease of reference. For example, microwaves and radio waves represent such categorizations.

DIATONIC SCALE												
1	2	3	4	5	6	7	8
C	C# D♭	D	D# E♭	E	F	F# G♭	G	G# A♭	A	A# B♭	B	C

Tonic — **Second** — **Third** — **Fourth** — **Fifth** — **Sixth** — **Seventh** — **Octave**

Tone — Tone — Semi tone — Tone — Tone — Tone — Semi tone

CHROMATIC SCALE												
1	2	3	4	5	6	7	8	9	10	11	12	13

Semitone | Semitone | Semitone | Semitone | Semitone | Semitone | Semitone | Semitone | Semitone | Semitone | Semitone | Semitone

1.6 IS THE GOLDEN NUMBER (SEQUENCE OF 1, 3, 5, 8, 13)
THE PERFECT CHORD RESPONDS TO THAT SEQUENCE

Figure 17: Nine Parallel Dimensions and Musical Notes

Added dimensions are spaced by harmonic images of the same fundamental frequency yet existing as different octaves. For example, one could have a fundamental frequency (termed drone frequency when playing a didgeridoo) of say note E_0 having a frequency of 20.60 Hertz and a wavelength of 1670 cm. This musical E note is in the first octave beginning with the subscript of zero. Repeated images of this note occur like the decreasing amplitude of a damped sinusoid. The next place in the spectrum where the energy of the note appears, the next harmonic, is E_1 whose frequency is 41.20 Hertz and an affiliated wavelength derived using the scalar ratio of the speed of light is 790 cm. The third harmonic of the E note, E2 has a frequency of 82.41 Hertz and a wavelength of 419 cm. We can continue this process noting the distance between the tonal E_i notes is simply N times the fundamental frequency. This repeated note images in various harmonics or octaves in the musical scale can continue indefinitely in theory. The reality is when a signal is created, its energy distribution and roll-off in the higher harmonics end up being so small in amplitude that it cannot be measured with scientific instruments, but exists anyway.

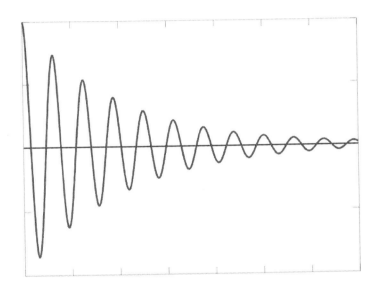

Figure 18: Damped Sinusoid and Harmonic Dimensions

This means there could be infinite dimensions, but according to both Thoth and modern String Theory, there seem to be NINE dimensions or worlds within worlds simultaneously accessible to the traveler operating apart from the confines of the LAW OF TIME.

Coupling the nine Mayan underworld frequencies that exist within the brainwave region for a human, and agreement showing nine dimensions in String Theory, along with this Emerald Tablet X taught by the DWELLER to Thoth, there may be some merit to String Theory, now mirroring ancient wisdom handed down from Enki's Atlantis.

The final correlation is that there were deemed nine rows of the evolution of consciousness in the Mayan Tzolkin Calendar and Dr. Carl Johan Calleman [25] cites the nine underworld Mayan frequencies which seem to coincide with the human brain waves segmented from Delta, Theta, Alpha and Beta and ranging from about 0.5 Hertz to approximately 20 Hertz in frequency.

Within the logic of the Mayan Long Count, he says, an auspicious end would have to be on a day which is 13 Ahau in the Tzolkin count. Since December 21, 2012 falls on 4 Ahau this is an unlikely end date. The 28 October 2011 is a 13 Ahau date.

Beginning with the Big Bang, he believes creation has continued through a series of waves, each one a factor of 20 times shorter in duration than the one preceding it. Each wave has driven the structure of the universe to a higher level. See Figure 19.

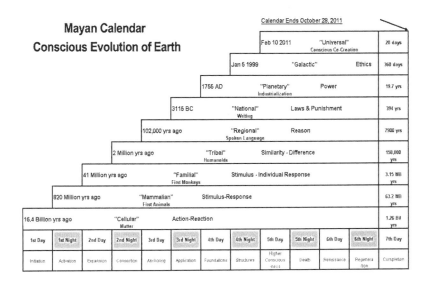

Figure 19: Mayan Calendar of Consciousness

The first wave drove the creation of physical cellular matter, and the second level of consciousness in the table produced mammals. The first monkeys were established in the third segment and in the fourth level we see the emergence of humans in tribal groups. During the fifth wave, we see humans organizing into regional groups and, then into national groups in the sixth. The seventh wave encompasses human awareness of the whole planet, and the eighth awareness of our place in the galactic structure. The final wave, the ninth and shortest of all, began on 8 March 2011 and will complete along with all the others on 28 October 2011 at which time an awareness of the whole of the cosmos is achieved

279

by the primitive workers transformed by wisdom into Gods. The importance of the telescoping scalar (20) is that in the final phase the time between our thoughts and the manifestation of their physical reality happens very quickly, essentially within 20 days. So, be very careful guarding your thoughts to direct them toward the LIGHT. You have become a hopefully conscious co-creator with the Creator of All during this ascension window of opportunity. Okay, back to the tablet analysis since we have gotten pretty deep with the LAW of TIME.

Next, Thoth discusses dressing himself in his Magician-Magus outfit and opening a portal via ritual, in an attempt to free ERESHKIGAL, a Lady of Light held captive by the dark prince of ARULU. This maiden in distress turns out to be Nergal's wife, as shown in my genealogy table. Nergal had the titles of King of the Netherworld as well as Metatron. ERESHKIGAL, the wife of Nergal, son of Enlil and Ninlil, was given the title *Queen of the Netherworld* in Sumer. It is my understanding that Enki had a son with ERESHKIGAL, Ningishzida. Thus, if this is the same being whom Thoth saves in this Tablet account, then he performed this act to save his mother! See Figure 20 below which depicts the relationships between the players.

The fact that Ningishzida is the captive's son, provides the motivation behind the Magus costume and the subsequent incantation to open the portal to space-time in an attempt to save her from some bad situation, which he achieves successfully. Interesting to see that a son of Enki married an offspring of Enlil, probably to mitigate family feuds.

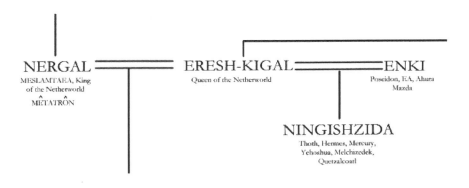

Figure 20: ERESHKIGAL Genealogy Tree

Thoth was the child of that union. Perhaps that is why Anu designated him to be the Messenger of the Gods.

List ye, O Man. Take of my wisdom.
Learn of his deep hidden mysteries of space.
Learn of the THOUGHT that grew in the abyss,
bringing Order and Harmony in space.

Know ye, O man, that all exists
has being only because of the LAW.

GERALD CLARK

Know ye the LAW and ye shall be free,
never be bound by the fetters of night.

Far, through strange spaces, have I journeyed
into the depth of the abyss of time,
until in the end all was revealed.
Know ye that mystery is only mystery
when it is knowledge unknown to man.
When ye have plumbed the heart of all mystery,
knowledge and wisdom will surely be thine.

Seek ye and learn that TIME is the secret
whereby ye may be free of this space.

Long have I, WISDOM, sought wisdom;
aye, and shall seek of eternity's end
for know that ever before me receding
shall move the goal I seek to attain.
Even the LORDS of the CYCLES
know that not yet have THEY reached the goal,
For with all of their wisdom,
they know that TRUTH ever grows.

Once, in a past time, I spoke to the Dweller.
Asked of the mystery of time and space.
Asked him the question that surged in my being,

saying: O Master, what is time?

Then to me spoke HE, the Master:
Know ye, O Thoth, in the beginning
there and VOID and nothingness,
a timeless, spaceless, nothingness.
And into the nothingness came a thought,
purposeful, all-pervading,
and It filled the VOID.
There existed no matter, only force,
a movement, a vortex, or vibration
of the purposeful thought
that filled the VOID.

And I questioned the Master, saying:
Was this thought eternal?
And answered me the DWELLER, Saying:
In the beginning, there was eternal thought,
and for thought to be eternal, time must exist.
So into the all-pervading thought
grew the LAW of TIME.
Aye time which exists through all space,
floating in a smooth, rhythmic movement
that is eternally in a state of fixation.

Time changes not,

but all things change in time.
For time is the force
that holds events separate,
each in its own proper place.
Time is not in motion,
but ye move through time
as your consciousness
moves from one event to another.

Aye, by time yet exist, all in all,
an eternal ONE existence.
Know ye that even though in the time ye are separate,
yet still are ONE, in all times existent.

Ceased then the voice of the DWELLER,
and departed I to ponder on time.
For knew I that in these words lay wisdom
and a way to explore the mysteries of time.

Oft did I ponder the words of the DWELLER.
Then sought I to solve the mystery of time.
Found I that time moves through strange angles.
Yet only by curves could I hope to attain the key
that would give me access to the time-space.
Found I that only by moving upward
and yet again by moving to right-ward

could I be free from the time of the movement.

Forth I came from out of my body,
moved in the movements that changed me in time.
Strange were the sights I saw in my journeys,
many the mysteries that opened to view.
Aye, saw I man's beginning,
learned from the past that nothing is new.

Seek ye, O man, to learn the pathway
that leads through the spaces
that are formed forth in time.

Forget not, O man, with all of thy seeking
that Light is the goal ye shall seek to attain.
Search ye for the Light on thy pathway
and ever for thee the goal shall endure.

Let not thine heart turn ever to darkness.
light let shine Soul be, a Sun on the way.
Know ye that eternal brightness,
ye shall ever find thy Soul hid in Light,
never fettered by bondage or darkness,
ever it shines forth a Sun of the Light.

Aye, know, though hidden in darkness,

your Soul, a spark of the true flame, exists.
Be ye One with the greatest of all Lights.
Find at the SOURCE, the END of thy goal.

Light is life, for without the great Light
nothing can ever exist.
Know ye, that in all formed matter,
the heart of Light always exists.
Aye, even though bound in the darkness,
inherent Light always exists.

Once I stood in the HALLS OF AMENTI
and heard the voice of the LORDS of AMENTI,
saying in tones that rang through the silence,
words of power, mighty and potent.
Chanted they the song of the cycles,
the words that open the path to beyond.
Aye, I saw the great path opened
and looked for the instant into the beyond.
Saw I the movements of the cycles,
vast as the thought of the SOURCE could convey.

Knew I then even Infinity
is moving on to some unthinkable end.
Saw I that the Cosmos is Order
and part of a movement that extends to all space,

a party of an Order of Orders,
constantly moving in a harmony of space.

Saw I the wheeling of cycles
like vast circles across the sky.
Knew I then that all that has being
is growing to meet yet another being
in a far-off grouping of space and of time.

Knew I then that in Words are power
to open the planes that are hidden from man.
Aye, that even in Words lies hidden the key
that will open above and below.

Hark ye, now man, this word I leave with thee.
Use it and ye shall find power in its sound.
Say ye the word:
"ZIN-URU"
and power ye shall find.
Yet must ye understand that man is of Light
and Light is of man.

List ye, O man, and hear a mystery
stranger than all that lies 'neath the Sun.
Know ye, O man, that all space
is filled by worlds within worlds;

aye, one within the other yet separate by Law.

Once in my search for deep buried wisdom,
I opened the door that bars THEM from man.
Called I from the other planes of being,
one who was fairer than the daughters of men.
Aye, I called her from out of the spaces,
to shine as a Light in the world of men.

Used I the drum of the Serpent.
Wore I the robe of the purple and gold.
Placed on my head, I, the crown of Silver.
Around me the circle of cinnabar shone.
Raised I my arms and cried the invocation
that opens the path to the planes beyond,
cried to the LORDS of the SIGNS in their houses:
Lords of the two horizons,
watchers of the treble gates,
stand ye One at the right and One at the left
as the STAR rises to his throne
and rules over his sign.
Aye, thou dark prince of ARULU,
open the gates of the dim, hidden land
and release her whom ye keep imprisoned.

Hear ye, hear ye, hear ye,

dark Lords and Shining Ones,
and by their secret names,
names which I know and can pronounce,
hear ye and obey my will.

Lit I then twith flame my circle
and called HER
in the space-planes beyond.
Daughter of Light return from ARULU.

Seven times and seven times
have I passed through the fire.
Food have I not eaten.
Water have I not drunk.
I call thee from ARULU,
from the realms of ERESHKIGAL.
I summon thee, lady of Light.

Then before me rose the dark figures;
aye, the figures of the Lords of Arulu.
Parted they before me
and forth came the Lady of Light.

Free was she now from the LORDS of the night,
free to live in the Light of the earth Sun,
free to live as a child of the Light.

Hear ye and listen, O my children.
Magic is knowledge and only is Law.
Be not afraid of the power within thee
for it follows Law as the stars in the sky.

Know ye that to be without knowledge,
wisdom is magic and not of the Law.
But know ye that ever ye by your knowledge
can approach closer to a place in the Sun.

List ye, my children, follow my teaching.
Be ye ever seekers of Light.
Shine in the world of men all around thee,
a Light on the path that shall shine among men.

Follow ye and learn of my magic.
Know that all force is thine if thou wilt.
Fear not the path that leads thee to knowledge,
but rather shun ye the dark road.

Light is thine, O man, for the taking.
Cast off the fetters and thou shalt be free.
Know ye that thy Soul is living in bondage
fettered by fears that hold ye in thrall.

Open thy eyes and see the great SUN-LIGHT.
Be not afraid for all is thine own.
Fear is the LORD of the dark ARULU
to he who never faced the dark fear.
Aye, know that fear has existence
created by those who are bound by their fears.

Shake off thy bondage, O children,
and walk in the Light of the glorious day.
Never turn thy thoughts to the darkness
and surely ye shall be One with the Light.

Man is only what he believeth,
a brother of darkness or a child of the Light.
Come though into the Light my Children.
Walk in the pathway that leads to the Sun.

Hark ye now, and list to the wisdom.
Use thou the word I have given unto thee.
Use it and surely thou shalt find power and wisdom
and Light to walk in the way.
Seek thee and find the key I have given
and ever shalt thou be a Child of the Light.

Tablet XI: The Key to Above and Below

Thoth begins this tablet by speaking to the contemporary people in Egypt, the land of Khem. He reminds them that they were primitive barbarians living in caves when he first arrived in Egypt, being raised up to higher consciousness by using his wisdom and instruction.

Thoth starts a relic scavenger hunt by telling the people of Khem that he hid the Keys to the Way into Life in the Pyramid at Giza. A relational map involving the Sphinx is used to point the way, aligned to the apex of the pyramid using two line segments along the same vector. Dig there to find his hidden Key to the underground hiding place in what seems like a hall of records.

We are suddenly interrupted looking for the underground hidden Key and informed of nine cycles above and fourteen below, set up to intersect like the hand of a clock at some future time. Clarity is provided about the masters of the nine cycle's mission, deemed discrete units of consciousness to help synchronize the future conjunction of intersecting cycles into one with the ALL. It is prophesied that the lords of the nine cycles will help merge the other cycles into a single unified whole leaving none above nor below at infinity. Consciousness is unique to the individuals path, thus one cannot simply copy someone else's life processes to take a shortcut. Truth is a pathless land only to be found by the efforts of a seeking soul.

Hear ye and list ye, O children of Khem,
to the words that I give that shall bring ye to the Light.
Ye know, O men, that I knew your fathers,
aye, your fathers in a time long ago.
Deathless have I been through all the ages,
living among ye since your knowledge began.

Leading ye upward to the Light of the Great Soul
have I ever striven,
drawing ye from out of the darkness of night.

Know ye, O people amongst whom I walk,
that I, Thoth, have all of the knowledge
and all of the wisdom known, to man since the ancient days.
Keeper have I been of the secrets of the great race,
holder of the key that leads into life.
Bringer up have I been to ye, O my children,
even from the darkness of the Ancient of Days.
List ye now to the words of my wisdom.
List ye now to the message I bring.
Hear ye now the words I give thee, and
ye shall be raised from the darkness to Light.

Far in the past, when first I came to thee,
found I thee in caves of rocks.
Lifted I thee by my power and wisdom
until thou didst shine as men among men.
Aye, found I thee without any knowing.
Only a little were ye raised beyond beasts.
Fanned I ever the spark of thy consciousness
until at last ye flamed as men.

Now shall I speak to thee knowledge ancient
beyond the thought of thy race.
Know ye that we of the Great Race
had and have knowledge that is more than man's.
Wisdom we gained from the star-born races,
wisdom and knowledge far beyond man.
Down to us had descended the masters of wisdom
as far beyond us as I am from thee.
List ye now while I give ye wisdom.
Use it and free thou shalt be.

Know ye that in the pyramid I builded are the Keys
that shall show ye the Way into life.
Aye, draw ye a line from the great image I builded,
to the apex of the pyramid, built as a gateway.
Draw ye another opposite in the same angle and direction.
Dig ye and find that which I have hidden.

There shall ye find the underground entrance to
the secrets hidden before ye were men.

Tell ye I now of the mystery of cycles
that move in movements that are strange to the finite,
for infinite are they beyond knowledge of man.
Know ye that there are nine of the cycles;
aye, nine above and fourteen below,
moving in harmony to the place of joining
that shall exist in the future of time.
Know ye that the Lords of the Cycles
are units of consciousness sent from the others to unify
This with the All.
Highest are They of the consciousness
of all the Cycles, working in harmony with the Law.
Know They that in time all will be perfected,
having none above and none below, but all One
in a perfected Infinity, a harmony of all in the Oneness of All.

Deep neath the Earth surface in the Halls of Amenti
sit the Seven, the Lords of the Cycles,
aye, and another, the Lord from below.
Yet know thee that in Infinity there is
neither above nor below.
But ever there is and ever shall be
Oneness of All when all is complete.

Oft have I stood before the Lords of the All.
Oft at the fount of their wisdom have drunken and
filled both my body and Soul with their Light.

Spake they to me and told me of cycles
and the Law that gives them the means to exist.
Aye, spake to me the Lord of the Nine saying:
O, Thoth, great are ye among Earth children,
but mysteries exist of which ye know not.
Ye know that ye came from a space-time below
this and know ye shall travel to a space-time beyond.
But little ye know of the mysteries within them,
little ye know of the wisdom beyond. Know ye that
ye as a whole in this consciousness
are only a cell in the process of growth.

The consciousness below thee is ever-expanding
in different ways from those known to thee.
Aye, it, though in space-time below thee,
is ever growing in ways that are different from
those that were part of the ways of thine own.
For know that it grows as a result of thy growth
but not in the same way that thou didst grow.
The growth that thou had and have in the present
have brought into being a cause and effect.
No consciousness follows the path of those before it,

else all would be repetition and vain.

Each consciousness in the cycle it exists in

follows its own path to the ultimate goal.

Each plays its part in the Plan of the Cosmos.

Each plays its part in the ultimate end.

The farther the cycle, the greater its

knowledge and ability to blend the Law of the whole.

Know ye, that ye in the cycles below us

are working the minor parts of the Law,

while we of the cycle that extends to Infinity

take of the striving and build greater Law.

Each has his own part to play in the cycles.

Each has his work to complete in his way.

The cycle below thee is yet not below thee

but only formed for a need that exists.

For know ye that the fountain of wisdom

that sends forth the cycles is eternally

seeking new powers to gain.

Ye know that knowledge is gained only by practice,

and wisdom comes forth only from knowledge,

and thus are the cycles created by Law.

Means are they for the gaining of knowledge

for the Plane of Law that is the Source of the All.

The cycle below is not truly below but only
different in space and in time.
The consciousness there is working and
testing lesser things than those ye are.
And know, just as ye are working on greater,
so above ye are those who are also working
as ye are on yet other laws.
The difference that exists between the cycles
is only in ability to work with the Law.
We, who have being in cycles beyond thee,
are those who first came forth from the
Source and have in the passage through
time-space gained ability to use
Laws of the Greater that are far beyond
the conception of man.
Nothing there is that is really below thee
but only a different operation of Law.

Look thee above or look thee below,
the same shall ye find.
For all is but part of the Oneness
that is at the Source of the Law.
The consciousness below thee is
part thine own as we are a part of thine.

Ye, as a child had not the knowledge

that came to ye when ye became a man.

Compare ye the cycles to man in his journey

from birth unto death,

and see in the cycle below thee the child

with the knowledge he has;

and see ye yourself as the child grown older,

advancing in knowledge as time passes on.

See ye, We, also, the child grown to manhood

with the knowledge and wisdom that came

with the years.

So also, O Thoth, are the cycles of consciousness,

children in different stages of growth,

yet all from the one Source, the Wisdom,

and all to the Wisdom returning again.

Ceased then He from speaking and sat

in the silence that comes to the Lords.

Then again spake He unto me, saying:

Oh Thoth, long have We sat in Amenti,

guarding the flame of life in the Halls.

Yet know, we are still part of our

Cycles with our Vision reaching unto them and beyond.

Aye, know we that of all,

nothing else matters excepting the growth

we can gain with our Soul.

Know we the flesh is fleeting.

The things men count great are nothing to us.

The things we seek are not of the body

but are only the perfected state of the Soul.

When ye as men can learn that nothing but

progress of Soul can count in the end,

then truly ye are free from all bondage,

free to work in a harmony of Law.

Know, O man, ye should aim at perfection,

for only thus can ye attain to the goal.

Though ye should know that nothing is perfect,

yet it should be thy aim and thy goal.

Ceased again the voice of the Nine,

and into my consciousness the words had sunk.

Now, seek I ever more wisdom

that I may be perfect in Law with the All.

Soon go I down to the Halls of Amenti

to live beneath the cold flower of life.

Ye whom I have taught shall nevermore see me.

Yet live I forever in the wisdom I taught.

All that man is is because of his wisdom.

All that he shall be is the result of his cause.

List ye, now to my voice and become
greater than common man.
Lift thine eyes upward,
let Light fill thy being,
be thou ever Children of Light.
Only by effort shall ye grow upward to
the plane where Light is the All of the All.
Be ye the master of all that surrounds thee.
Never be mastered by the effects of thy life.
Create then ever more perfect causes
and in time shalt thou be a Sun of the Light

Free, let thine soul soar ever upward,
free from the bondage and fetters of night.
Lift thine eyes to the Sun in the sky-space.
For thee, let it be a symbol of life.
Know that thou art the Greater Light,
perfect in thine own sphere,
when thou art free.
Look not ever into the blackness.
Lift up thine eyes to the space above.
Free let thine Light flame upward
and shalt thou be a Child of the Light

Tablet XII: The Law of Cause and Effect and the Key of Prophecy

Thoth the Atlantean reminds us that he has conquered the laws of space-time providing encouragement that we too will merge and become ONE with the ALL. The future declared to be known, an open book for the literate, as he calls it. Ironically, the future is stated as changeable, not fixed, but knowable. This would be true if the LAW of TIME were halted and all events go to their default state stacked in the space in a clump with no separation or distinction.

Cause and Effect, arising from the first cause, are reversed to demonstrate the result of this timeless condition where one leads back to the other, the ALL. Recall the first cause detailed in Tablet X is initiated when the INFINITE BRAIN sending a sound vibration into the great VOID created the LAWS OF TIME as a thought manifestation. Physics terms this event the BIG BANG THEORY.

Cause and effect are related to fate and destiny. Take the right fated steps (cause) and one's destiny (effect) may come into view. Luckily we are encouraged by Thoth that although our life path is cloaked in shadows, Light shall be All and darkness shall fall. Reading this tablet is like a breath of fresh air, stumbling outside escaping the body odor and sweat pouring from a 100 degree

Fahrenheit Bikram Yoga studio after an hour and a half session. What a relief knowing that the New World Order criminals will fail, it has been pre-ordained by the CREATOR OF ALL, the INFINITE BRAIN.

We are warned that most will forget the knowledge of the Gods and that in the future we will be gods to others given our knowledge shared by Thoth. The DARK BROTHERS initiate a terrible great war between the Light and the Night, altering Earth's course causing earthquakes and trembling. This is predicted to occur when man has learned to conquer global transportation via sea and air and has scientifically progressed to harness the power of lightning. The prerequisites have been met here on Earth and the war is on the verge of expanding to a world wide scale. My prediction is that the DARK BROTHERS are focused on Ukraine's destruction to draw in Russia, a hook in the jaw long prophesied by Enlil in the Biblical account in Revelations, the Gog and Magog war.

CAUSE: Invade a sovereign nation installing a puppet government which distracts the populace while their resources are stolen. This is a repeating pattern worldwide.

EFFECT: Trigger national populace's instinctive territorial imperative to protect one's homeland, leading to war. Conflict spills over borders to allies sworn to defend each other increasing the carnage; a DARK BROTHER Special Forces operation right from the CIA handbook. Weapons of force shall wipe out half of the Earth's humans. At this point we are told that Thoth and the Sons of the Morning intervene in the war. Exposure to the Gods halts striving against thy brother leading to Atlantis rising and an age (Aquarius) of Light. We are told that we will receive a new home, a place in the stars, a different dimension. Thoth heads back to the Halls of Amenti to await the coming future age of Light with words of encouragement, providing us with three names to call him by three times in a row when in need.

Call thou on me when thou dost need me.
Use my name three times in a row:
Chequetet, Arelich, Volmalites.

List ye, O man, to the words of my wisdom,
list to the voice of Thoth, the Atlantean.
Conquered have I the Law of time-space.
Knowledge have I gained of the future of time.
Know I that man in his movement through
space-time shall ever be One with the All

Know ye, O man,
that all of the future is an open book
to him who can read.
All effect shall bring forth its causes
as all effects grew from the first cause.

Know ye the future is not fixed or
stable but varies as cause brings forth an effect.
Look in the cause thou shalt bring into being,
and surely thou shalt see that all is effect.

So, O man, be sure the effects that ye bring
forth are ever causes of more perfect effects.
Know ye the future is never in fixation but
follows man's free will as it moves through
the movements of time-space toward
the goal where a new time begins.

Man can only read the future through
the causes that bring the effects.
Seek ye within the causation and
surely ye shall find the effects.

List ye, O man, while I speak of the future,
speak of the effect that follows the cause.
Know ye that man in his journey light-ward
is ever seeking escape from the night that surrounds him,
like the shadows that surround the stars in the sky
and like the stars in the sky-space, he, too,
shall shine from the shadows of night.

Ever his destiny shall lead him onward
until he is One with the Light.
Aye, though his way lies midst the shadows,
ever before him glows the Great Light.
Dark though the way be yet shall he conquer
the shadows that flow around him like night.

Far in the future, I see man as Light-born,
free from the darkness that fetters the Soul,
living in Light without the bounds of the darkness
to cover the Light that is Light of their Soul.

Know ye, O man, before ye attain this that
many the dark shadows shall fall on your Light
striving to quench with the shadows of darkness
the Light of the Soul that strives to be free.

Great is the struggle between Light and darkness,
age old and yet ever new. Yet, know in a time, far in the future,
Light shall be All and darkness shall fall.

List ye, O man, to my words of wisdom.
Prepare and ye shall not bind your Light.
Man has risen and man has fallen as ever new
waves of consciousness flow from the great
abyss below us toward the Sun of their goal.

Ye, my children, have risen from a state

that was little above the beast,

until now of all men ye are greatest.

Yet before thee were others greater than thee.

Yet tell I thee as before thee others have fallen,

so also shall ye come to an end.

And upon the land where ye dwell now,

barbarians shall dwell and in turn rise to Light.

Forgotten shall be the ancient-wisdom,

yet ever shall live though hidden from men.

Aye, in the land thou callest Khem,

races shall rise and races shall fall.

Forgotten shalt thou be of the children of men.

Yet thou shalt have moved to a star-space

beyond this leaving behind this place where thou has dwelt.

The Soul of man moves ever onward,

bound not by any one star.

But ever moving to the great goal before him

where he is dissolved in the Light of the All.

Know ye that ye shall ever go onward,

moved by the Law of cause and effect

until in the end both become One

Aye, man, after ye have gone,

others shall move in the places ye lived.

Knowledge and wisdom shall all be forgotten,

and only a memory of Gods shall survive.

As I to thee am a God by my knowledge,

so ye, too shall be Gods of the future

because of your knowledge far above theirs.

Yet know ye that all through the ages,

man shall have access to Law when he will.

Ages to come shall see revival of wisdom

to those who shall inherit thy place on this star.

They shall, in turn, come into wisdom

and learn to banish the darkness by Light.

Yet greatly must they strive through the ages

to bring unto themselves the freedom of Light.

Then shall there come unto man the great warfare

that shall make the Earth tremble and shake in its course.

Aye, then shall the Dark Brothers

open the warfare between Light and the night.

When man again shall conquer the ocean and fly

in the air on wings like the birds;

when he has learned to harness the lightning,

then shall the time of warfare begin.

Great shall the battle be twixt the forces,

great the warfare of darkness and Light.

Nation shall rise against nation

using the dark forces to shatter the Earth.

Weapons of force shall wipe out the Earth-man

until half of the races of men shall be gone.

Then shall come forth the Sons of the Morning

and give their edict to the children of men, saying:

O men, cease from thy striving against thy brother.

Only thus can ye come to the Light.

Cease from thy unbelief, O my brother,

and follow the path and know ye are right.

Then shall men cease from their striving,

brother against brother and father against son.

Then shall the ancient home of my people rise

from its place beneath the dark ocean waves.

Then shall the Age of Light be unfolded

with all men seeking the Light of the goal.

Then shall the Brothers of Light rule the people.

Banished shall be the darkness of night.

Aye, the children of men shall progress

onward and upward to the great goal.

Children of Light shall they become.

Flame of the flame shall their Souls ever be.
Knowledge and wisdom shall be man's
in the great age for he shall approach the eternal flame,
the Source of all wisdom,
the place of beginning,
that is yet One with the end of all things.

Aye, in a time that is yet unborn,
all shall be One and One shall be All.
Man, a perfect flame of this Cosmos,
shall move forward to a place in the stars.
Aye, shall move even from out of this space-time
into another beyond the stars.

Long have ye listened to me,
O my children,
long have ye listened to the wisdom of Thoth.
Now I depart from ye into darkness.
Now go I to the Halls of Amenti,
there to dwell in the future when Light
shall come again to man.
Yet, know ye, my Spirit shall ever be with thee,
guiding thy feet in the pathway of Light.

Guard ye the secrets I leave with thee,
and surely my spirit will guard thee through life.

Keep thine eyes ever on the pathway to wisdom.

Keep the Light as thy goal evermore.

Fetter not thy Soul in bondage of darkness;

free let it wing in its flight to the stars.

Now I depart thee to dwell in Amenti.

Be thou my children in this life and the next.

The time will come when ye, too, shall be deathless,

living from age to age a Light among men.

Guard ye the entrance to the Halls of Amenti.

Guard ye the secrets I have hidden among ye.

Let not the wisdom be cast to barbarians.

Secret shall thou keep it for those who seek Light.

Now depart I.

Receive thou my blessing.

Take thou my way and follow the Light.

Blend thou thy Soul in the Great Essence.

One, with the Great Light let thy consciousness be.

Call thou on me when thou dost need me.

Use my name three times in a row:

Chequetet, Arelich, Volmalites.

Tablet XIII: The Keys of Life and Death

We are told that when we discover the oneness of all, that higher access to the ALL occurs, conquering death. Essentially repeating what happened in his path is available to us as well, including access to the Halls of Amenti in spirit (OOBE?).

The Gateway to life is through death, but not as we understand the term, instead involving fire and light (law of conservation of energy). We are told the secret is within us, reminding us of the lessons taught by Jesus in the New Testament Gospel of Luke.

Luke 17:1

"Neither shall they say, Lo here! or, lo there! for, behold, the kingdom of God is within you."

Thoth teaches that the Flower of Life mechanism in the Halls of Amenti is broadcasting the energy that is the source of the Spirit that acting as a template from which all matter is formed, everything from planets to people.

Next a discussion of what I term the human antenna model is presented. The statement is made that we die because the balance in polarity (an electrical term) in our bodies is out of kilter, shaken if you will, negating the connection to the positive or negative pole.

From Structural Integration and the Chakra system we know the body is malleable and electric. Thoth tells us that if we keep both poles active (Chakras open) that all exists therein. This is where energy and matter collide, terming it the Spirit of Life. The Mayan underworld frequencies are alluded to as being generated by the Flower of Life in the Halls of Amenti. This would make sense since the lord of the cycles were stationed within the flower of life matter generating device.

We are told that during the Earth's transformation we will hold our energetic form until all matter passes away. We are told to maintain our electrical polarity by spending one hour with our positive head (Sphenopalentine Ganglia behind the nose is positive pole of electrical body) to the North locating our consciousness from the chest to the head (upper Chakras) and then change positions of the body to the reverse pole charging position and repeating the hour with head to the South, consciousness focused from the chest to the feet. This is essentially close (chest versus pelvic bipole axis) to the model Structural Integration (SI) uses, except the pelvis is used to distinguish the upper from the lower body girdle based on the lines and plane referenced to the gravity field. The energy body division of the chest by Thoth into upper and lower halves follows the location of the Chakras whose perspective is energetic re-charging, like a battery. Thoth insinuates that if we live past the age of 100 years old, this recharge technique becomes life-sustaining, stop the practice and surely die.

The relationship between structure (gravity distribution mechanism) and energy (Chakra quantized consciousness model) together compose the two models whose intersection parameter is gravity. Structure as function and energy were presented to the reader previously discussed in detail in The Anunnaki of Nibiru [3, Ch. 6]

Finally we are taught how to preserve our consciousness when our mission in the holographic simulator comes to an end. When at death's door, lie down with the head facing eastward. Fold your hands across the solar plexus, placing the consciousness in the life seat (behind the belly button), spawning the head to toe vibration used to initiate an OOBE leading to a merging of your body, connected by the silver thread of light that remains attached, heading towards the Sun dawning on the eastern horizon, destined to blend with the source of all, Light. There one waits until desiring to take on a body at a location of choice, referring to the past soul Masters who have experience the process as Avatars, determining when to incarnate and when to return to the Light. Masters of life and death if you will.

Next we are taught how the Masters of Time have access to past lives using this process. It is a memory preservation technique essentially, used just prior to death so that when reincarnating in a new body, one retains all the memory from the past life.

While relaxed lying down with head to the East and with arms still crossed over the solar plexus, move the flame of the soul (consciousness) to the heart Chakra then move the energy rapidly whirling (pulsating North to South) to the seat of the triangle (pelvic bowl or Chakra symbol). This is the OOBE maneuver as taught by Robert Monroe.

List ye, O man, hear ye the wisdom.
Hear ye the Word that shall fill thee with Life.
Hear ye the Word that shall banish the darkness.
Hear ye the voice that shall banish the night.

Mystery and wisdom have I brought to my children;
knowledge and power descended from old.
Know ye not that all shall be opened
when ye shall find the oneness of all?

One shall ye be with the Masters of Mystery,
Conquerors of Death and Masters of Life.
Aye, ye shall learn of the flower of Amenti
the blossom of life that shines in the Halls.
In Spirit shall ye reach that Halls of Amenti
and bring back the wisdom that liveth in Light.
Know ye the gateway to power is secret.

Know ye the gateway to life is through death.

Aye, through death but not as ye know death,

but a death that is life and is fire and is Light.

Desireth thou to know the deep, hidden secret?

Look in thy heart where the knowledge is bound.

Know that in thee the secret is hidden,

the source of all life and the source of all death.

List ye, O man, while I tell the secret,

reveal unto thee the secret of old.

Deep in Earth's heart lies the flower,

the source of the Spirit

that binds all in its form.

or know ye that the Earth is living in body

as thou art alive in thine own formed form.

The Flower of Life is as thine own place of Spirit

and streams through the Earth

as thine flows through thy form;

giving of life to the Earth and its children,

renewing the Spirit from form unto form.

This is the Spirit that is form of thy body,

shaping and moulding into its form.

Know ye, O man, that thy form is dual,
balanced in polarity while formed in its form.
Know that when fast on thee Death approaches,
it is only because thy balance is shaken.
It is only because one pole has been lost.

Know that the secret of life in Amenti
is the secret of restoring the balance of poles.
All that exists has form and is living
because of the Spirit of life in its poles.

See ye not that in Earth's heart
is the balance of all things that exist
and have being on its face?
The source of thy Spirit is drawn from Earth's heart,
for in thy form thou are one with the Earth

When thou hast learned to hold thine own balance,
then shalt thou draw on the balance of Earth.
Exist then shalt thou while Earth is existing,
changing in form, only when Earth, too, shalt change:
Tasting not of death, but one with this planet,
holding thy form till all pass away.

List ye, O man, whilst I give the secret so that
ye, too, shalt taste not of change.

One hour each day shalt thou lie
with thine head pointed to the
place of the positive pole (north).
One hour each day shalt thy head be
pointed to the place of the negative pole (south).
Whilst thy head is placed to the northward,
hold thou thy consciousness from the chest to the head.

And when thy head is placed southward,
hold thou thy thought from chest to the feet.
Hold thou in balance once in each seven,
and thy balance will retain the whole of its strength.
Aye, if thou be old, thy body will freshen
and thy strength will become as a youth's.
This is the secret known to the Masters
by which they hold off the fingers of Death.
Neglect not to follow the path I have shown,
for when thou hast passed beyond years
to a hundred to neglect
it will mean the coming of Death.

Hear ye, my words, and follow the pathway.
Keep thou thy balance and live on in life.

Hear ye, O man, and list to my voice.
List to the wisdom that gives thee of Death.

When at the end of thy work appointed,

thou may desire to pass from this life,

pass to the plane where the Suns of the Morning

live and have being as Children of Light.

Pass without pain and pass without sorrow

into the plane where is eternal Light.

First lie at rest with thine head to the eastward.

Fold thou thy hands at the Source of thy life (solar plexus).

Place thou thy consciousness in the life seat.

Whirl it and divide to north and to south.

Send thou the one out toward the northward.

Send thou the other out to the south.

Relax thou their hold upon thy being.

Forth from thy form will thy silver spark fly,

upward and onward to the Sun of the morning,

blending with Light, at one with its source.

There it shall flame till desire shall be created.

Then shall return to a place in a form.

Know ye, O men, that thus pass the great Souls,

changing at will from life unto life.

Thus ever passes the Avatar,

willing his Death as he wills his own life.

List ye, O man, drink of my wisdom.
Learn ye the secret that is Master of Time.
Learn ye how those ye call Masters are
able to remember the lives of the past.

Great is the secret yet easy to master,
giving to thee the mastery of time.
When upon thee death fast approaches,
fear not but know ye are master of Death.

Relax thy body, resist not with tension.
Place in thy heart the flame of thy Soul.
Swiftly then sweep it to the seat of the triangle.

Hold for a moment, then move to the goal.
This, thy goal, is the place between thine eyebrows,
the place where the memory of life must hold sway.
Hold thou thy flame here in thy brain-seat
until the fingers of Death grasp thy Soul.
Then as thou pass through the state of transition,
surely the memories of life shall pass, too.

Then shalt the past be as one with the present.
Then shall the memory of all be retained.
Free shalt thou be from all retrogression.
The things of the past shall live in today.

Supplemental Tablet XIV:

We are told that the Earth is a portal with access to heaven guarded by Dark Lords known to the Dwellers here long ago. The portal was hidden by the Dark Lords to prevent access to heaven (Nibiru) and Arulu which appears to be the spherical boundary limits for Light-born man's travels (OOBE).

We are coached that we must be cleansed of darkness in order to use the portals of Light. Man of the future (now) will deny the mysterious information, but the seeker will find the way. Admonishments are given to not cast his pearls of wisdom to the untested so that the pure are not corrupted and that Truth may prevail.

Duat is described as a space composed of two regions that exists between the Earth and the Great One (CREATOR OF ALL dimension?) Duat is considered home of the powers of illusion, House of the Gods located at Sekhet Hetspet within the Duat. This appears to be two higher dimensions from our own, accounting for three occupied of the nine declared "worlds within worlds" previously cited by Thoth. Osiris's role is disclosed at the guard of the portal (Earth's) that turns back the souls of unworthy men.

Arulu, a place where the Great Ones have passed, is mentioned as being accessible from the Earth prison portal if one can get by Osiris the gate guard. Thoth declares when he has completed his mission of awakening humans, that he will join his ancestors, the Great Ones in his ancient home in the House of the Gods. Arulu is discussed as having the heaven-born powers. This is also the location where Thoth entered the gates of the Netherworld, controlled by Nergal according to my genealogy table, with ERESKIGAL as his spouse, to save his mother. This is consistent. The writer states that the Mighty or Great Ones on Arulu have seven mansions with three guards each against dark forces. The two dimensions in the Duat that separate Earth from Arulu has fifteen access points or openings. Not to be outdone, the Lords of Illusion have twelve unique houses oriented in different directions. It is claimed there are forty two judges of the Dead on Arulu, controlling access to Earth's dead seeking to leave the portal to the Duat that Osiris guards.

We are told that four of the judges are the Sons of Horus, and that Isis has two guards oriented east and west. She garners a new name, Queen of the Moon to add to her AKA list.

A very significant key to the mysteries is provided regarding energy differentiated into two types: *Ba* and *Ka*. *Ba is eternal essence* and *Ka is the illusion of matter that man knows as life.* After a human being is incarnated living according to *Ka*, then is infused. *Ba* is the hidden soul connection back to the SOURCE of ALL. This hidden connection is our birth right, providing the keys to the portal to the Sacred Land separated by what appears two dimensions described as the Duat. Thus, we here on Earth are living in a third dimensional reality with two additional dimensions to get to the home of the of the Great Ones, a soul repository being located there

Three universal principles attributed to GOD are disclosed: These are the equilibrium that comprise the Source of Creation:

1. *One God*: *source of all life*
2. *One Truth*: *source of all good*
3. *One point of freedom*: *source of all power*

This information most certainly is the source of the special nature of the number three. This is the first use of the term GOD versus the other terms used. Note that the Trident has three prongs. Is this a coincidence given the fact that Poseidon founded Atlantis and was dwelling in his Temple there, his symbol being the Trident?

The three qualities of God in his Light Home are:

1. Infinite **Power**
2. Infinite **Wisdom**
3. Infinite **Love**

Masters (ascended) are given three powers:

1. Transmute **evil**
2. Assist **good**
3. Use **discrimination**

The Three Powers that create all things

1. Divine Love possessed of perfect knowledge
2. Divine Wisdom knowing all possible means
3. Divine Power possessed by the joint will of Divine Love and Wisdom

We are told there are three states or circles of existence

1. The circle of **Light** where only GOD dwells
2. The circle of **Chaos** where all things by nature arise from death (*ka*)
3. The circle of **Awareness** where all things spring from life (*ba*)

Three are the paths of the Soul

1. **Man:** *ka* and the circle of chaos
2. **Liberty:** *ba* and potential ascension
3. **Light:** access to Arulu- heaven if found worthy

Three are the impediments to ascension

1. No motivation to obtain knowledge
2. Atheistic beliefs about god (not sure why god is lower case here?)
3. Attachment to evil

We are warned that even though light-born man may make it past Osiris guarding the Earth portal to the Duat, proceeding to the sphere of Arulu (heaven, sacred land), more tests await. If found unworthy, it is better to have been consumed by fire than waste the trip and their time evaluating your soul.

The next portion of the supplemental tablet is addressed to those who are liberated meaning that the *ba* is active, aware of and potentially living beyond the illusion of *ka*. The chronology indicates that the Dweller in Ancient Atlantis (Enki?), existed prior to the creation of man (220,000 years ago). The Dweller has the power to issue the key to the Earth portal for ascending souls. The Dweller is described to be the Holy One enthroned in the Flower of (Fire) Life that eventually was taken by Thoth to the land of Egypt (Khem) and was placed in the Great Halls of Amenti. An additional clue as to the identity of the Dweller in Atlantis is provided indicating that his countenance was so bright that it had to be veiled in order that visitor's Souls would not shatter from the Glory emanated. Wow!

The Flower of Life symbol has very special meaning to sacred geometry researchers and is the source of the two volume series *The Ancient Secret of the Flower of Life* [32-33] described in the bibliography and authored by Drunvalo Melchizedek. I attended a sacred geometry workshop based on this work in 2004, after having read Volumes 1 and 2, and having spent significant time assimilating Drunvalo's work. I now understand why Thoth was cited as the being that imparted much of the wisdom taught in the weekend seminar, profound unveiling of the ancient mysteries was in print for all to see. Fundamental to Drunvalo's teachings is the activation of the **ba** and **ka** energy which I now equate to the **Mer-Ka-Ba** meditation whose name contains both **ka** and **ba** energies mentioned in this supplemental tablet [32, Chapter 13].

Drunvalo provides his understanding of the place where energy meets matter to us as detailed below:

1. **Chakra** Energy feeds Chi in the body's meridians down to the cellular level.
2. **Prana** energy field close to the body arises, this is what PIP and RFI instrumentation are able to depict which I describe in my first book [3].
3. **Auric** field, spherical egg-shaped energy emanating from thoughts and emotions reaching about two feet.

Later in the fourteenth tablet, a near cinematic unveiling occurs. The Atlantis Dweller, with his countenance dampened for Thoth's safety, morphs out of another dimension (from Arulu?) with fire, Spirits of Heaven, Wonder of wonders, and clouds *materializing* into the world of man. The palace is described as starry and another name is ascribed to the Dweller of Atlantis, that of Holy One. This reminds me of the scene in the Immortals when Hades appears among the populace in the film, complete with clouds, smoke and fire.

A demonstration of the First Cause is initiated by the Dweller causing energy to infuse into Thoth's body. This light is termed the Spirit-Sun, the Sovereign of the Sun spheres. This appears to be the *ba* energy that permits ascension via the Earth portal to Arulu, home of the Ancient Gods, and the God of all Gods, GOD. Thus, the Dweller gave Thoth the words to say to open the portal. But first he had to take a tour for his edification.

Next Thoth is transported via the space-time to see Arulu, learning the secrets of the cosmos. Primeval chaos is witnessed on Arulu, noting that is why guards are necessary to watch over God's creation, keeping destruction at bay. Eight of those permitted to ascend from Earth via the portal were encountered in a splendor of light on Arulu. After his tour of the Great God's abode, Thoth returns to his body on Earth. It is at this point that Thoth renounces his birthright to return to Arulu, choosing instead to remain on Earth helping mankind until the *age of darkness* has elapsed. This could very well be the same story in which Thoth-Ningishzida accompanies the Adam to Nibiru to meet Anu. As pointed out in my research, the Anunnaki were limiting their rulership terms by Zodiacal house division. The age of darkness most likely is referring to the Age of Pisces which was a negative polarity house, alternating each sign from positive to negative.

Thoth returns to the Halls of Amenti after receiving instructions from the Dweller as to how the sacred knowledge is to be used, symbolized, and guarded. A very profound statement is made about the precondition necessary to ascend, in which Thoth advises that if one has passed all the trials of the outer, to summon him with the key (*ba* light-spirit) that you possess, implying that when out of the body access to the Halls of Amenti is possible. Thoth promises the words of power to the initiate, calling himself the Initiator. A warning is issued to the potential traveler to the Halls of Amenti. Calling on Thoth when not seeking wisdom, having an impure heart, or being weak willed in purpose may revoke portal access permanently.

List ye, O Man, to the deep hidden wisdom,

lost to the world since the time of the Dwellers,

lost and forgotten by men of this age.

Know ye this Earth is but a portal,

guarded by powers unknown to man.

Yet, the Dark Lords hide the entrance

that leads to the Heaven-born land.

Know ye, the way to the sphere of Arulu

is guarded by barriers opened only to Light-born man.

Upon Earth, I am the holder of the keys

to the gates of the Sacred Land.

Command I, by the powers beyond me,

to leave the keys to the world of man.

Before I depart, I give ye the Secrets of how

ye may rise from the bondage of darkness,

cast off the fetters of flesh that have bound ye,

rise from the darkness into the Light.

Know ye, the soul must be cleansed of its darkness,

ere ye may enter the portals of Light.

Thus, I established among ye the Mysteries

so that the Secrets may always be found.

Aye, though man may fall into darkness,
always the Light will shine as a guide.
Hidden in darkness, veiled in symbols,
always the way to the portal will be found.
Man in the future will deny the mysteries
but always the way the seeker will find.

Now I command ye to maintain my secrets,
giving only to those ye have tested,
so that the pure may not be corrupted,
so that the power of Truth may prevail.

List ye now to the unveiling of Mystery.
List to the symbols of Mystery I give.
Make of it a religion for only thus will its essence remain.

Regions there are two between
this life and the Great One,
traveled by the Souls
who depart from this Earth;
Duat, the home of the powers of illusion;
Sekhet Hetspet, the House of the Gods.
Osiris, the symbol of the guard of the portal,
who turns back the souls of unworthy men.

Beyond lies the sphere of the heaven-born powers,

Arulu, the land where the Great Ones have passed.

There, when my work among men has been finished,

will I join the Great Ones of my Ancient home.

Seven are the mansions of the house of the Mighty;

Three guards the portal of each house from the darkness;

Fifteen the ways that lead to Duat.

Twelve are the houses of the Lords of Illusion,

facing four ways, each of them different.

Forty and Two are the great powers,

judging the Dead who seek for the portal.

Four are the Sons of Horus,

Two are the Guards of East and West of Isis,

the mother who pleads for her children, Queen of the Moon,

reflecting the Sun.

Ba is the Essence, living forever.

Ka is the Shadow that man knows as life.

Ba cometh not until Ka is incarnate.

These are mysteries to preserve through the ages.

Keys are they of life and of Death.

Hear ye now the mystery of mysteries:

learn of the circle beginningless and endless,

the form of He who is One and in all.
Listen and hear it, go forth and apply it,
thus will ye travel the way that I go.

Mystery in Mystery,
yet clear to the Light-born,
the Secret of all I now will reveal.
I will declare a secret to the initiated,
but let the door be wholly shut against the profane.

Three is the mystery, come from the great one.
Hear, and Light on thee will dawn.

In the primeval, dwell three unities.
Other than these, none can exist.
These are the equilibrium, source of creation:
one God, one Truth, one point of freedom.

Three come forth from the three of the balance:
all life, all good, all power.

Three are the qualities of God in his Light-home:
Infinite power, Infinite Wisdom, Infinite Love.

Three are the powers given to the Masters:
To transmute evil, assist good, use discrimination.

Three are the things inevitable for God to perform:
Manifest power, wisdom and love.

Three are the powers creating all things:
Divine Love possessed of perfect knowledge,
Divine Wisdom knowing all possible means,
Divine Power possessed by the joint will of
Divine Love and Wisdom.

Three are the circles (states) of existence:
The circle of Light where dwells nothing but God,
and only God can traverse it;
the circle of Chaos where all things
by nature arise from death;
the Circle of awareness where
all things spring from life.

All things animate are of three states of existence:
chaos or death, liberty in humanity and felicity of Heaven.

Three necessities control all things:
beginning in the Great Deep, the circle of chaos, plenitude in
Heaven.

Three are the paths of the Soul:
Man, Liberty, Light.

Three are the hindrances:
lack of endeavor to obtain knowledge;
non-attachment to god; attachment to evil.
In man, the three are manifest.
Three are the Kings of power within.
Three are the chambers of the mysteries,
found yet not found in the body of man.

Hear ye now of he who is liberated,
freed from the bondage of life into Light.
Knowing the source of all worlds shall be open.
Aye, even the Gates of Arulu shall not be barred.
Yet heed, O man, who would'st enter heaven.
If ye be not worthy,
better it be to fall into the fire.
Know ye the celestials pass through the pure flame.
At every revolution of the heavens,
they bathe in the fountains of Light.

List ye, O man, to this mystery:
Long in the past before ye were man-born,
I dwelled in Ancient Atlantis.
There in the Temple,
I drank of the Wisdom,
poured as a fountain of Light
from the Dweller.

Give the key to ascend to the
Presence of Light in the Great world.
Stood I before the Holy One
enthroned in the Flower of Fire.
Veiled was he by the lightnings of darkness,
else my Soul by the Glory have been shattered.

Forth from the feet of his Throne like the diamond,
rolled forth four rivers of flame from his footstool,
rolled through the channels of clouds to the Man-world.
Filled was the hall with Spirits of Heaven.
Wonder of wonders was the Starry palace.

Above the sky, like a rainbow of Fire and Sunlight,
were Formed the Spirits.
Sang they the glories of the Holy One.
Then from the midst of the Fire came a voice:
Behold the Glory of the first Cause.
I beheld that Light, high above all darkness,
reflected in my own being.
I attained, as it were, to the God of all Gods,
the Spirit-Sun, the Sovereign of the Sun spheres.

There is One, Even the First,
who hath no beginning,
who hath no end;

who hath made all things,

who govern all,

who is good,

who is just,

who illumines,

who sustains.

Then from the throne, there poured a great radiance,

surrounding and lifting my soul by its power.

Swiftly I moved through the spaces of Heaven,

shown was I the mystery of mysteries,

shown the Secret heart of the cosmos.

Carried was I to the land of Arulu,

stood before the Lords in their Houses.

Opened they the Doorway so I might

glimpse the primeval chaos.

Shuddered my soul to the vision of horror,

shrank back my soul from the ocean of darkness.

Then saw I the need for the barriers,

saw the need for the Lords of Arulu.

Only they with their Infinite balance could

stand in the way of the inpouring chaos.

Only they could guard God's creation.

Then did I pass around the circle of eight.

Saw all the souls who had conquered the darkness.

Saw the splendor of Light where they dwelled.

Longed I to take my place in their circle,

but longed I also for the way I had chosen,

when I stood in the Halls of Amenti

and made my choice to the work I would do.

Passed I from the Halls of Arulu

down to the earth space where my body lay.

Arose I from the earth where I rested.

Stood I before the Dweller.

Gave my pledge to renounce my Great

right until my work on Earth was completed,

until the Age of darkness be past.

List ye, O man, to the words I shall give ye.

In them shall ye find the Essence of Life.

Before I return to the Halls of Amenti,

taught shall ye be the Secrets of Secrets,

how ye, too, may arise to the Light.

Preserve them and guard them,

hide them in symbols,

so the profane will laugh and renounce.

In every land, form ye the mysteries.
Make the way hard for the seeker to tread.

Thus will the weak and the wavering be rejected.
Thus will the secrets be hidden and guarded,
held till the time when the wheel shall be turned.

Through the dark ages, waiting and watching,
my Spirit shall remain in the deep hidden land.
When one has passed all the trials of the outer,
summon ye me by the Key that ye hold.

Then will I, the Initiator, answer,
come from the Halls of the Gods in Amenti.
Then will I receive the initiate, give him the words of power.

Hark ye, remember, these words of warning:
bring not to me one lacking in wisdom,
impure in heart or weak in his purpose.
Else I will withdraw from ye your power
to summon me from the place of my sleeping.

Now go ye forth and summon thy brothers
so that I may impart the wisdom to light thy
path when my presence is gone.
Come to the chamber beneath my temple.
Eat not food until three days are past.

There will I give thee the essence of wisdom

so that with power ye may shine amongst men.

There will I give unto thee the secrets so that

ye, too, may rise to the

Heavens, God-men in Truth

as in essence ye be.

Depart now and leave me while I summon

those ye know of but as yet know not.

Supplemental Tablet XV: Secret of Secrets

The path to Eternal life is discussed first by receiving power to reveal the God-man. Darkness and light are asserted to be from the same nature only perceived differently, given the fact that the Creator of All permits both for duality contrast. Light is order and darkness is disorder.

We are told that our purpose for being is to transmute the darkness in our incarnation into light.

Man is deemed to have a three-fold composition which is a subset of nine (9) total elements, as above, so below on Earth:

4. **Physical** -Blood movement facilitates the heart beating. Magnetism traveling through nerve ganglia and pathways is claimed to provide energy for cells and tissue. The *Akasa* flows through subtle channels in the body for a complete system. The three work in unison allowing life in the body. The skeletal system is formed from the system where the *Akasa* subtle energy flows, like an antenna as I have posited. Mastering the elements allows the Secret of Life in the body (*ba*?) to be activated, enabling one to choose to relinquish the body only when the mission is accomplished on Earth! Based on the three energy body

distinctions provided by Drunvalo (Chakra, Prana, Auric) these fall under Physical.

5. **Astral** -This energy component has three aspects

    a. **Mediator** between the above and below

    b. **Non-Spiritual.** Not sure how Spirit and the energy nature are differentiated. I often use the term Spirit and Energy interchangeably. The energy field that has the potential to use the Earth portal is the *ba*. The Mer-Ka-Ba star tetrahedron field has the key elements cited for this access, the *ba* and the *ka*.

    c. **Non-Physical.** Able to move above and below which is what we here on Earth term an out of body experience or OOBE.

6. **Mental** -The mind also has three natures:

    a. **Carrier of the Will of the Great One**

    b. **Arbiter of Cause**

    c. **Arbiter of Effect**

We are told that in addition to these three natures, is the Spiritual Self which is composed of four qualities penetrating all parallel dimensions, worlds within worlds (9 total). The number *thirteen* (13) is denoted as a *mystical number of the Great One*, based on the nature of the dimensions appearing as one, separated by the LAW of TIME. This number is composed as a summation of the **nine** dimensions, **three** natures of man, plus the infinite nature of the SOURCE for a total of thirteen. Is this why the thirteenth Zodiacal sign has been occluded, that of Ophiuchus?   Also significant is the Mayan Tzolkin Calendar division of the creation account into seven days and six nights which totals thirteen columns in their representation. Also significant, while assigning importance to numbers is the fact the nine rows in ascending consciousness is a map to the nine underworld frequencies according to the Mayans. A final correlation is that Thoth discloses nine worlds within worlds or parallel dimensions exist.

The account continues stating that we are held in bondage by a frequency vibration alluded to by Drunvalo as a false Mer-Ka-Ba field [32, Pg. 103], obviously set up by the Dark Lords. This false field binds the consciousness of mankind to the third dimension. The way out is embedded in us all, which is not stated but implied, to be the Light-born birthright we received from our genetic archetype, Lord Enki-Poseidon himself.

We are told that during an OOBE, we are to rise to the outermost limits of the Earth's plane or third dimensional sphere discussed more fully in Chapter 12, Reality's Bounds: Spherical Energy Layers.

This dimensional boundary limits is discussed by the OOBE

pioneer Robert Monroe labeling the accessible boundaries Locales 1-3 [30].

Next we are given the Earth portal activation words separating the third dimension from the Duat, which connects via fifteen pathways to Arulu ending up in the sixth dimension by inference. Speak ye the word *Dor-E-Lil-La*, after a short time your Light will be lifted allowing passage through the space barrier. A time limit of six hours is provided to go to Arulu to visit those who occupy the sacred land, seeing and knowing the destination of one's Sun-soul at the end of the third dimensional cessation (willed or otherwise?) and of the need for an Earth suit energy container.

An OOBE process is specified in order to leave the body and access the portal out of the prison planet Earth. Lie down and relax the mind and body. Make your intention of leaving the body, focusing on the portal as one's destination. Repeat the thought to be free of the body. Then think of the word *La-Um-I-L-Gan* letting it resonate as a sound in your mind, *drifting* with the energy vibration subsequently leaving the body and visualizing the 3rd dimensional Earth boundary sphere as the destination where the portal is to be accessed. Enjoy your six hour visit in Heaven so that you will know your destiny as a Light being, a birthright inherited from the CREATOR OF ALL. It is not stated in the Tablet, but simply thinking of returning to the body will automatically initiate the end of one's astral voyage. Be sure to write down a transcript of your experience as soon as you are able in order to capture all the details for later analysis. When I was a teenager the OOBE process began to happen to me spontaneously resulting in my fascination for flying like a bird without any aircraft. I had what I thought were just vivid dreams of standing on a railroad tie fencepost at a corner position supporting the gate to our farm pasture and barn, turning into the wind and taking off like a bird at will. This went on unidentified as an OOBE until the age of seventeen, while attending Point Loma High School in 1982. Professor Dick Englehart offered a mysticism class as part of the humanities requirement wherein we were asked to keep a diary. An entry in my diary caught his attention concerning an OOBE that I had recently recorded while living in Ocean Beach, a community near my high school that is famous for its pier and Newport Avenue hippie scene. Commonly when leaving the body, especially as a newbie, fear limits the duration in this unknown realm, often resulting in very short trips, certainly not six hours, more like seconds. On this particular diary entry, I relayed the fear felt when re-entering the body and being fully awake and aware of my otherworldly experience. I found myself unable to speak or move for some time. It was mortifying as no sound could be generated and my back was in a strange position on a foldout bed, resting across the metal support bar uncomfortably at the lumbar spine.

Dr. Englehart kept me after class to discuss the diary entry about my OOBE. He noted that it was treated as a recurrent event in my life and told me emphatically that I needed to read Robert Monroe's book *Journeys Out of the Body* [30]. I found great comfort in the shared experiences and techniques disclosed in the book, knowing that this explained what was happening to me spawning the zeal for flight. For those who have not been exposed to my radio interviews and lectures, I chose to leave college right after high school to pursue my once in a lifetime chance to fly like a hummingbird, choosing to serve in the military from 1982-1989 as a Chief Warrant Officer 2. My assigned aircraft qualifications after completing flight school (Light Blue class 85-13) included both AH-1S Cobra attack and OH-58 Aero scout helicopters. However, my experience flying for the Army did not fully satisfy the experiences I had during an OOBE. Later in 1999, ten years as a civilian, the skies reached out to me again pulling me back heavenward. My qualification as a hang glider pilot began and soon I was flying free like a bird in the various sites sponsored by the San Diego Hang Gliding and Paragliding Association which can be investigated online for the air enthusiast. My real life experience, as close as it gets in my book, was one of my last flights at glass off (about 5pm at that time of year) at one of my favorite places: Horse Canyon. The rocky and mountainous terrain just north of Interstate 8 (Buckman Springs Road exit) is a unique site in that the prevailing westerly coming off the Pacific Ocean meet the warm dry air of the East County desert causing a lift zone that runs north and south for a substantive distance. This convergence zone is easily accessed by hang gliders and some brave paraglider pilots as well. On this particular day, I was one of only two pilots present. My paraglider pilot and friend, Ron Smith, took off from the upper peak of Horse Canyon during the smooth flying conditions caused by a more even radiation of terrestrial trapped solar energy. This showed up as a uniform smooth flying experience, almost effortless and devoid of the violent wind gusts and turbulence present in altitudes achieved there, sometimes over 10,000 feet above ground level (MSL).

For some reason, to my surprise, given that paragliders can fly in far less wind than hang gliders can, Ron got flushed out and had what we in the hang gliding business term a sled ride to the landing zone (LZ). My expectation was that I, too would get a sled ride lasting no more than 3-5 minutes and begin to break down my glider with Ron after an uneventful attempt at experiencing the wonders of an effortless flight in the beautiful mountains of East County, San Diego.

I launched with little to no wind, relying on the ridge lift that I had located and used many times before, envisioning the lifting force of the thermals as a liquid medium that, when striking an object, would have resultant flow vectors (directions). Seeing the terrain using this etheric water model helps anticipate staying ahead of the glider as decisions must be made rapidly to avert deadly accidents. Following the ridge to my left, remaining in close proximity to the lift envelope created by the 4,000 foot MSL mountainous ridge line, my secret serpent friend lay waiting. There is a rock feature called the rattlesnake, used by glider pilots who know Horse Canyon well. This vertically winding rock feature located at the apex of an upward sloping canyon creates an impediment to the thermals drifting with the wind. As a drifting and rising column of warm air impacts a terrestrial feature like the rattlesnake, strong thermal vents often lead to cloud formation at the dew point temperature for water at some altitude we term thermal equilibrium. Rising to this location is usually not possible in glass off conditions at day's end. But the lift being generated at the special snake rock led to my solitary experience which most closely approximated the feeling of an OOBE.

Arriving at the rattlesnake, just barely high enough be useful, I found the sacred breath of the snake. Its hissing but mellow breath raised the kite, fashioned from fabric and aluminum poles, with me suspended in a cocoon below. The rattlesnake trigger point produced enough upward lift that I was able to make it to a set of twin peaks which were just visible north of Buckman Springs rest area. The LZ for the club is located very near the rest area. The twin peaks are often a good place to head when the wind is coming more out of the North, although at glass off time there was very little wind, just enough to cause one to turn left and not right toward the rock pile at launch.

Ron was asked via radio if he needed to return to town, and indicated he did not, allowing me to explore the twin peaks in my glider until the magical flying conditions ended near sundown. While circling the peak of the first twin granite pyramid-shaped mountain, a raptor caught my eye leaving its nest atop the rock. Triggering its territorial imperative to protect its hunting grounds, the red-tailed hawk joined me in a counterclockwise circle as I intruded on its domain. The encounter could have gone very badly, as predatory birds will attack an intruder without notice, often climbing high above, then suddenly diving on the prey with the added force of gravity to facilitate a mortal wound imparted at very high speed. Hang gliders are very aware of such dangers when flying in remote mountain sites where raptors nest. Suddenly, the hawk came very close to me, both of us circling the same direction, eye to eye looking in the direction of the coordinated turn. Mystically, possessed of a meta-awareness with time seemingly standing still, at this very moment I felt a complete transcendent sensation that this was truly the closest spiritual experience in waking life that I had during an OOBE. Soaring with a creature I was mimicking was the penultimate experience for me, unconcerned about the Greek legend of a fellow flight aspirant who met a mortal end by getting his wings too close and subsequently melted by the heat of the sun.

Returning back to Thoth's process, after a long-winded story, we are instructed to stand before the gates of the Duat and command the guardians by these words:

I am the Light. In me is no darkness. Free am I of the bondage of night. Open thou the way of the Twelve and the One, so I may pass to the realm of wisdom."

Expect the gate guards to refuse you, then say:

I am the Light. For me are no barriers. Open, I command, by the Secret of Secrets "Edom-El-Ahim-Sabbert-Zur Adom."

Then if thy words have been Truth of the highest, then the barriers will open for you. The tablet closes with encouragements to win ye the way to me, my children. This is an open invitation only to those that seek his wisdom. Thoth states I am the Key and the Way. Does this last statement sound familiar to you, Bible scholars? It should now that you know the AKA list for Thoth also included the person known as Yehoshua or Jesus to Christians. The keys to the kingdom of heaven rest in Thoth's control, which is provided to you here. Now for the actual tablet text.

Now ye assemble, my children,
waiting to hear the Secret of Secrets
which shall give ye power to unfold the God-man,
give ye the way to Eternal life.

Plainly shall I speak of the Unveiled Mysteries.
No dark sayings shall I give unto thee.
Open thine ears now, my children.
Hear and obey the words that I give.

First I shall speak of the fetters of darkness
which bind ye in chains to the sphere of the Earth.

Darkness and light are both of one nature,
different only in seeming,
for each arose from the source of all.
Darkness is disorder.
Light is Order.
Darkness transmuted is light of the Light.
This, my children, your purpose in being;
transmutation of darkness to light.

Hear ye now of the mystery of nature,

the relations of life to the Earth where it dwells.

Know ye, ye are threefold in nature,

physical, astral and mental in one.

Three are the qualities of each of the natures;

nine in all, as above, so below.

In the physical are these channels,

the blood which moves in vortical motion,

reacting on the heart to continue its beating.

Magnetism which moves through the nerve paths,

carrier of energies to all cells and tissues.

Akasa which flows through channels,

subtle yet physical, completing the channels.

Each of the three attuned with each other,

each affecting the life of the body.

Form they the skeletal framework through

which the subtle ether flows.

In their mastery lies the Secret of Life in the body.

Relinquished only by will of the adept,

when his purpose in living is done.

Three are the natures of the Astral,

mediator is between above and below;

not of the physical, not of the Spiritual,
but able to move above and below.

Three are the natures of Mind,
carrier it of the Will of the Great One.
Arbitrator of Cause and Effect in thy life.
Thus is formed the threefold being,
directed from above by the power of four.

Above and beyond man's threefold nature
lies the realm of the Spiritual Self.

Four is it in qualities,
shining in each of the planes of existence,
but thirteen in one,
the mystical number.
Based on the qualities of man are the Brothers:
each shall direct the unfoldment of being,
each shall channels be of the Great One.

On Earth, man is in bondage,
bound by space and time to the earth plane.
Encircling each planet, a wave of vibration,
binds him to his plane of unfoldment.
Yet within man is the Key to releasement,
within man may freedom be found.

When ye have released the self from the body,
rise to the outermost bounds of your earth-plane.
Speak ye the word Dor-E-Lil-La.

Then for a time your Light will be lifted,
free may ye pass the barriers of space.
For a time of half of the sun (six hours),
free may ye pass the barriers of earth-plane,
see and know those who are beyond thee.

Yea, to the highest worlds may ye pass.
See your own possible heights of unfoldment,
know all earthly futures of Soul.

Bound are ye in your body,
but by the power ye may be free.
This is the Secret whereby bondage
shall be replaced by freedom for thee.

Calm let thy mind be.
At rest be thy body:
Conscious only of freedom from flesh.
Center thy being on the goal of thy longing.
Think over and over that thou wouldst be free.
Think of this word La-Um-I-L-Ganoover
and over in thy mind let it sound.

353

Drift with the sound to the place of thy longing.
Free from the bondage of flesh by thy will.

Hear ye while I give the greatest of secrets:
how ye may enter the Halls of Amenti,
enter the place of the immortals as I did,
stand before the Lords in their places.

Lie ye down in rest of thy body.
Calm thy mind so no thought disturbs thee.
Pure must ye be in mind and in purpose,
else only failure will come unto thee.

Vision Amenti as I have told in my Tablets.
Long with fullness of heart to be there.
Stand before the Lords in thy mind's eye.

Pronounce the words of power I give (mentally);
Mekut-El-Shab-El Hale-Sur-Ben-El-Zabrut Zin-Efrim-Quar-El.
Relax thy mind and thy body.
Then be sure your soul will be called.

Now give I the Key to Shambbalah,
the place where my Brothers live in the darkness:
Darkness but filled with Light of the Sun
Darkness of Earth, but Light of the Spirit,
guides for ye when my day is done.

Leave thou thy body as I have taught thee.
Pass to the barriers of the deep, hidden place.
Stand before the gates and their guardians.
Command thy entrance by these words:

I am the Light. In me is no darkness.
Free am I of the bondage of night.
Open thou the way of the Twelve and the One,
so I may pass to the realm of wisdom.

When they refuse thee, as surely they will,
command them to open by these words of power:
I am the Light. For me are no barriers.
Open, I command, by the Secret of Secrets
Edom-El-Ahim-Sabbert-Zur Adom.

Then if thy words have been Truth of the highest,
open for thee the barriers will fall.

Now, I leave thee, my children.
Down, yet up, to the Halls shall I go.
Win ye the way to me, my children.
Truly my brothers shall ye become.

Thus finish I my writings.
Keys let them be to those who come after.
But only to those who seek my wisdom.

CHAPTER 6: Alchemy Past and Present

Recall from Lawrence Gardner's research that the five pointed star was a very important symbol that goes way back in history, connecting the Biblical Ham to Thoth. The genealogical path demonstrating this occult secret connection has been closely edited out of the annals of history by the Papacy and its tentacles.

Our goal is to try to understand the connection between Thoth the Atlantean and first alchemist, to societies with secrets as the Masons like to be called. The motivation for me to make this connection was sparked by seeing and visiting Washington, DC in 2009. After walking the symbol of an inverted pentagram, visible on any local tourist map, with its astral fire-emitting jewel located at Scott Street Circle, just south of the Scottish Rite Temple Headquarters, 1633 17th Street. See Figure 21 below. This was clearly Ningishzida-Thoth's symbol, so why is the double eagle symbol of Ninurta now boldly emblazoned over the All Seeing Eye at the Scottish Rite 33rd Degree Temple?

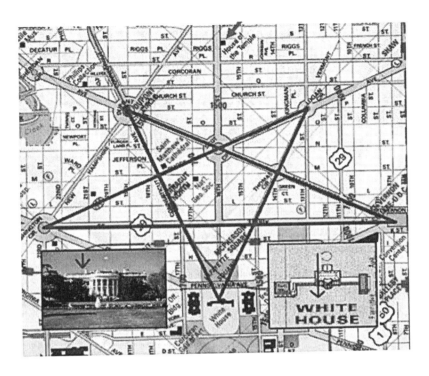

Figure 21: Inverted Pentagram in the Streets of DC

First we have to revisit Atrahasis-Ziusudra-Noah's family drama to find the connection which has been intentionally suppressed. Noah and his spouse Emzarah had sons named Shem, Ham and Japhet according to *Genesis 5:32*.

Masons and Alchemy

There is a very strange story in the Bible involving Noah's kids and a supposed drinking binge in the account. After Enlil, Enki, Ninharsag and fellow Anunnaki crew had their encounter with Noah on Mount Ararat following the Great Flood, we change context to a short time thereafter when life begins to normalize, or so it seems. Noah supposedly gets drunk and falls asleep in his tent, sans clothing, and is encountered by his boy Ham who witnesses his father naked. So what? The story continues by involving Shem and Japhet who save Dad's dignity by covering his nakedness with a garment as if he was violating an indecent exposure municipal ordinance at a populated beach during high season. He is treated like a random streaker who must be covered with the flag during a media frenzied football game.

It gets stranger, as all three kids saw their fathers sleep naked. One of them didn't cover him and seems to have earned a curse on his offspring. What kind of crazy weird ritual is being used to justify some evil deed? When Noah wakes up and finds out that Ham saw him disrobed he places a curse on Ham's son Canaan. Let me understand better, Ham sees his supposed father naked and subsequently Ham's son, Canaan gets cursed for it? There is no intelligent way to address this cloaked idiocy over such a simple circumstance. Canaan was not even in the story, so why was he punished for an imaginary infraction from the accused peeping Tom, I mean Ham?

Let's see if we could fashion a better cover story than the one provided, given that we are told that Ham accidentally stumbles onto a naked, passed-out drunk and failed to have covered him up in his own tent (bed). Perhaps a more believable cover story could be fashioned to simply blame Ham for poisoning his fermented grape juice, subsequently leading to his inebriation state of drunkenness or perhaps fabricate a lie that leads to the theft of his wine making apparatus, probably a distillery. This would really infuriate a hillbilly in the mountains of the American deep south, where raiding a fella's still is up there with cattle rustling. Not a good idea. So why all the fibbing? It happened all throughout history.

This form of namesake occlusion and obscuration was a trick often used in the bible to cover for Enlil, the Lord of the Command's lies. It usually had to do with powerful people with a noble mission who needed to be removed from the narrative. Reminds me of Genesis 1:26 where a committee of folks were involved in the creation story for man, yet only one of the players, Enlil, gets promoted as God, getting all the praise and glory. Enki, Ninharsag, and Ningishzida as well as the rest of the Anunnaki Council of Twelve are curiously missing from the main Bible narrative regarding the Gods interaction with mankind. Taking credit for other's work is sycophantic and dishonorable, a low character mark. Is this the example that was intended for the followers of Zeus? If so, then he must have a cadre of lawyers, nihilists, and marauders to implement his destructive and deceiving will. Whereas the twin pillars on Atlantis, home of Poseidon-Enki, promoted character development and ascension.

GERALD CLARK

This is why, in my humble opinion, that the Greek hero Solon was seeking information about the Atlanteans, leading him to Egyptian city of Sais, seeking to know of the noble race and civilization that came before him. The Atlantean society, recorded by Plato in the Critias, were seen as the model of choice for the leader Solon, seeking a better governing method. Enki established *Paradise* conditions wherever he went, it seems. That included his first city on Earth featuring Eridu's famed Garden of Eden, then Atlantis and later Persia where we recover the Avestan language phrase (*Pairi Daize*) from its original source. [45, Pg. 199] The carved image of Ahura Mazda on the temple of Persepolis is worth seeing. This image of Enki also appears in Iran on the cliffs of Behistun, the Mesopotamian Rosetta Stone found to be written in three languages which led to the decipherment of Sumerian Cuneiform tablets found all over Iraq, Syria, and elsewhere in the Middle East.

How many Biblical scholars have read that silly Noah deceptive story and agreed that Ham should have covered up his drunken fool father, lest Shem and Japhet nark on Ham for his oversight? Failing to protect dad from potential bad public relations due to his over indulgence, although done in the confines of his own damn tent, was the basis for the curse! You've got to be kidding me. Who has a breathalyzer handy so we can document the extent to which Noah should be fined, his permit to distill alcohol from the grapes of his vineyard revoked, and furthermore to be in compliance with the BLM, all crops to be sprayed with toxic pesticides immediately (no evacuation necessary, fumes are harmless) as a Department of Agriculture reports there is a potential Mediterranean Fruit Fly infestation now upwind of his vineyard and must be stopped!!!

Checking my digital genealogy table, published on my website www.geraldclark77.com, one will find a different family composition for Noah and Emzarah, showing only two boys, Shem and Japhet as offspring. A table of nations shenanigans to help erase the lineage that ended up affiliated with Marduk in Babylon, should be obvious at this point. In fact, it is so critical to understand.

The importance of this quirky story involves the only Great Flood-surviving family to exist in spite of the Anunnaki Council's sworn oath that everyone would perish in the flood. No life was to survive. Note that Ham is deemed to be Noah's youngest son in Genesis 5:32 and 6:10. A clue to the true family structure is exposed at the time of that the curse is irrationally enacted. As a result of the family disharmony due to the heinous incident, only Shem was allocated access to Jehovah-Enlil, while Ham's accursed son Canaan (Genesis 9:25-26) was demoted to being his brother's low level servant. So what happened to Ham directly? Nothing, how odd.

According to Gardner [45, Pg. 193], referencing the Anchor

Bible, the crazy story appears to be a red herring. According to this more accurate source, **Canaan was the son, not a grandson of Noah, whose offspring became the kings of Babylon.** Also corrected is the fact that **Ham was not a member of Noah's family at all.** Turns out that Canaan's descendant is the 1st dynastic ruler of Babylon, Marduk's gateway for the Gods. This Enkiite connection to Marduk via Canaan's offspring was a big problem for the Hebrew priests held captive in the same city, as well as for Enlil whose territory the enemy was occupying. A smear campaign against the Babylonian heritage was initiated by the Enlilites, and placing a curse on Ham served to demonize the Canaanites, while simultaneously promoting the Shemite line into Syria through Aram, Lud, Elam just to name a few.

If Ham had been correctly detailed in the genealogy showing his actual father to be Tubal-Cain, this intentional kingly line obscuration would be exposed and Ham's historically significant grandson, Nimrod, could not have been thwarted by the Sethian false promotion that followed. Canaan receives little attention in the Biblical account once he was cursed by Noah, with only passing mention in Genesis 10:9-10, because **he was the source of true Grail Kingship.**

The Sethian line had lower aspirations obtaining governorship positions in the generations prior to Abraham. Ham's heritage was so important to the Messianic history than an escutcheon (coat of arms) was fashioned and held in high regard symbolically showing up in prominent documents as late as the Stemma Jacobi of the 1630 Genethliacon. Ham's coat of arms symbol, composed of a dragon and a goddess, was circulating circa 1645 AD, evidenced in Britain's scientific Royal Society which came from the parent organization, the Invisible College.

An important link in Nimrod's chronology is provided in the Targum, a collection of ancient Aramaic writings relating to the Old Testament, aggregated into a single document during the 1st century establishment of the Babylonian dynasty. Here we find out that Nimrod was the father of an Egyptian pharaoh who goes nameless. Ethiopian texts disclose that Nimrod's contemporary in Egypt was Anedjib (pronounced Yanuf), called out as the king of the 1st dynasty of Egypt, reigning about 3000 BCE.

Shortly after Anedjib's reign in Egypt circa 2890 BC, a new dynasty emerged. King Raneb, the second pharaoh of the Egyptian dynasty, introduced the veneration of the Goat of Mendes to Egypt. This highly significant ritual was important in the Grail and Dragon traditions (claimed to be the same by Gardner) as the Goat of Mendes had historically been affiliated with Nimrod's grandfather Ham. Mendes was a city slightly north and west of the Egyptian delta city of Avaris where the Sacred Goat took on several names which included Khem, Chem or Ham. This is the zodiacal goat of the sign Capricorn assigned to Ham and was used in accordance with the Dragon Court Tradition. There he had an added designation as the Archon of the Tenth Age of Capricorn. The shocking part is the escutcheon shield became a five-pointed star. This star, in its inverted form is known to us as the pentagram. See Figure 22.

In the inverted form of the star, the two uppermost points represent the ears of the sacred Goat of Mendes. The two downward points at the sides represent the ears and the single point at the very bottom is the chin and beard [45, Pg. 194].

Using a pentagram in its inverted form (male position) symbolically identifies Khem who is personalized by the addition of an emerald jewel set centrally between the horns. Recall who wrote the Emerald Tablets as a possible alternative connection for the symbol. When inverted to the commonly recognized star on the US Flag, this represents the female entity with the uppermost point becoming the goddess' head in the Venus affiliation. The upward facing points to the side represent her arms, while the downward points are her legs. Adding the jewel of Venus where the legs conjoin at the vulval position signifies the goddess shown in the Hammite shield, whereas the dragon is affiliated with the male pentagram, Ham.

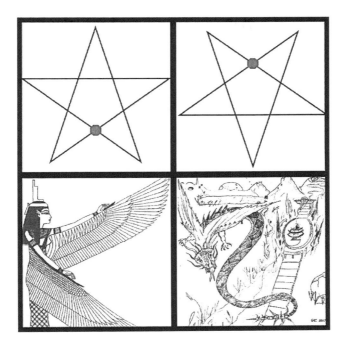

Figure 22: Male and Female Pentagram

Figure 22 above depicts the male and female five-pointed star affiliations with the dragon and pentagram and the goddess with the inverted pentagram.   Ningishzida and Ninharsag together composed the twin archetypal energies, encapsulated by Thoth the hermaphrodite as indicated on the Tarot Magician or Magus card.

The Goat of Mendes is directly associated with alchemy, the spelling of which is derived from the word *al-khame*, meaning *the science of overcoming the blackness*. Its secondary root was al-Khem, specifying the Khem to be the black ruler of Mendes, also known as Azazel of Capricorn. The book of Enoch discusses Azazel, leader of the Watcher rebellion. The lead Watcher was punished for disclosing metallurgy and the use of antimony or stibium [Sb] appearing on the periodic table of elements as number 51. As previously disclosed by me, antimony had to be added to gold during the smelting process in the right quantity and time to transform gold into a talcum-like powder. Later the alchemy formula for the Philosopher's Stone included the use of antimony.

We have another Bible story involving Azazel which is almost as puzzling as the story of Noah's drunken cursing. According to the Vulgate book of Leviticus 16:8, an early ritual involving sacrificing a goat was detailed. *"Aaron shall cast lots upon two goats, one for the Lord and the other for Azazel"*. The Lord's goat was deemed a sin offering whereas the goat allocated to Azazel was to be freed in the wilderness as a nature atonement. This is the source of the English mistranslation and term scapegoat, which misrepresented and hid the name Azazel.

The hidden reason why the English translation substituted *scapegoat* for the actual name Azazel was that the alternative biblical text stated in no uncertain terms that the offerings were made to both **Jehovah-Enlil** and to **Khem-Azazel**.

We know from the nature of the material that Azazel was punished for teaching the primitive workers how to make Star Fire gold using element number 51, stibium or also known as antimony.

This forbidden knowledge provides us a direct linkage to the field of alchemy and the hermetic tradition. This term alchemy and its affiliated traditions came from the teachings of Hermes Trismegistus (Hermes the Thrice Great). It was Thoth-Hermes who disclosed in his writings, "The Book of Thoth", that through the process of the mysteries, the brain could be stimulated to augment and extend the limits of human consciousness. This is why the Mystery Schools that he established along the Egyptian Nile, were highly esteemed as academic and spiritual powerhouses. They were under the careful watch of the grand master Thoth, himself.

The gold-smelting that has been shown to have taken place at Hathor's temple lead to the Anunnaki consumption of the life-prolonging effect of Star Fire gold. As discussed and promoted by my wife and me, this product is known to have an effect on the brain's pineal gland, the secret eye or *ayin*, as taught in hermeticism. The writings of Thoth represent gold using the solar hieroglyph represented by a dot inscribed in a circle. This symbol is identical to the *ayin*. The genealogical unveiling occurs when we see the direct link between Thoth and Cain (Q'ayin) [45, Pg. 197] and the Biblical Ham. Recall the fact that Tubal-Cain, AKA Mes-Kalam-Dug in my chart, was the King of Ur and known to the locals as a hero of the good land.

This sounds like a benevolent title versus the one earned by

Enlil as reported in the Lamentation account during the Second Dynasty of Ur. Recorded in the annals of history, Nannar and his spouse Ningal disclose in the Lamentation that Enlil has decided to nuke their kingdom, primitive workers and all. I doubt Nannar-Allah's father Enlil had the same title, "hero of the good land" as was ascribed to Tubal-Cain. More likely his epithet would read *"he who brings the nations low"*, alluding to a similar and obscure (only one reference to this name) biblical lambasting of Lucifer. The text is provided using the King James Version. Later versions altered the translation eliminating the name Lucifer all together. Enlil's editorial oversight resulted in many translations, an obvious proverbial lid put on the truth.

In Isaiah 14:12 in the KJV we read:

"How art thou fallen from heaven, O Lucifer, son of the morning! how art thou cut down to the ground, which didst weaken the nations!

Knowing that heaven and Nibiru are one and the same planet (not an ethereal cloud as propagandized), we see the same spirit witnessed by Nannar in the Chaldean Ur, where Enlil gets the destructive label, deservedly so, just as he earned it in the Atrahasis [2, Tablet 1] account as a genocidal murderer. An examination of the number of times the kingship changed locations in Enlil's assigned region of Mesopotamia is telling, giving the reason for the move from the destruction of Ur as well as many other Sumerian cities as, **"then Ur was defeated and kingship was taken to Adab."** Hmm, the insinuation is that a battle took place and that upon losing, the kinship was transferred in some controlled fashion to a new city. Nothing could be further from the truth. Enlil nuked an unsuspecting population, for no known reason, peacefully residing in the heavily occupied city of Ur. The destroyer ensured complete success by hitting the city with nuclear assaults on both flanks, using an advanced energy weapon which enveloped the unwanted kingdom occupied by his son and daughter-in-law (and their citizens) which poisoned the terrain in a deadly nuclear radiation blast. I guess genocidally eliminating a kingdom can be more accurately recorded in the annals of history for the regime change. It might go something like this: "Ur was decimated with weapons of the Gods and I, Zeus-Yahweh subsequently moved kingship (a mere vice devised by us to allure unconscious power and pride seekers to the next city, sans radiation.) They will get to know some new heroes, and after much torturing, they will also know the beastly side of themselves, thanks to me. Hope they learn and change, and if not, destruction is so much fun."

In alchemical circles, Cain was affiliated with the priest-king Melchizedek, king of Salem, the same name used in Paulo Coelho's fabulous book "The Alchemist" [22]. Coelho's main character has a series of transformative encounters with the mystical king of Salem, named Melchizedek, on his archetypal heroic journey to fulfill his destiny. Clearly Coelho understood the variety of names that Thoth used in his many incarnations affiliated with alchemy.

Cain was the ancestor of the Magian priestly dynasties called Zarathustra or Zoroaster. Chem-Zarathustra, our Biblical Ham was the credited founder of the Persian Empire. The kingdom was described as *Pairi Daize*, which later became the term paradise, just as was rumored on Atlantis under Poseidon-Enki.

This linkage makes sense given the fact that the chief deity venerated by the Zoroastrians was Ahura-Mazda or Chem-Zarathustra's father Enki. Thus, it should not be surprising to find Thoth involved in helping to found his father's ancient domain of Persia, modern day Iran. Could this hidden historical connection linking Thoth to modern day Iran have geopolitical implications? Consider the propagandizing and bullying Iran is enduring from the USA at this present time, accusing the nation of pursuing nuclear weapons while hypocritically housing thousands of the missiles in its own stockpile. Is the eagle attempting to smite the trident, Poseidon, and both beings, male and female, affiliated with the five pointed star, Ningishzida and Ninharsag?

Is this major conflict representative of the forces of light and dark colliding just as was believed in the Zoroastrian religion? It is happening again and is the source of the conflict which will most likely result in a great culling as predicted. The Enlilites and Enkiites are at war.

Could this explain why the Arab armies led by Enlil's son Allah replaced Zoroastrian beliefs? After all, the territory was given to Enlil as a result of casting lots with Anu and Enki in Africa [3 Atrahasis, Tablet 1]. A disturbing pattern of subversion is surfacing relative to the Enkiites and Enlilites rewriting history. Making up an irrational story about Noah getting drunk and cursing a kid who is not his son now makes more sense. Bet that most supposed modern Bible scholars still swallow Enlil-God's deceptive lies. This is why the genealogy table efforts were put forth by me to make palatable the name soup tables of nations and ancient astronauts, all mixed together.

Recall from the Bible that Abram was asked by Jehovah-Enlil to sacrifice his son on an altar, being saved at the last minute by a ram caught in the brush, which got axed instead. This was the famous land deal promising his offspring Jacob the land of Israel. Clearly Enlil likes the smell and possibly the taste of burnt flesh, whereas the goat offered to the alchemist Khem-Azazel was not harmed, but rather released to nature as an atonement. The fact that the Book of Enoch was left out of the Canonical Bible, probably to hide the alchemy link to Azazel and the additional data that tied alchemy back to the Grail king lineage descending from Ham to his son, Canaan's dynasty in Babylon, is now an understandable omission.

Masonic tradition supports that their craft origins can be traced back in time to discover that the early lodges credit the children of Lamech as the founders. Tubal-Cain was one of the three children of Lamech, who we now know was the father of Noah from the Bible. Although, evidence offered in my first book shows that Enki was the father of Noah and he received eternal life from Enlil on Mount Ararat. According to Gardner [45, page 199], they recorded the Wisdom of Lamech on two pillars, one that would resist fire and the other impervious to water. This wisdom was derived from Enki's Table of Destiny which held 'all that humankind had ever known, and all that would ever be known'.

The reason this historical detail is provided is because according to historians, the script etched into the pillars by Lamech's kids was later translated to an Emerald Tablet by Tubal-Cain's grandson Ham, also known to the Egyptians as Khem or Thoth. This is an incredible linkage, connecting the pillars described on Atlantis which specified how to live well and build character traits necessary to advance in the holographic simulator with the original Masonic order Pillars of Wisdom. English Masonic traditions, corrupted according to Gardner, relays that the Pillars of Wisdom were accredited to the biblical patriarch Enoch, not

Lamech. He further states that by the 18th century, the English Masons supplanted Thoth the Great Architect and Guardian of the Emerald Tablets with their Judeo-Christian God (Enlil) as discussed in detail herein.

Due to this historical genealogical replacement of the name Lamech for Enoch, this falsification is claimed as the basis for why the organization has become a place to participate in meaningless rituals versus seeking conscious evolution via an alchemical transformation. This is unlike its original teachings from Thoth's Mystery Schools along the Nile. Thus, it should not surprise us to see Egyptian symbols all over Washington DC, along with Thoth's symbolism built into the streets. After all, it is common knowledge that Masonry played a pivotal role planning and building the nation's capital buildings and many other monuments as well. Some symbols affiliated with the Masonic order, specifically the one seen on the temples at this present time are clearly visible. This is the same reason that my path separated with the modern Church; no transformation taking place given the original plan by Ningishzida-Thoth to elevate humans symbolized by his energy-matter symbol of the Caduceus.

Figure 22 above depicts the male aspect of this symbol's affiliation with the early Masonic Order that was involved in the design and building of Washington DC, to include street design.

This is the symbol for Ningishzida-Thoth the Atlantean in its male star orientation, complete with the jewel representing Astral Light landing on Scott Street Circle. I walked this pattern and lingered long enough to meditate at the Scott Street Circle where the emerald green jewel would be located. This is the very spot, were this to be a pentagram necklace, that the attachment point would be located for the chain.

The emerald used in the male pattern has been affiliated with Astral Light whereas the jewel of Venus emanates uterine flames indicative of the universal essence of the goddess, Star Fire (based on a hormone from menstrual flow).

Thus, whether symbolizing Astral Light or Star Fire, the pentagram symbol was affiliated with the concept of enlightenment and the pre-Jewish Sabbath. This is why Saturday (Sabado in Spanish) was designated as a time of reflection and recovery. For you see, Khem of Mendes was also called the Sabbatical Goat, which denotes a work stoppage and short hiatus in which to recover. This same designation of Saturday as the day of rest, is noted in the ancient record. The serpent and goat were both used to symbolize spiritual attainment.

The pentagram and the Sabbatical Goat tradition later became part of the heterodox Christians such as the Cathars during the Middle Ages. Alternatively the orthodox Christian Church ran a smear campaign against the heterodox heretics. They strove to obscure the ancient wisdom of the mystery schools by creating a hybrid religion based upon salvation accessible only via the Papal authority. The religious disparate system increased, later landing the Gnostics on the heterodox bad list, and who were declared blasphemous by the Inquisition. This point in history is where Ham's pentagram and goat symbolism were denounced as black magic and witchcraft.

It has been my personal experience, which coincides with the trashing of the pentagram and the dragon affiliated truth seekers seen in the Middle Ages, is that the authority behind the Churches does not want one to seek personal attainment and learning, especially outside of the Bible. This started with the Inquisition and continues to this very day. Personal attainment and learning which does not conform to religious authorities' dogma has historically been labeled heretical leading to ex-communication and often torture, to include burning at the stake and drowning. Water boarding was too good for these dissidents to the truth-suppressing Church authorities. Individually acquired occult knowledge and wisdom was so feared by the PTB that the Goat of Mendes and affiliated symbols were demonized as the epitome of the Devil. The result of this smear campaign is still evident even to this day, evidenced by a wealth of printed and theatrical material proliferating in our culture.

====

Lessons presented by Thoth in the Emerald Tablets, one of the most ancient documents I have ever encountered, describes what is called the "Perennial Philosophy". This historical thread of truth at the basis of the philosophy, has appeared throughout history and been suppressed by governments as well. The basic idea is that the physical (material) world is created by energetic forces, a higher "spiritual reality". For an electrical engineer like me, this can be thought of as an energetic template from which matter is stimulated to form matter in the physical world. Our job is to make the physical body match the energy template from which it is specified. *This in my humble opinion is another way to view the alchemical transition process for humanity's archetypal journey through one's life.* We are encouraged to do a deep dive into the lessons our benefactor and teacher Ningishzida-Thoth encoded in the Emerald Tablets, a hundred times if necessary. This is relevant here as Thoth was considered the original alchemist.

Since authoring my first book and discussing the research on Starfire gold therein, many people contacted me to find out more about this Anunnaki life-extending product, ultimately equating it to the famed Philosopher's Stone. This famed Stone was most likely a bread/cake-like coagulation of the white substance that has the consistency of very fine flour. Images described by Lawrence Gardner decorating Hathor's temple located by archeologists atop Mount Serabit El Khadim, or Mount Sinai to the locals, show the formation of conical bread cakes from the monoatomic gold dust. Gardner describes the temple wall paintings showing Hathor, her priests, and ritual attendants partaking of the conical-shaped bread cakes. This superconductive power was fashioned from the alchemical admixture of gold and antimony exposed to a fiery smelting process, thus the smoke Moses saw from the base of the mountain.

Moses Feeds the Followers Starfire Gold

Starfire Gold was discussed by me as it relates to the Biblical Moses account. Using detailed analysis of the Biblical Exodus account, it is found that Moses was invited by the Anunnaki to Hathor's temple for an encounter, while his followers waited below with the metallurgist Aaron. Moses must have discussed the method to produce the orbitally rearranged monoatomic elements

(ORMES) with the Anunnaki during his Hathor temple visit. ORMES is just another name representing the same product as the Philosopher's Stone, Starfire Gold. The mystery of the verse should be dispelled by understanding who the Anunnaki gods were, that they had an aging issue on Earth, and that heightened energy body Chakra, Auric, and *Akasa* subtle energies effectively prevented Telomere decay and thus they were deemed immortals.

Exodus 32: 20-28 King James Bible

And it came to pass, as soon as he came nigh unto the camp, that he saw the calf, and the dancing: and Moses' anger waxed hot, and he cast the tables out of his hands, and brake them beneath the mount.

[20] And he took the calf which they had made, and burnt it in the fire, and ground it to powder, and strewed it upon the water, and made the children of Israel drink of it.

[21] And Moses said unto Aaron, What did this people unto thee, that thou hast brought so great a sin upon them?

[22] And Aaron said, Let not the anger of my lord wax hot: thou knowest the people, that they are set on mischief.

23 For they said unto me, Make us gods, which shall go before us: for as for this Moses, the man that brought us up out of the land of Egypt, we do not know what is become of him.

24 And I said unto them, Whosoever hath any gold, let them break it off. So they gave it me: then I cast it into the fire, and there came out this calf.

25 And when Moses saw that the people were naked; (for Aaron had made them naked unto their shame among their enemies:)

26 Then Moses stood in the gate of the camp, and said, Who is on the LORD's side? let him come unto me. And all the sons of Levi gathered themselves together unto him.

27 And he said unto them, Thus saith the LORD God of Israel, Put every man his sword by his side, and go in and out from gate to gate throughout the camp, and slay every man his brother, and every man his companion, and every man his neighbour.

28 And the children of Levi did according to the word of Moses: and there fell of the people that day about three thousand men.

It seems that Enlil imparted commands for Moses to give to his followers, deemed unworthy revelers in sin, and gave them the elixir of the gods, smelting the life-extending Starfire gold that the primitive workers mined for them in the fiery furnace located in the

Anunnaki gold mines of Enki's Abzu (Africa). Once Moses had given the people the colloidal gold to drink, it seems he was hoping they would wake up and be righteous immediately. He was proven wrong in verse 26 as the ultimatum was given: you are either for Enlil-El Shaddai-Yahweh (Lord God of Israel) or against him. Only the Levites (priestly class) joined the ancient astronaut who summarily orders the execution of all opposed to him in verses 27-28. Is this the deity you venerate? Not me! Anyway, the point here is that monoatomic gold shows up in the Bible as part of the famed Ten Commandment genocidal encounter with Enlil, in his territory near the Anunnaki space port. The Sinai Peninsula was named after Enlil's son for whom the land was named. Sinai means *in the wilderness of Sin*, (Nannar-Sin), who we currently know as Allah, god of the crescent moon.

Moses and his paramilitary band of thieving marauders landed at the base of Mount Sinai, subsequently allowing Moses to have an encounter with Hathor's crew in the temple where he saw the smoke rising up from the furnaces. This is where the Anunnaki elite were concocting life-prolonging alchemical substances used to optimize their biological functions while they were here on the Seventh Planet, Earth.

Interest in longevity and energy body optimization were keen on the minds of those who made contact with us, both before and after experiencing the monoatomic products. Since that time we have studied the patent positions, researched the alchemical marketplace, and conferred with alchemists on product development issues. This investigation led to the creation of the products and the issues involved in this venture. Much deserved credit has to be given to my wife Christa, whose path has been transformed alongside mine, now serving humanity as the "The Artistic Vegan Alchemist", my twin flame soul mate!

For Kindle readers, the links are active and may be used to gather more information on these stellar products, made with love by the alchemist!

Alchemical Elixir of the Anunnaki – Powder

Alchemical Elixir of the Anunnaki – Liquid

Monatomic Gold Powder 4gms
Alchemical Powdered Elixir of the Anunnaki
Made from Vulcanized Artesian Mineral water Gold, Dead Sea Salt, Mineral salt powders, Glacial milk sediment dust. Take as needed. Very Potent

www.artisticvegan.com

Spagyric Alchemical Elixir of the Annunaki

Colloidal Silver Line

The last product that we have been alchemically producing is colloidal or nanosilver as the marketing gurus have termed the age old product in order to differentiate, divide, and conquer versus cooperating effectively. That said, it has been shown by researchers and doctors interested in natural health care that positively charged Ag ions used in a ten part per million (10 PPM) solution kills all known pathogens to include Ebola, HIV, Anthrax, and all others tested in Army and Government laboratories.

Silver, Gold, and Red Tape...

Christa Clark states that "Colloidal Silver is likely one of the most profound health benefactors out there in my opinion". I wish I would have known about it growing up but am thankful it's in our lives now. It is my hope that you discover this gem either through our product, others' products, or by making it yourself which is preferred.

Over the past year we've encountered numerous road blocks in providing our products to market for both the <u>Starfire Gold</u> and <u>Colloidal Silver</u>. This last road block affected the community and not just my husband and I so that is why I decided to disclose information on the propagandized assault on colloidal silver, citing the health concern termed *Argyria*.

We received the following note from eBay recently (bold and *italics* added for emphasis!

"You listed **colloidal silver**. Because of **FDA concerns** with this product, and documented cases of colloidal silver causing **argyria**, we have decided to **prohibit all listings for colloidal silver**. While we appreciate that you have chosen to utilize our site, we must ask that you please not relist this particular item.

... Keep in mind that if further items aren't listed in accordance with our policy, it could result in additional actions including account restrictions or loss of buying and selling privileges on eBay"

Figure 23: eBay Letter RE: Colloidal Silver

The reasoning behind eBay's decision is OUTRAGEOUS and quite frankly done on invalid terms. I recently found this wonderful article that is meaty with great resources from Doctors and even from the FDA. Here is the LINK (for book readers with inactive HTML, http://www.silvergen.com/argyria1.html). This work was compiled from a researcher in Ontario named Terry Chamberlin. Thank you, Terry, for your great work!

I encourage taking the time to read his article, it was a great compilation of work. Let's get to the heart of the matter. We were unable to offer this product to the community via eBay:

> *"Because of **FDA concerns** with this product, and documented cases of colloidal silver causing **argyria**, we have decided to **prohibit all listings for colloidal silver.**"*

NOW, please read the smoking gun below found from this article, copy and posted from this link with bold added for emphasis: http://www.silvergen.com/argyria1.htm

The following two letters to and from the **FDA** are most informative:

October 14th, 1999

Food and Drug Administration

U.S. Department Of Health and

Human Services Public Health Service

5600 Fishers Lane Rockville, MD 20857

Dear Sirs/Madam,

Pursuant to the Freedom of Information Act and in regard your August 17th, 1999 ruling regarding colloidal silver, could you please supply the following documentation on which you based your decision?

1. The number of deaths related to the consumption of colloidal silver.

2. The number of allergic reactions to the consumption of colloidal silver.

3. The number of harmful drug interactions from both OTC and prescription drugs when combined with colloidal silver.

4. The number of reported cases of Argyria from colloidal silver made with the AC or DC electrical process.

5. The number of cases of Argyria from colloidal silver that did not contain protein stabilizers.

Thank you for your time and consideration of this request.

Sincerely, Brent Finnegan

Figure 24: Letter to FDA Regarding Colloidal Silver

Here is the FDA response to Brent's letter:

Public Health Service Center for Drug Evaluation and Research Office of Training and Communication Freedom of Information Staff HFD-205

5600 Fishers Lane 12 B 05

Rockville, Maryland 20857

DEPARTMENT OF HEALTH AND HUMAN SERVICES

November 3, 1999

In Response Refer to File: F99-22589 Brent Finnigan Takoma (sic), WA 98408

Dear Mr. Finnigan:

This is in response to your request of 10/14/99, in which you requested adverse events associated with the use of Colloidal Silver. Your request was received in the Center for Drug Evaluation and Research on 10/25/99.

We have searched the records from FDA's Adverse Event Reporting System (AERS) and have been unable to locate any cases that would be responsive to your request.

Charges of $3.50 (Search $3.50, Review $0, Reproduction $0, Computer time $0) will be included in a monthly invoice. DO NOT SEND ANY PAYMENT UNTIL YOU RECEIVE AN INVOICE.

If there are any problems with this response, please notify us in writing of your specific problem(s).

Please reference the above file number.

Sincerely,

Hal Stepper Freedom of Information Technician

Office of Training and Communications

Freedom of Information Staff, HFD-205

In spite of the road blocks and red tape, we are offering the products currently on Amazon and alternative arrangements can be made with the Alchemists to obtain access. Switching gears from our recent product focus, we now turn to others that have added significantly to the field.

Two published alchemists have truly affected both Christa and me. These modern alchemists have provided insight into the esoteric and occluded path, writing in a language and style that has archetypal worldwide appeal. A few of my favorite inspirational alchemical pioneering authors will now be explored.

The Alchemist (Paulo Coelho)

There is a reason that this book has had such wide popularity as it takes the reader to the forks in their alchemical path. A lowly shepherd boy has the courage to live his personal legend, following his dreams. Having been trained to listen to the omens, the boy has a divine encounter just when his fated journey appears to be ending. None other than the King of Salem, Melchizedek in disguise as an old beggar, empowered the seeker to be a finder. The symbology alluding to the first alchemist, Thoth, is fantastic. [22].

Most folks who have heard of alchemy think it is about transforming common metals like lead into precious gold. Part of this story is true as we see in Exodus 32:20. Moses makes a batch of colloidal monoatomic gold which we now know involves the alchemical knowledge of Antimony (Stibium element 51) which was taught to humans by Azazel. This being was lambasted for teaching humans alchemy. Wonder if the angst came from the Lord of the Command, Enlil? You bet it did. The elixir of life, Starfire gold, could elevate consciousness which as you see in the next section activated the *ba* field, potentially freeing the primitive worker slaves from their skewed perception of reality.

The conversion of a dull metal like lead into something precious like gold is merely a symbolic representation of the lifting of a barbarian consciousness to an ascended Light Being . This being becomes aware of his SUN-soul birthright to return home to the land of the Ancient Great Gods residing in Arulu, two or more dimensions closer to the CIRCLE OF LIGHT, the SOURCE OF ALL including the holographic boundaries between dimensions which are guarded by the likes of Osiris et al.

Sorcerer's Stone (Hauck)

Dennis Hauck is one of the world's leading experts on the ancient art of alchemy. *Sorcerer's Stone: A beginner's Guide to Alchemy* [1] is a must-have book for those on a transition path. In the second chapter titled *The Golden Thread That Runs Through Time*, he lays the background connecting Thoth and his sacred Emerald Tablets to the alchemical transformation that we as seekers undergo.

Alchemy's consistent teachings are based on the idea that the physical world is a manifestation of a greater spiritual reality.

"The nature of this reality is that it cannot be directly or immediately apprehended except by those who have chosen to fulfill certain conditions, making themselves loving, pure in heart and poor in spirit."

Getting past the trappings of one's ego and becoming an empty vessel is a fundamental condition for experiencing this higher reality. As we saw in Chapter 5, the Emerald Tablets teach that we can activate the *ba*, connecting with the higher reality (dimensional frequency?) through the purification of consciousness. Physical reality (holographic simulation) can be altered by changing the higher spiritual ideal or archetype on which it is based. The mind over matter principle stems from the saying "As Above, so Below" which originated in Egypt. Thoth created a précis version of the Emerald Tablets that was circulating in Europe around the time of the Middle Ages.

The earliest known copy of Thoth's Emerald Tablet exists as a copy of an Arabic book circa 650 A.D. which was later translated into Latin in Spain around 711 A.D. The book does a great job explaining the significance of the liquid metal Mercury, most likely the reason that Thoth affiliated himself with the unusual Earth element, as well as the ninth planet in their cosmogony detailed in the Enuma Elish.

Mercury has no color of its own and reflects whatever light or image is cast upon it. The odorless liquid metal extinguishes fires and absorbs other metals placed into it, including gold as all prospectors know. Once the gold is absorbed into the Mercury, it is heated to its vapor threshold temperature evaporating into the air. What is left is the sought after gold. Note, Mercury vapor is highly toxic, be warned! To alchemists, Mercury represents the watery, occult properties expressed in plant and metals, which also include Sulfur.

Here again we see the number nine, which we now know represents the number of worlds within worlds, parallel holographic realities to which our *ba* SUN-soul can travel. The *ba* can then manifest an intermediate form (quasi body) such that the experience in that dimension can be realized.

Mercurial Synchronicities

During a twelve day period starting September 1st, 2013, a

series of strange symbolic coincidences or synchronicities began occurring in my life. This unexplained sequence of events happened only 5 days after conducting my first national radio interview on Coast to Coast Radio with George Noory at the microphone. The conversation we had catapulted my book *The Anunnaki of Nibiru...* onto the national stage where mankind's true origins are still a hot topic today. It took me about 3 synchronicities before it became evident they needed to be recorded for later analysis, checking for omens and clues as to how the destiny map will unfold. When we are on a journey, it is natural to seek to know the details of the destination.

Synchronicity 1, Date: 09.01.13

Infatuation with my first car, a 1967 Mercury Cougar XR7, came up recently. So much so that I want to get one and restore it. Watched several YouTube videos of restored autos and was highly intrigued. I also want my Jade Tiger back that was sold under duress. This object was purchased at the Ming Dynasty Burial Grounds craft village in China. One of my spirit animals. Mercury and Cougar in the same car name!!! How telling of my path.

Synchronicity 2, Date: 09.02.13

Gold panning and treasure hunting also started coming up regularly as well. Recollections of prospecting by myself in my dune buggy with my metal detector and my dog were epic. I recently made my own *aqua regia* solution to leach gold from computer parts in a 5 gallon bucket. First attempt was successful. Need lots of supply...Also been gathering ore samples, crushing it, panning it, separating out black sand with a magnet, and bought a smelting kit to include the ingot mold and the ceramic crucible and graphite stir rods to play with smelting my own metals. While panning at Torrey Pines State Beach, collected a couple of sea shells that led to a renewed interest in jewelry making, wearing one of my creations now. Found significant Mercury in the pan and was quite alarmed at how much there was...Hg synchronicity number two.

Synchronicity 3, Date: 09.03.13

After releasing my book on August 4th, conducted a 3-hour radio interview on Coast to Coast with George Noory. This launched my book to best-selling status on Amazon.com. A fan from LA, noted that my background was as an aviator and that I was bringing the ancient symbol of the Caduceus forward as a messenger, insinuated this was the role for the winged messenger Hermes. She then sent me two articles on Mercury: "Mysterious Mercury", by Lisa Alexander, and a Toastmaster by her titled "Mercury-The Magical Poison". Lisa works in LA for the Department of Environmental Protection (DEP). Synchronicity number 3.

Synchronicity 4, Date: 09.04.13

At the end of August, shortly after the George Noory Radio Show hosted on 8.21.13, I was contacted by Rick Solinsky from Truckee, CA. He indicated that they were involved with the Sierra club, a controversy over Mercury disruption caused by mining, versus the $9,000,000 allocated to a cleanup effort, $3,000,000 of which was spent by Sierra trying to recover Hg. Rick invited me to Truckee, where I am presently located, to peruse the mines and check out the issue. Again, Mercury was at issue for the gold mining Western Alliance that Rick is president of. Rick is going to be my first SI client since leaving Arkansas October, 2011.

Synchronicity 5, Date: 09.05.13

Was channeled 08.25.13 for the umpteenth time to watch "*Jason and the Argonauts]*", 1963 version. This is the year of my birth. Significant German origins to this film? German is the language I studied in College and had an Eastern German manufacturing division under my watch in Dresden, while VP Engineering at LightPointe Communications. The scene where Jason encounters the temple priest who morphs into a 35 foot tall Caduceus carrying Hermes that takes Jason to meet the Gods on mount Olympus. Mercury rose and shocked my inner spirit, to the point I saw myself clearly as Jason did, awestruck in disbelief.

Synchronicity 6, Date: 09.06.13

Just before the show on 8.21.13, I felt led to research a link between my book and George Noory's interest. This occurred only hours before the show, as a last minute thought so that I had a nugget for George, which he would not expect. While reading Edgar Cayce's work, having been familiar with it from past readings and owning his books, I found the information on the body as the temple of God the most fascinating, as it crossed over to the Structural Integration domain. I had a biased reason to look into the work of Edgar Cayce, the most famous sleeping-healing prophet, with thousands of channeled books on display in the Cayce ARE institute in Virginia. The nugget that I found within an hour of the Coast to Coast radio show was the linkage between the "word" and "flesh", indicating that the message became flesh for the benefit of humanity. In this Cayce document, of which there were five (5) separate and supporting positions, that *Hermes-Mercury was the being whose words became flesh to deliver a message to humanity. This was referenced to George on air along with the John 1:12 verse from the Bible, indicating that the word became flesh (Jesus). This was one of the pivotal points in my research to positively identify whose Anunnaki energy represented Jesus. It was undoubtedly Ningishzida, Enki's second born son, the Caduceus carrying scientist like his father.* I am the second born son of my father, my brother Donny was killed in a head on collision in Arkansas on his way from Mountain Home to Fayetteville Arkansas, where he resided with his wife Terrie and ten year old daughter Becky, who was also killed in the crash. The significant connection between Ningishzida-Thoth-Hermes-Mercury-Jesus were obvious to me at this point, both logically and emotionally. I knew that I knew and have had that feeling many times before as an inventor.

Synchronicity 7, Date: 09.07.13

My sons, Matthew and Michael have very telling email accounts that were their earliest email forays. Matthew has maximus_ruler@yahoo.com and Michael has moomoo@yahoo.com. My personal reflections on the connotations of the meaning in those chosen names are such: the maximum ruler would be the next zodiacal ruler in the Enkiite lineage, foretold by the Christian tradition that the coming *messah* (Kingly Mesopotamian and Egyptian term for he who was anointed by Draco, the sacred fat of the Egyptian crocodile.) This is Jesus-Ningishzida-Thoth-Hermes-Mercury, the winged messenger. From Michael's unorthodox nomenclature, I glean the word *mummu*, pronounced exactly the same way, which was the planet Mercury in the Babylonian Epic of Creation, the Enuma Elish, as decoded in my book, *The Anunnaki of Nibiru: Mankind's Forgotten Creators, Enslavers, Destroyers, Saviors, and Hidden Architects of the New World Order*, currently selling very well on Amazon.com, a Middle

East History best seller since inception, 8.4.13. Two more confirmations that Hg is rising.

Synchronicity 8, Date: 09.08.13

Another enthusiastic book fan, Victor Mason, hailing from Victorville, CA, contacted me about getting into the audio book narration loop. He had a studio at home from his now downsizing Mojave Amplifier operation. We agreed to have him be one of two audio test customers to provide feedback as to what needed to be improved on my audio recording, being a new hack to this domain. I also had the audio book narration script out for solicitation on ACX, a company that feeds Audible.com, owned by Amazon.com. Agreed to stop by in Victorville (Nike=Victory in Greek) to see the Victor, with a last name allegory to the Masonic Temple in Washington, D.C. about which I was writing supplemental information on my Facebook page for book fans. My step father was a Mason and his son, whom I have been in frequent contact with suddenly, is a 32 degree active and a current Mason in Wiggins, Mississippi. Just sent him my autographed book. Wow! The amplifier links that Victor sent me to rival my Roland MicroCube portable amplifier were the Coyote Hg (high gain or Mercury abbreviation) and the Sidewinder (snake symbol). This synchronicity about Mercury again and the Mesopotamian snake allusion to a god or king kept coming up, since I had just written that on my Facebook page and had the idea of Dragons and a

Tattoo in my head. Still do to this day. We arrived in Victorville on 09.07.13, eight synchronicities in as many days in the month. Two more occurred there (not recorded) and we left on 09.09.13 for the mountains, having slept on the floor with two Boxers, Sheila and Roscoe, amazing love those dogs had.

Synchronicity 9, Date: 09.09.13

"*Mercury Rising*" was chosen by me as the title of my next book when someone asked me during a chat session over Facebook, what my next book was titled. So, spontaneously, without thought, my next book title manifested: "*Mercury Rising*". Number 9.

Synchronicity 10, Date: 09.10.13

Arrived by vehicle on the 09.09.13 in Truckee, CA, with host Robin Wilcox. Decoding her phone number (removed from the original document for privacy reasons) turns into 6 sevens. Coincidence given all the sevens showing up and being decoded by me, connected to Enki. Hey dad. In a conversation with her, Robin brought up the concept of *Mercury Rising ver batum,* something that she first encountered 20 years ago. She brought it up in reaction to a picture Victor Paul, a Facebook book fan, sent me on 09.10.13. The image was of a winged messenger holding out his hand with light coming out enveloping the Earth. It was clearly Hermes-Mercury the messenger, another synchronicity.

Synchronicity 11, Date: 09.10.13

A few days ago, a fellow pilot contacted me having read my book. In the book, I listed the Warrant Officer Flight program I participated in the Army, being class 85-13 Light Blue Flight. The pilot that contacted me graduated about 1 year before I did, but was stationed at almost the same places. He now resides in Illinois, where he is VP of an Electronics outfit. Sound familiar? Anyway, he sent me a burning question about who in Revelation I thought was analogous to in the Anunnaki hierarchy. The image he had was of a being with seven stars in his hand and a sharp double-edged sword coming out of his mouth. I gave it some thought, and it clearly came to me by the next day that the image was Mercury holding the Earth, seventh planet in his hand, and speaking the divining truth as a message for mankind. This one hit me right at home from a brother in arms. Synchronicity number 11.

Synchronicity 12, Date: 09.12.13

Neil Freer is a fellow researcher and close friend with Marshall Klarfeld, whom I have on my list to contact. Neil sent me an email to contact him. I did. We had a long conversation about many topics, to include his use of Starfire gold. We ended the conversation by me honoring his years on this Earth and asked his advice on the best method to deliver this message given where we are in the unveiling. He indicated the big screen, although he was aware that the movie *"The Anunnaki" that* was killed in 2010. He then stated that he was close friends with Timothy Leary and that he had a write-up in his third book on Futants. I asked if he was indicating that I should read that material, and he emphatically stated I should, offering to .pdf a copy of it and send it to me immediately. I took the liberty to look up Tim Leary's lecture on YouTube regarding the definition of a Futant. Here is the link on YouTube (http://www.youtube.com/watch?v=rAmi9kDQe7U). It seems I am one of the 1.5-2% Futants on the planet, without question. My title is Herr Futant Hg. Jawoll, and my Mercury is Rising!!! Ha ha...The winged messenger is back, the aeroscout observer preparing mankind for the coming of the new Kingdom from Nibiru has delivered his double-edged words on Amazon.com: Paperback, Kindle, Hardback, Audio book on eBay, soon to be on Audible.com. Movie script first draft completed today.

I wanted to share the twelve synchronicities that occurred for me immediately following the release of my book, and especially after the first national radio show with Coast to Coast AM hosted by George Noory. My exposure to the original alchemist starting in the Sumerian cuneiform tablets up to the present time is inspiring and provides me with the knowledge that I stumbled onto the right path for my current incarnation, lumps and all. As you can see, the book title was augmented later with the prelude "The (7th) Seventh Planet..." It is due to these events and their embedded lessons when unthreaded that make this path so *interesting*. My encounters with Mercury continue to this day, filling me with the inspiration to live life to the fullest knowing that a benevolent being has our backs on the way home to the LIGHT.

CHAPTER 7: The Anunnaki Virtual Environment

Mankind has been observing his environmental physical reality during his primitive worker existence here on the seventh planet, Ki to the Anunnaki, Earth to us. The terrestrial environment encountered on our slave planet is often quite distinct with some terrain featuring rocky crags and steep cliffs, while other areas of the Earth provide flat fertile plots like river deltas. Each circumstance one traverses in life could be modeled as a simulator.

Simulation Required

Consider the complexity that modern electronic gamers enjoy, navigating a personal virtual world now presented in amazing 3D with animated sprites that are hard to distinguish from actual human beings. The participants explore complex contrived simulation mazes which create a feeling of being there. Technical advances in the software modeling domain have been applied to a vast set of problems to determine the most optimal simulator solution. Drug companies utilize complex biogenetic and chemical reactions (a different domain expert needed here versus the cockpit of a helicopter at war) in a rule-based design environment in order to discover new agents to be deployed in the name of healthcare.

Simulations are used to establish the complex electronic design process. Software models of each circuit element, their capacitive, resistive, and inductive parameters stored in a component library, are used to develop printed circuit boards, logic within programmable devices like the Field Programmable Gate Array (FPGA) and the Complex Programmable Logic Device (CPLD). Computer hardware modeling software was designed specifically to simulate the clock timing, setup and hold times for signals, as well as the transitional changes spawned within the complex parallel process that must be synchronized and coordinated in order to turn a blueprint into a tangible multi-layered electronic circuit board. Now add all the surface mount and through-hole components to the simulator and one can determine where not enough current is available, the ringing of an inductor resonating at the output of a power transformer fed by a closed loop magnetically decoupled flyback converter. Simulations used to be a nice thing to have to verify design constraints like thermal cooling and air flow. Now, with the complexity of interaction and logic density in today's modern electronics, not using simulation is no longer not an option. Making a mistake that takes months to correct in the electronic design domain is a firing offense in our highly competitive technical skills market. Best practicing engineers not only simulate unknown components to establish the theoretical performance curves, but often prototype risky parts of an electronic circuit to ensure that the iteration time to get to production quality is minimized. Simulations are a necessary part of modern technical life for designers in most domains, which include mechanical engineering, chemical engineering, communications and systems engineering, the stock market gurus, and even epidemiologist tracking and predicting pandemic outbreaks, like Ebola, among many others.

Rat Maze Motives

If we attempt to codify a simulation model of a human being for simulation purposes, would not the Anunnaki have had a similar inclination to utilize the tool as a means to test various hypothesis as to how the primitive workers will respond to various stimuli? Earlier an analogy was made to humans existing in a similar state as a rat in a complex maze. The stimuli posited in the thought experiment involving the rat simulated a hazardous environment to assess the rodent's intelligence and learning ability to survive. Various "mine fields" and hazardous choices are added to the maze to make the process of finding food, avoiding risk, and locating a way out alive more interesting to the lab researcher; most likely an avid gamer.

Hollywood and Virtual Life

Hollywood has been busy releasing films recently like The *Truman Show, The Hunger* Games, and the *Thirteenth Floor*. Each cinematic offering approaches the idea of a virtual reality in a different method. In the Truman Show, Jim Carey is placed as a young child into a very large half-dome simulated environment large enough to contain a small rural town fully equipped with all-seeing electronic eye surveillance cameras. Every person in the town is aware of the simulated city except for Truman, the primitive worker under test and analysis. The ceiling of the half dome has a holographic projection of the sky to include the sun, the moon, and the ephemeris in motion. A weather-generating device is used to add reality to the sea, along with wave action and real storms. Was the simulated archetypal-challenging tempest at sea created with an extreme low frequency (ELF) focal beam-arrayed radio transmission system which can heat the ionosphere creating storms? If so, it would be like that which author Jerry Smith discloses in the high amplitude acousto-aural research program (HAARP) detailed in his book "HAARP: The Ultimate Weapon of the

Conspiracy" [39]. The ELF brain wave and earthquake fault-perturbing ultimate weapon of the conspiracy as HAARP has been deemed, was recently decommissioned by the Air Force indicating that they had an even better system that can be deployed on an aircraft carrier. How convenient [38]!

Or, was a mechanical wave generator along with hurricane force Venturi effective turbo fans being implemented? Truman is terrified of dying at sea, as this is how he believes he lost his father. It was a false flag event to plant the archetypal fear of drowning into Truman's memory.

The Hero with a Thousand Faces

Consider the concept of reincarnation for a moment as the ascended beings that help orchestrate the next life plan for the reincarnated soul. Together they conjure up future life events designed to transform the primitive worker into the archetypal Hero destined for them as a species. This reminds me of the movie *"Defending Your Life"*, in which the protagonist finds himself in the quasi netherworld after dying, the location in space-time where one's archetypal journey is assessed and a plan is reformulated for the almost-graduating aspirant in anticipation of returning to Earth. Then the energy is reincarnated into a mutually decided upon body for another go at succeeding in the simulation vignette. The need to rise up to overcome the dark night of our soul and achieve an enlightened victory was genetically embedded in us by Thoth. Joseph Campbell's assertion that the Hero archetype story can be told and retold using different players and scenes, with a thousand different faces, is proven as we still are drawn to the story. Even Hollywood requires a precisely formulated script that follows the Hero archetype story without deviation.

A brief description of the template is presented here. The archetype story told Hollywood style has been done so many times that producers have adopted a standardized template for its retelling in movies. The basic concept of a beginning, middle, and ending form the foundation.

In the beginning the setup, conflict, and resolution for the hero is presented in three stages: Acts 1-3 which span the entire story. Act 1 is allotted 30 pages (minutes), Act 2 takes an entire hour with 60 pages, and Act 3 is also allocated 30 pages (minutes) to complete the template. The story is to be told in exactly 120 pages with each page taking one minute or so when performed. This creates a duration limit of 2 hours maximum, probably because the mind can only absorb what the bottom can endure. [42, Pgs. 215-216]

The Hunger Games Pushes Holographic World

Katniss Everdeen, the female heroine featured in the *Hunger*

Games movie series, discovers the secret behind the control mechanism used by the powers that be (PTB) to control the senses of the brutally governed populace. The all-seeing eyes of the elite overlords seem to be everywhere. In this movie, the holographic nature of our environment is pushed to the edge of reality. A holographic remote viewing simulation room is operated by a master gamer. It all comes down to moves and counter moves, like a chess game. The heroine, after many forks in the winding fateful road, gets some help from a "sponsor" to improve her chances of finding her way out of the deadly rat maze. The game imposed on the populace is a competitive culling device to rid the land of heroes and dissidents. Instead of a virtual dome which Truman escapes by overcoming his fear of drowning at sea, Katniss forms alliances with some peers who have a more scientific leaning in their environmental negotiation skills. With some technical input, the protagonist is spurred to understand and ultimately destroy the holographic projector being used to manifest the predatory conditions for the hunt. We ask ourselves, how can a simulated animal have the ability to actually interact with and potentially kill one of the game participants? The only way that is possible is that we, too are simulation objects that share the same sensors and perception. This point was brought out more astutely in the movies *The Matrix* and *Avatar* where the idea of our energy having the ability to animate a remote host is another important element in the holographic nature of reality.

The Thirteenth Floor is a World within Worlds

Finally, the movie *The Thirteenth Floor* is discussed as it relates to the holographic claims made by modern physicists attempting to tie together multidimensional String Theory to the concept of a holographic universe. This movie is for those nerds who have written a line or two of software computer code in a multitude of languages. The software engineers involved in an "avatar time traveling" simulation come to the realization that they too, are caught in a simulator, having discovered a glitch in the holographic program that exposes the truth. They are brought to the same troubling realization that faces us today in the highly technical information age. What if we are just containers that can interact with energy to animate physical matter as is implied? Is this scientific concept really new?

Religion, Energy, and Quantized Consciousness

Various spiritual disciplines like Buddhism and Hinduism recognize the complex relationship between energy and matter. The concept of a quantized state of consciousness that coincides with the degree to which energy is synthesized with our carnal bodies is the key to finding a way to experience a higher dimension of reality than we normally do. Seeing beyond the veil of our imposed reality (think brain waves here) during our waking consciousness seems to be a stumbling block for us. How could what we have been perceiving with our Anunnaki designed sensors, our eyes, not be the true nature of reality?

Human Sensor Limitations

Consider that human optical sensors, our eyes, have been significantly functionally constrained. If you doubt this, simply observe how much better the optical sensors are are in other creatures of nature. Owls clearly see better at night and possess the deadly acquisition, tracking, and focusing ability of a predatory bird on the lookout for its next meal. Adding insult to injury regarding human focal range limitations, eagles and hawks can spot their prey from very high altitudes while simultaneously circling in a warm summer thermal draft or effortlessly surfing the rising air currents that add invisible buoyancy to a wind facing cliff or trigger point. Clearly nature has the upper hand in the optical sensor department. Additionally, some snakes are able to use a form of thermal sights to facilitate their sneaky death strikes when the victim least expects it, in the dark. Their sense of hearing is so keen, along with their ability to smell the victim's odor in the air with their tongue, they simply follow the sound of the poisoned future meal's heartbeat listening for it to stop before eating. Hopefully, my point about our limited sensors contributing to our holographic enslavement has been made.

What is Interesting?

As an electrical engineer having created and worked with complex six degree of freedom simulations models, the idea of a simulated reality is not so far-fetched. In 1989 I received an honorable discharge from the United States Army in which I served for seven years contiguously since 1982. My exposure to the attack helicopter environment as a pilot in command created the attention necessary to obtain small business innovative research grants while working as a systems engineer at Reticular Systems, Inc. At the time I did not understand the significance of the field of data mining, which is essentially the initial role I played at the company having just left the cockpit of a complex helicopter with over 1500 flight hours accumulated in all weather conditions. I was tasked to operate under night vision goggle operations using a multitude of terrain masking techniques. This experience could be codified into a rule base which could serve as the basic survival and mission-oriented intelligence an experienced pilot learns over the course of intensive training and combat preparedness.

Once the rules were derived from the domain expert, they could be tested in a simulator mimicking a mission plan to determine the effectiveness at task completion and survival impacts. During the development of the software simulation model, the concept of sensor fusion came to the forefront. On the biological human pilot level, a subset of the five sense are fully engaged in environment assessment. How does one take in all the objects in the environment and determine whether they have the potential to help the mission succeed or impede its efficacy? A stunning realization occurred to me at that technical juncture in the program development. The question was posed, "What is interesting?" This is the first constraint the objects in the simulator had to meet in order to allocate the onboard sensors toward the object to make this assessment. This forced me to determine how I would convey the concept of *interesting* to the computer. In order to answer this question, I simply asked myself in the most general terms possible, what I find interesting and why. The answer not only surprised me but led to a life lesson so profound that I enjoy sharing this story zealously with others. Before I give away my conclusion and definition of the term interesting, think of how many times this term is used, most likely by you the reader as well. Have you ever taken the time to define what interesting means to you and how those unique desires seem to distinguish each person one from the other. We sometimes meet folks with similar interests in a particular domain and are happy to have encountered birds of a feather that flock together, at least for a while. The solution to this thought experiment query was elusive when dealing with real life scenarios, with all the emotion and overhead of life occluding the generic definition desired. Alternatively, when attempting to illustrate the sensor focusing concept that can identify a friend or foe mentality which an attack helicopter pilot relies on instinctively in the cockpit for survival, the solution was found.

The key to whether an external entity is interesting to a pilot is an assessment of the potential that it has to affect specific mission parameters. For instance, if the sensors detect that a S300 ground to air anti-aircraft radar has detected them, this would be an interesting entity given its potential as a hostile threat, one that could alter the mission plan by shooting down the chopper. Other less drastic examples can be cited. For instance, consider flying close to the ground at night with limited lighting, an external entity of interest may be anything that can impact the rotor blades like foliage or blowing debris. A proximity warning sensor can alert the pilot that a very damaging object, the ground, is fast approaching. Even the time to get from the start point to the object we can be parameterized with time, distance, and many other plan specific expectations. In general then, when teaching the computer simulation about assessing the environment for a plan altering one of entities of interest, the generic definition of the term interesting started to emerge.

What is interesting to us as humans, in general, is that which has the potential to alter our life mission. The specific assumptions that predicate mission success are those that are necessary to do route planning. In the Army Aviation, business, this had a direct correlation to the definition of interesting it seemed. Let's try to apply this interesting definition to our biological lives and then see how it is possibly an underlying primitive fight or flight type intelligence that is endemic to all humans. When we ask ourselves if we find a particular song or theory interesting and why, the answer is seemingly more elusive than the life or death cockpit decisions a helicopter pilot uses to negotiate a hostile environment and achieve mission success. A final generalized statement about what is interesting in life is now posited. What an individual finds interesting is that which has the potential to change your fate into destiny. This endemic archetypal genetic programming within an Enki-Ningishzida fashioned primitive worker, is attracted to any person, place, or thing in their current incarnation due to the potential to learn a lesson that will lead to spiritual growth.

We find certain music interesting because of the way it makes us feel, and do not realize that as a species we are attracted to beauty. We instinctually seek a mate who exhibits the proper bilateral symmetry affiliated with a Bo Derick "10". This hidden attraction has interesting benefits, perceived to be the result of choosing the best looking mate with the potential to produce progeny without survival threatening defects.

Interesting Forks in the Road

Life circumstances are similar to the various vignettes composed for a simulation run to determine the survivability and effectiveness of the pilot's expert system rule set. This is very much like the application envisioned where the aircraft operates autonomously, like an unmanned drone as an example. The environment is hostile to our mission. When we are faced with critical life decisions at the proverbial forks in the road, we as intelligent beings endowed with reflective consciousness, are solely responsible for the direction we take at the junction.

If we listen to our heart's council, seeking to find a higher state of consciousness in order to navigate our way through fated decisions in our individual paths, the lessons learned when encountering something interesting can be brought to bear at the decision point. This sharpens our character and resolve to choose what is at least "perceived" to be good in this world. A lesson learned during nap-of-the-earth terrain navigation training in a helicopter is applicable to your spiritual path toward your destiny. If you get off course from your mission path, the safest and most effective way to get back on course, to make your fated decisions work in the direction of your destiny, is to go back to the location (event or life circumstances) where you clearly knew you were on course. This may mean backtracking the current path all the way back to the last known fork in the road or checkpoint. Once arriving at this known "good" place, applying the lessons learned on the wrong path helps making the correct choice more obvious at the road junction. As a budding chopper pilot, the evaluator established the parameter that getting more than 50 yards off your planned course is a check ride failure. Thus, matching the terrain to the map and not the other way around was highly interesting to me and is even more profound when applying this principle to one's life path. Each of us has a story to tell about how an ill-fated path led to catastrophe. Hopefully there is a redemption story to go along with each of the bad decisions such that the ultimate destiny for one's life is obtained. I challenge the reader to use these simple parable analogies to make one's fate meet their destiny.

Destiny Dreams in the Hologram

While we are tossing about definitions, I would like to make an attempt at defining generically the destiny for each of us. We have been designed by Enki, Ninharsag, and upgraded genetically by Ningishzida as primitive workers, 'tis true. Our way out of the holographic slave planet universe, to rise up from tyranny and to become an enlightened being, aware of our true origins and capabilities, can occur. It is the Creator of All's plan for free-will beings (SUN-souls intact) to achieve the GOD-given endowed rights which include the right to life, liberty, and the pursuit of happiness, just like it used to be in America. Happy are those who dream

GERALD CLARK

dreams and are willing to do what it takes to make them come true. ***Thus, if you are not fervently chasing your unavoidably interesting dream, you have lost your way at one of the forks in the road.***

Interesting Leads to Destiny

The magical part about paying attention to what is interesting to you and defining it in your own terms relative to your path is that the creative FORCE, the SOURCE OF ALL, fashioned the archetypal inherent distinction ability in us all. This is the ability to recognize the difference between the concept of good and evil and is an understandable duality construct given our fallen state. Recall that if we can detect what is interesting, the reason it is interesting is that the entity has the potential to change course. Another way of saying the same thing is to pay attention to what you are paying attention to. There is a reason, whether the potential for change is beneficial or harmful to your path is what forms your decision at that fork in the road. In a simplistic pilot model, it comes down to identifying the entity as friend or foe (IFF) and then taking action appropriately. Isn't that interesting!!!

Interesting Synchronicities

David Wilcock in his book *The Synchronicity Key* [42] alludes to the hidden forces that are behind our experience of synchronicity events. Leonardo Di Caprio starred in the movie *Inception* in which he carried a dimensional identification device that he would use to

416

establish whether he was awake or dreaming. This is similar to the famous French philosopher Renee Descartes' question of how one could differentiate whether they were awake or dreaming. Renee simply needed to have a personal talisman which he could deploy, like a spinning gyroscope, to answer his own question.

Physicists Claim Proof for a Holographic Universe

Nature magazine's article "Simulations back up Theory that Universe is a hologram" dated December 10, 2013, asserted that physicists provided some of the clearest evidence yet that we could be actually operating in a Holographic Universe, one massive spherical layered projection.

In 1997, theoretical physicist Juan Maldacena proposed [14] a gravitational model of the Universe. His theory postulates that gravity arises from infinitesimally thin, vibrating strings could be reinterpreted in terms of well-established physics. The mathematically intricate world of String Theory states that we exist in nine dimensions of space coupled with one dimension of time. If true, then our perception of what is out there in the multidimensional simulation environment, is by definition a hologram.

Maldacena's theory was appealing to quantum physicists because it solved apparent inconsistencies between quantum physics and Einstein's theory of gravity. It provided physicists with a mathematical tool that allowed them to translate back and forth between the two languages, and solve problems in one model that seemed intractable in the other and vice versa. This ability to simulate complex cause and effect vignettes like a chess game is invaluable to those that require rapid decision making with advanced sensor fusion intelligence.

In two papers posted on the arXiv repository, Yoshifumi Hyakutake of Ibaraki University of Japan and his colleagues now provide compelling evidence that Maldacena's theory is true.

In one paper [15] Hyakutake computes the internal energy of a Black Hole, the position of its event horizon, its entropy and other properties based on the predictions of String Theory as well as the effects of so-called virtual particles that continuously pop into and out of existence. A related paper agreed [16] in which collaborators calculate the internal energy of the corresponding lower-dimensional cosmos with no gravity. The two computer calculations are highly correlated claiming the same results were obtained mathematically. "It seems to be a correct computation," says Maldacena, who is now at the Institute for Advanced Study in Princeton, New Jersey.

The findings "are an interesting way to test many ideas in quantum gravity and String Theory", declares Maldacena, and he elaborates further stating "The whole sequence of papers is very nice because it tests the dual nature of the universes in regimens where there are no analytic tests."

"They have numerically confirmed, perhaps for the first time, something we were fairly sure had to be true, but was still a conjecture — namely that the thermodynamics of certain black holes can be reproduced from a lower-dimensional universe," says Leonard Susskind, a theoretical physicist at Stanford University in California who was among the first theoreticians to explore the idea of holographic universes. See the Scientific American periodical cover page positing the holographic nature of reality as a possible actuality in Figure 25 below.

The cosmos with a black hole has ten dimensions, with eight of them forming an eight-dimensional sphere. The lower-dimensional, gravity-free one has but a single dimension, and its menagerie of quantum particles resembles a group of idealized springs, or harmonic oscillators, attached to one another.

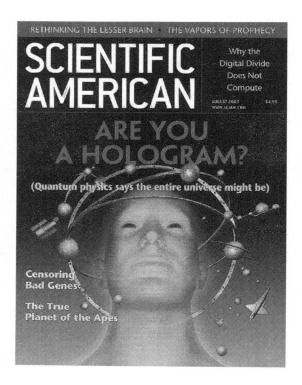

Figure 25: Holographic Reality

Now that we have considered the mathematical and quantum basis for the potential holographic reality and reviewed the simulation capabilities we now enjoy in many fields, along with significant advances in our understanding of the physical world, why is it so shocking to people to accept the holographic nature of reality? An interesting correlation that will be added to the hillbilly memory of mine is that the number of worlds within worlds spoken of in the Emerald Tablets herein matches the nine dimensions of space and one dimension of time the researchers derived mathematically. Seems like modern scientists are approaching a place in our unveiling of the truth in which reconstructing the CREATOR OF ALL's LAW OF SPACE and LAW OF TIME simulation parameters are instantiating in simulation variables happening now! These models confirm the understanding of our holographic reality. Several reasons can be proffered why this peek behind the GRAND SYSTEM ARCHITECT's curtain is being allowed at this seminal time in processional wobbling history, one of which forces us to address the nature of energy and matter as it applies to each of us. As our understanding of energy and matter improves at an exponential manner, it is high time that industrialized peoples of the world begin asking themselves how the law of conservation of energy might apply to them. The physics law, taught in all universities around the world, is that energy is neither created nor destroyed, it merely changes state. As an extreme example consider all matter that is gravitationally tugged on by our Milky Way Galaxy gargantuan black hole. All matter that trespasses beyond the event horizon threshold, is completely transformed into energy, specifically a large portion of which is emitted at the black hole poles as gamma rays. Recall that Albert Einstein offered us the simple equation that stated energy equals the mass of an object times the speed of light squared. Thus the derived energy from Uranium or Plutonium can be precisely determined. Both civil and military uses exist for matter that is extremely dense as this translates to the most potential energy latent therein. Choosing these rare heavy earth metals, versus far less dense aluminum, produces the biggest bang for the buck using Einstein's simple equation. Matter is converted to energy and not destroyed. This applies to meteors as well.

Suppose that two meteors, occupying the same volume in space, hypothetically strike the earth or the lower atmosphere. Let one hypothetically be made of Plutonium which is very dense, and let the other be composed of loosely compacted sandstone for a less destructive rival. Depending on the size and impact angle, both may do damage but the denser Uranium meteor could cause an extinction level event whereas the sandstone meteor may disintegrate as it heats up coming into contact with the parasitic drag imparted by earth's dense atmosphere.

A frightening expansion of man's inhumanity to man through war has culminated in the export and positioning of weaponry into space. What must our Galactic neighbors think about this hostile offensive and defensive posture on such an unevolved planet filled with primitive beings barely even aware of the electromagnetic spectrum? Consider further the threats that a nation like North Korea have leveraged against its perceived enemies like the United States. A rogue nation like North Korea could launch what appears to be a harmless low earth orbiting weather satellite. This has already occurred. Further suppose that in their attempt to be taken seriously in the world, they install a 10 foot long spear shaped Uranium rod into an enclosed and hidden chamber onboard the satellite. Low earth orbiting (LEO) satellites are put into this non-geosynchronous orbit to move along certain earth oriented axis, often times in polar orbit. This was the case for the Globalstar satellite constellation that I was involved with during my tenure at Loral Telemetry and Instrumentation based in San Diego's overpopulated defense contractor menagerie. If the North Koreans were allowed to maneuver their harmless weather satellite equipped with a simple metal dart, it could be dropped from orbital altitude like a downward pointing arrow. It would appear to be just another meteorite given its small profile and would most likely not be detectable or categorized as a threat to the earth or perceived as a weapon of mass destruction. If this unfortunate Uranium dart-dropping incident were to occur over a densely populated area like Los Angeles or New York City, it could have the same potential energy releasing destructive capability as our modern guided nuclear weapons. A constellation of weather monitory satellites armed with heavy metal darts could turn out to be one of the most devastating space weapon capabilities a small nation like North Korea can contrive. Given the threats that have been made, and the statements leaked during highly intense saber rattling media rants, it seems that this is exactly what North Korea is up to. They even went so far as to state which American cities would be targeted, coinciding with the Korean's LEO satellite. The orbital path chosen for the North Korean LEO does in fact traverse the United States. See Figure 26 below. As can be seen from the orbital lines overlaid on the United States, perhaps Philadelphia and New York were included on the target list given the flight paths over land.

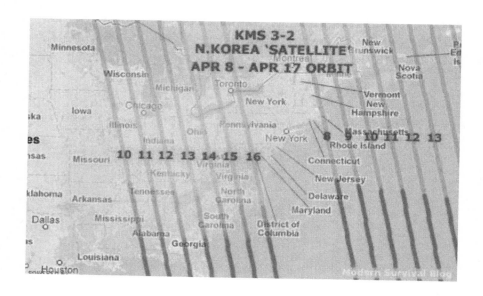

Figure 26: North Korean LEO Satellite Path

Another feature that LEOs possess is the ability to be re-vectored using onboard thrusters to change course to a different orbit and altitude when desired. The only way to counter a dart dropping satellite is to closely monitor their movement, especially if they are allowed to overfly terrestrial targets.

For those who have forgotten their physic equations, the density is equal to the volume divided by the mass.   The weight is defined as the mass of an object times the supposed accelerative force of gravity. Density variation in metals is affected by molecular bonding as a function of temperature and motion.   Simulated annealing uses both to create hardened steel. Settling molten metal ions group closer together in a molecular bond affecting the resultant density which translates to energy potential as the Japanese living in Hiroshima and Nagasaki discovered first hand. Robert Oppenheimer knew he failed in his archetypal journey when he quoted the ancient Sanskrit texts where he got his inspiration building the first atomic bombs. He quotes the realization that he has become the destroyer of worlds, just like the ancient Gods in Sumer and India had demonstrated they were willing and capable of achieving. Returning the reader back to metallurgy issues, the tighter the metal's molecular bond, the denser the material will be. Heavy unstable metals are dangerous in that they emit radiation for long periods of time. They are also the weapon making material of choice given the latent potential to convert the periodic element into a massive Hiroshima sized blast. In my last book, a detailed discussion of the energetic makeup of the Galactic center established various levels of radiation that humans can tolerate up to a limit.   The Mayan dark rift is a dangerous place and the radiation therein can be fatal.

GERALD CLARK

Energy production capabilities in a power-generating nuclear reactor or the destructive power of an unstable heavy metal isotopes can unleash given that the mass of the weapons grade material contains massive potential. Could the North Koreans have simulated all possible outcomes for their plan? We shall see. I spent a year of my life serving my country deployed to South Korea as an aspiring helicopter pilot and stationed overseas at such an early age. I celebrated my 21st birthday on deployment to Chun Chon, Korea 1984, don't ask me about my Combat mission encounter with Soju that night.. The Army experience in Korea from 1983-1984 feels almost like a misty dream, although a brutal one, so long ago. As part of our sensitivity training to the hostile situation that existed between the North and the South Koreans, we were taken to the divided building that straddles the 38th parallel designated as a demilitarized zone or as we in the Army called it, simply the DMZ.

For those who are not aware, the North and South Korean governments only signed a truce at the close of the Korean War, leaving hostile forces staring each other down in Panmunjom, game face on both sides, across an imaginary line separating generations one from another.

Panmunjom, located in Gyeonggi Province North Korea, is an abandoned village on the *38th Parallel* that separates North and

426

South. This location marked the place where the 1953 Korean Armistice Agreement that paused the Korean War was signed. The building where the armistice was signed still stands, although it is north of the Military Demarcation Line, which runs through the middle of the DMZ, accessible only by the single bridge of no return. This place is considered one of the last vestiges of the Cold War. After entering the one way building that straddled the border with the North, I realized the severity of the potential resurgence of violent conflict, the point of the Military-sponsored escorted mission to view the shattered remnants of a nation accomplished.

Next we will spend time going over some theory, but given the breadth and depth of the material provided in the book, a brief summary will be offered with more in depth discussions to follow.

Holographic Theory

Michael Talbot offers in his book, *The Holographic Universe* [47], some credible evidence that helped to convince me that our limited sensors were not producing a realistic interpretation of the outside world. He further pointed out that during brain injury assessments, research and clinical case studies showed that patients who suffered brain traumas or had large tumors removed from the cerebral cortex experienced memory functions that were often affected as were lingual abilities. Visual after effects that limited focal range and field of view were often present as well. One study was cited in which lost memory that was affiliated with a surgically removed brain tumor unexpectedly returned bringing into question science's brain functional mapping models and theories. It seems that the brain stores all memories as a hologram, such that if one part is lost that the whole can exist in any other part.

TJ Hegland, author of *The Virtual Earth Graduate [12]*, discusses the correlation between Robert Monroe's locales (1-3) with the findings in Quantum physics. In Emerald Tablet X, I take the correlation even further adding the mathematics from the String Theory domain and connecting it to the nine dimensions postulated by holographic universe proponents. The number nine seems to be in agreement with Thoth's teachings as well. There you have it folks, there are eight additional dimensions for us to explore with hopefully no TSA guards at each! However, we learned that Earth's portal is guarded by Osiris, and he cannot be bribed!

Constructing the 3D Earth Simulation Model

Definitions

Sensor: Electromagnetic receiver, biological or mechanical

Affecters: Object features that can change the state space variables of another object. An example is a robotic arm on a rover or your own multi-levered biological arm.

Sensor Fusion: Data captured from the sensor suite (bodily and augmented like radar and cameras) is compiled into an aggregate whole so that a perceived image of the external entity of interest is understood. Battlefield commanders rely on a meta-view given the data set in order to assess the situation, rapidly making life or death decisions during realistic training exercises or combat.

Software Constructs

Our goal here is to demonstrate a basic approach to how a simulator is constructed. Hopefully my enthusiasm here will not translate to actual code but remain understandable as natural language, hillbilly and all. We will choose an object oriented programming language like C++ to demonstrate the data constructs and relationship between objects for our Earth simulation, complete with a portal at the Duat and a variable holding the key to ascend.

Object Oriented Programming

This programming language category is very useful for simulations, which can be seen as objects (entities of interest?) that have the potential to interact or statically represent a three-dimensional map. Some features we need to pull this off are necessary to make it real.

1. **Inheritance**: Objects inherit the class attributes from the parent. Suppose one of the attributes was a SUN-soul that gets inherited by the spawned child objects inheriting the feature...

2. **Polymorphism**: Multiple instances of a class object acting as independent agents in the simulator of life. Consider that some of the instantiated objects from the parent class have the variable luminescence which can be either LIGHT or DARK. Now we have the opportunity to have heroes and villains just like real life, assuming you still think we do not live in a holographic reality. Each object can take its own actions simultaneously, in parallel. This would be helpful if we defined a class called *Dimension* and summarily made nine instances of it for our simulation agent to explore. This could represent the nine dimensions we now know exist.

3. **Encapsulation**: Simulation objects can be given accessibility levels like *public* or *private* controlling which objects can communicate with each other.

Now let's examine a basic object class of PrimitiveWorker to see how the variables and functions give life to the slave.

Primitive Worker Class Sample

class PrimitiveWorker

```
{
  private:
    int age_limit = 120;
    int luminescence = 1;                 // 1=LIGHT, 2=DARK
    char* name;
  public:
    int luminescence (void)
    {
      return luminescence =1;
    }
    char* getName()
    {
      name = "Thoth the Atlantean";
      return (char*) name;
    }
};
```

The class object can be defined with as many functions and attributes as desired. The keywords from the C++ programming language are shown in bold, the rest of the code is either variable names or function names which provide the data structure needed for the simulation object desired. I promised this would not turn into a computer programming lesson, so will stop with merely the class object.

A fundamental part of our simulation model is the map. A three-dimensional terrain model with relief topology layers like trees and buildings create a playground for the simulation agents. Modern gamers are used to complex environments requiring beefed up graphics hardware to crunch all the polygons and get them drawn so the hero has something to look at during the journey. Now imagine that instead of limiting our terrain model to our Earth dimension (third) we allow the worlds within worlds parallel nine dimensions.

In general we can instantiate objects and provide them with tweakable plans that expose the mission agent under observation to external entities of interest that have the potential to alter the plan. Then the simulation can be reviewed to establish effectiveness for the life test function among many other simulation constructs one might find interesting.

Modeling Populations

Genetic Algorithms are a class of routines that are based on population dynamics. Suppose that you create a parent object that has certain genetic features you want the child populace to inherit. No problem with an object oriented computer programming language like C^{++} as shown. Now all we have to do to simulate the theory of natural selection is to establish what life test function the children (and the parent) are exposed to, specifying survivability like in nature. The idea is to use random genetic recombination to show up in the progeny then see if they survive. If so, then after some time specified, they, too can become parents passing on their genetic code and possibly a Futant mutation to see how the new feature survives the life test function. Using this simulation, one can change the life test function such that it rewards certain attributes that move the child closer to completing the assigned mission objective, perhaps to more than just survival. Extrapolate this simulation capability to a planetary and beyond to infinity scale and you are most likely witnessing the CREATOR OF ALL class object definitions and functions occurring right before your eyes! Welcome to the holographic simulator. Learn the rules, and graduate! *"To infinity and beyond"* we ascend, as aptly stated by Buzz Lightyear.

DNA is an interesting material seed, capable of specifying the instantiation of animate material objects for our simulation. Given what must be true, Light augments the human DNA to enliven it, potentially changing the code to activate features for the mission agent. In short, light can alter your DNA. I suggest that this is symbolized with the double helix rising serpents shown on Thoth's symbol the Caduceus. DNA features may be latent or acquired due to environmental stressors, much like a barnyard pig becomes feral in the wild - which Arkansans lovingly call The Razorbacks. This pig is the University of Arkansas mascot. No wonder the world thinks of us as hillbillies!

Light is now known to be the most unmanifested energy source that composes all matter as an illusion of *ka*. From the Emerald Tablets we find that by using a multi-tonal vibration, the CREATOR OF ALL established the LAW OF TIME so that simulation objects could be spaced out and sequenced. This gives us the perception of a moving clock hand, even though it is circular. Perhaps we need to add a new function to the class object PrimitiveWorker who performs the Mer-Ka-Ba meditation. This would activate its private variable *ba* to add a new ascension feature, timed with the Great Year. Ever wonder why it was called the Great Year? Perhaps one would understand the wheels of TIME more pragmatically if suddenly a large portal opened up on the horizon, aligned to Ophiuchus that has a sign stating: *Exit the hologram here, Duat Earth portal this way out.* At least the hero from the *Truman Show* had the courage to sail toward the potential mirage as his personal legacy demanded, overcoming the stormy seas to find the exit from his enslavement in the virtual world he inhabited.

Sensing the Simulation Environment

As discussed many times on radio programs, the eyes give away our enslaved condition as they are limited range sensors. This immediately inhibits the simulator participant with this designed receptor limitation. Primitive workers were designed with five senses. Our eyes are sensitive to the visible spectrum which ranges from 400 nanometers to 700 nanometers. What if an object like a predatory saber tooth tiger could be instantiated into the simulator with visibility parameter set such that it is viewable in the human eye range. No problem here, we see the threat, run back to the cave, and look for a flint tipped spear to respond to the fight or flight instinct programmed into the parent object received by inheritance.

Similarly, if the predatory cat were accidentally instantiated in the simulator with a visibility attribute that was only visible at 850 nanometers in the near-infrared region, then the cave-dwelling hero would not even be able to detect the threat unless finding a pair of infrared goggles located during a scavenger hunt in the forbidden zone. Hopefully my point has been made about the infinite simulation possibilities without salivating at the opportunity to code up the simulator now! The key point to make the simulator believable to the participants is the mystery of how to create an object from light that the other objects can interact with as if they are real. In the Hunger Games, the heroine Katniss has an encounter with several simulation objects that can kill. This makes the holographic reality real, or so it seems. How can a simulation object have form such that it can alter the form of another supposedly real person playing the survival game? This is the secret. Light is the answer. When one delves deeply into physics, it becomes clear that all matter is composed of energetic bonds using the periodic table of the elements as building blocks in the simulator. It is hard to fathom having knowledge about the properties of light that perform this function, creating matter from photons. I am not claiming to understand how this is done, but by analogy to the field of Cymatics and understanding of the Platonic

Solids, the idea of matter forming from vibration seems true. This is the same WORD spoken by GOD to instantiate the LAW OF TIME. This is the SECRET OF SECRETS, held closely guarded by those working for the game master, the GRAND ARCHITECT. The Anunnaki took on functional roles in the evolution of consciousness simulation set up by GOD in the CIRCLE OF LIGHT. Thoth is our simulation game agent that can appear at the forks in the road of our mission plan, facilitating those with the luminescence attribute defined in their private class as either LIGHT or DARK. It is our choice how that variable gets filled. Review the temporal overview you have of the Earth simulator thus far and decide which one you want to emulate, LIGHT or DARK and it will be updated dynamically for you. Fill your class object variables with those taught by Thoth in the Emerald Tablets and the magical interventions from the grand game will meet you on the illuminated path back to the LIGHT.

Luckily you were given more than just one sensor to experience the simulator. Use them all in your quest to identify what is interesting and how the lesson takes you home to your destiny as a SUN-soul lost in an intentionally destructive maze we call life. It is your job to encounter the DARKNESS and transmute it into LIGHT. Turn lemons into lemonade until the lemons turn to gold! Do so enough times and you may make it past level 3 potentially all the way to level 9 in the simulator.

CHAPTER 8: Atlantis and the New World Order

The only written account we have leading us to Enki's Atlantis comes to us from the Critias by Plato. From the book *The Ancient Atlantic* [43, Pgs. 25-32], we have the recounting of Solon's findings told by Plato in both the Timaus and the Critias stories.

Solon's Quest for LIGHT

Like a good leader, as opposed to those that fill the seats in our current governments in the global simulator state, Solon searched the world over looking at various governing models that could improve the life for the citizens in Athens and all of Greece. Myths about the heroes of old who occupied his lands catalyzed him to see if there was a better way to rule. His assigned heroic journey involved high level kingly-type actions, similar to those performed by the son of the King of Thessaly. We know him as Jason, our archetypal Hero leading his fellow Argonauts to the symbolic communal destiny they pursued to recover the Golden Fleece, a relic of the Great Gods that had the power to heal.

Almost made it Solon, Persistence Counts

From the Timaeus, also by Plato, Critias holds dialogs with

Plato about Solon's legacy. In Critias' judgment, Solon was not only the wisest of men but the noblest of poets. He continues Solon's character analysis by stating *"...if Solon had only like other poets made poetry the business of his life, and had completed the tale which he brought with him from Egypt, and had not been compelled by reason of the factions and troubles he found stirring in his country when he came home to attend to other matters, he would have been as famous as Homer or Hesiod or any other poet"* *[43, Pg. 25].*

Are you distracted by other matters and troubles that are causing you to bind your LIGHT? We all have different legacies to live which involve facing fears, overcoming, striving for wisdom, and doing it in the spirit of love. Each path is unique and must be approached by living according to character building principles espoused by many of the world's great spiritual traditions.

Kingly Actors on the Atlantean Stage

Some really key names show up as Enki's five pairs of sons, ten males total, who became the kings and princes ruling Atlantis. The eldest boy, Atlas, was the son of Poseidon and Cleito, and from him the whole island and the ocean received his name. Atlas' twin brother Gadeirus was given as his lot the extremity of the island toward the Pillars of Hercules, which he called Gades or in the Hellenic language, Eumelus. Atlas had a large and honorable family, but his eldest branch always retained the kingdom, which the eldest son handed to his eldest for many generations.

The palaces in the interior of the citadel were constructed in the following manner: The center was a holy temple dedicated to Cleito and Poseidon, which remained inaccessible, and was surrounded by an enclosure of gold. Poseidon's own temple, of a stadium (600 feet) in length and a half a stadium (300 feet) in width and of proportionate height. It had a barbarian splendor for all of the outside of the temple and covered in silver except for the pinnacles which were of gold" [43, Pg. 30]. The temple interior roof was of ivory, adorned everywhere with gold, silver and orichalcum. Walls, pillars, and floors were also lined with orichalcum. A golden statue of Poseidon standing in his chariot pulled by six winged horses was of such size they touched the roof of the temple.

In regard to the relations of the ten kings to one another, they were regulated by the injunctions of Poseidon as they had been handed down in a covenant of laws. These laws were inscribed by the first men on a column of orichalcum, which was situated in the center of the island, at the temple of Poseidon. Every fifth and sixth years alternatively, where the people gathered to consult on public affairs. This process may be the alluring element to Solon, leading him to find out more about the heroes of old.

1. Laws written on the public pillars outside Poseidon's temple
2. People gathered at the temple every 5th or 6th year alternating turns for odd-even jury duty.
3. The people gathered and consulted as a community, soliciting any transgressions against the communally adopted laws which were posted in plain sight in a public place. No secrecy allowed
4. If anyone had transgressed the law, the process to bring judgment began.
5. Before they passed judgment they hunted a bull, sacrificed it and poured the blood over the sacred inscriptions on Poseidon's Pillars, and burned the remains in fire.
6. Next the ten leaders purified the temple and then conducted a ritual vowing to uphold the laws on the column, and punish anyone who had previously transgressed, reviewing the matter eliciting vows not to repeat the failing. They would not command or obey any ruler who had commanded them to act otherwise than according to the laws of their father Poseidon.
7. They then dined until dark, when they dressed up in their finest robes and sat on the ground at night around a fire, sacrificial embers of the bull still smoldering to remind

them of their oaths. This is a solemn reflection as a community

8. After discussing the issue around the camp fire, if any judgments were to be brought, they were written down the next morning on golden tablets and submitted to the temple guardians along with their robes.

Societal Collapse, What Went Wrong?

From the Critias report by Plato, we discover that the SUN-soul of the original Atlanteans was corrupted by a long period of inbreeding. They lost their connection to the *ba*, falling back into the illusion of *ka* and materialism. At this point Plato's account ends as Zeus is brought into the scene to begin destroying that which went awry on Enki's watch. Here is the actual account as told by Plato.

"By such reflections, and by the continuance in them of the divine nature, all that which we have described waxed and increased in them, but when the divine portion began to fade away, and became diluted too often, with too much of the moral admixture, and human nature got the upper hand, then they, being unable to bear their fortune, became unseemly. To him who had an eye to see, they began to appear base, and had lost the fairest of their precious gifts, but to those who had no eyes to see the true happiness, they still appeared glorious and blessed at

the very time when they were filled with unrighteous avarice and power. Zeus, the god of the gods, who rules with law, and is able to see into such things perceiving that an honorable race was in a most wretched state, and wanting to inflict punishment on them that they might be chastened and improved, collected all the gods into his most holy habitation, which being placed in the center of the world, sees all things that partake of generations. When he had called them together, he then spake as follows…"

Here the manuscript of Plato ends. This strange legend ends leaving us hanging as to the outcome, which is the reason the account has haunted men for over two thousand years.

From the Emerald Tablets we discover a clue about what happened as Thoth reports that the Atlantean Dweller in the Temple (Enki IMHO) discovers the fact that the Dark Lords have perturbed the Earth simulator, attempting to cause a large flood (It was Enlil the agent provocateur as he asked Enki to bring a flood according to the Atrahasis account, wherein he refused, but it happened anyway) by destabilizing the rotational axis wobble. The DWELLER intercedes and brings their own destructive ploy to a halt and directs the destruction toward the Dark Lords instead. The DWELLER survives the catastrophe on the Island of Undal as told in the Tablets.

Dark Lords Simulated in America

As I pointed out in my first book, it appears that some subset of the Dark Lords has taken over America and the European Union. These New World Order forces are motivated by greed and power. Recall that the Roman Caesar's downfall vices were overweening pride and ambition. As we noted in Chapter 6 <u>Alchemy Past and Present</u>, the primary precondition to participate in the higher order reality involved with ascension is to subjugate the ego and purify the consciousness thus creating a clear vessel for the CREATOR OF ALL to fill with **ba** energy designed to lead the hero back home to the LIGHT.

From my genealogy table and disclosures from the likes of Paul Hellyer, former Canadian Defense Minister, along with the changes that came to America following WWII involving space and weapons programs (see Table 8), Zeus and Ninurta are definitely playing the destructive entity of interest role attempting to avert the path of the Light beings. They seem to be sleeping on the couch covered in processed food wrappers, beer cans, and the HDTV remote and sporting schedule slipped beneath the cushions. If you are not seeking to live an extraordinary life as Jason decides to do, enrolling Argonauts to help, passionate about achieving your dream, then as I stated earlier, you have missed an omen or sign at a previous fork in the road. You now know that to get back on track finding your personal legend and your way back to the LIGHT, you have to get out of the bleachers and get back on the field of life facing your fears of failure, judgment, and all the rest. Each time I stood at the edge of a Hang Glider launch point in the mountains of San Diego, the butterflies in my stomach alerted me that I was violating a primitive instinct that even human babies are born with, jumping off the edge of a cliff. Once you get past your fear of death or failure, the adrenaline can be channeled toward your new reality, soaring over the simulated terrain, free like a bird. Only in retrospect, after taking your leap of faith, will you see how silly it was to imprison yourself with fearful limitations. Your energy container (body) is only a construct in the simulator to allow you to explore the maze and learn the rules of the game to move on to the next level. Perhaps it is the guarded Duat gate with key memorized (Rote step in Gerald Clark's Learning Model) so that it can be recalled under duress or during an OOBE, leading to our destined home on Arulu, in the presence of the Great Gods, men of renown and the heroes of old.

Masonic Order Changed Gods

The influence of the Masons, demonstrated in the proliferation of United States Presidents who were members of the organization throughout the nation's history cannot be ignored. As specified in Lawrence Gardener's exceptional book *Genesis of the Grail Kings* [45, Pgs. 192-199], the offspring of Noah played a vital role in the historical origins of the Masonic Order. Recall that the connection between Atlantis and the New World order was previously clarified by Tubal-Cain's accursed Ham obscuration lie given in the Bible such that the alchemical connection between Thoth-Azazel, AKA Chem-Zaranthustra, AKA The Black Goat of Mendes, the Sabbatical (Saturn's Day Saturday), AKA Thoth the Atlantean, was removed from the Masonic Order and replaced with the Judeo Christian God, Lucifer-Enlil himself in England circa 1885. Couple this fact along with the newly added double eagle symbol attributable to the Sumerian deity Ninurta also known as Apollo to both the Greek and the Roman peoples. Could this be the reason that Albert Pike's veneration for Lucifer and the prophecy for the third culling war in his letter to Mazzini sponsored by the Illuminati? We now know the Illuminati infiltrated the Masonic Order circa 1776 in Bavaria under the leadership of Adam Weishaupt. Thus, the Masons are serving Lucifer now too. Wonder if those below 33rd degree are aware of that fact? This leads to the next chapter where we will discuss the infiltration impact of the Dark Lords in America's imminent collapse.

CHAPTER 9: America's Collapse

Alien Agenda and the Military Industrial Complex

Table 5 below lists the Greek Olympian God names correlated with their function and symbols. The reason this table is provided is to then link them to the space and weapons programs that followed the German scientists after WWII to America via the Paperclip Project [44].

The United States was interested in the technical capability of the Germans. A team of American scientists was dispatched to Europe on August 14, 1945, to collect information and equipment related to German rocket progress. As a result, the components for approximately 100 V-2 ballistic missiles were recovered and shipped from Germany to White Sands Proving Grounds in New Mexico. Also recovered was an invaluable cache of documentation. During October 1945, the Secretary of War approved a plan to bring the top German scientists to the United States to aid military research and development. Near the end of the year, more than 100 Germans, who had agreed to come to the United States under Project Paperclip, arrived at Fort Bliss, Texas. Their assignment was to begin work at nearby White Sands on the V-2 rockets that had

already arrived from Germany. The Olympian gods are shown
below in Tables 5-7. They seem to have been instrumental in this
move. One should recognize some of these names there as well.
This is a telling piece of evidence.

Greek Name	Consort	Father	Mother	Roman Name	Sumer Name	Role	Remarks	Symbol
Aphrodite				Venus	Inanna	Goddess of Love, Beauty, Desire and Pleasure	Often depicted partially nude. Sacred animal doves and sparrows.	Roses and flowers, scallop shell, and myrtle wreath
Apollo		Zeus	Leto		Ninurta	God of music, arts, knowledge, healing, plague, prophecy, poetry, manly beauty and archery	Embody physical perfection. Twin sister Artemis (moon symbol). Cruel and destructive. Half-brother to Hermes?	Sun, Laurel Wreath, and Lyre Sacred animals Roe Deer, Swans, Cicadas, Hawks, Ravens, Crows, Foxes, Mice, and Snakes
Ares		Zeus	Hera	Mors		God of war, bloodshed, and violence.	Depicted nude with helmet and spear.	Sacred animals are the vulture, venomous snakes, dogs, and boars
Artemis		Zeus	Leto	Diana		Virgin goddess of the hunt, wilderness, animals, young girls, childbirth, and plague	Depicted as a young woman dressed in a short knee-length chiton with bow and arrows. Attributes are hunting spears, animal pelts, deer and other wild animals.	Scared animals are deer, bears, and wild boars.
Demeter		Cronus	Rhea	Ceres		Goddess of grain, agriculture, and the harvest, growth and nourishment.	Sister of Zeus, mother of Persephone. Depicted as a mature woman, often crowned and holding	Symbols are cornucopia, wheat-ears, winged serpent, and the lotus staff. Sacred

Table 5: Olympian God Table 1

							sheafs of wheat and a torch.	animals are pigs and snakes.
Dionysus	Ariadne			Bacchus		God of wine, parties, and festivals, madness, chaos, drunkenness, drugs, and ecstasy.	Hails from Chios. Depicted as an older bearded god or effeminate youth. Attributes include the thyrsus (pinecone-tipped staff), drinking cup, grape vine, and a crown of ivy.	Sacred animals include dolphins, serpents, tigers, and donkeys.
Hades	Persephone	Cronus	Rhea	Pluto	Dumuzzi?	King of the underworld and dead, and god of regret.	Attributes and the drinking horn or cornucopia, key, scepter, and the three-headed dog Cerberus. Ambiguous place among Olympians as he was a chthonic god with Hades being the place called "the Rich Father"	Sacred animals are the screech own.
Hephaestus	Aphrodite	Zeus	Hera	Vulcan		Crippled god of fire, metalworking, and crafts.	Depicted as a bearded man with hammer, tongs and anvil.	Sacred animals are the donkey, the guard dog, and the crane.
Hera	Zeus	Cronus	Rhea	Juno		Depicted as a regal woman wearing a diadem and veil holding a lotus-tipped staff. Goddess of marriage.	Jealous and revengeful for Zeus's infidelity.	Sacred animals are heifer, the peacock, and the cuckoo.
Hermes	?	Zeus	Maia	Mercury	Ningishzida	Hermes is the messenger of the gods of boundaries, travel, communication,	Depicted as handsome and athletic beardless youth or an older bearded man. Attributes include	Scared animals are the tortoise, the ram, and the hawk.

Table 6: Olympian God Table 2

						trade, language, and writing.	the herald's wand or caduceus, winged sandals and a traveler's cap.	
Hestia		Cronus	Rhea	Vesta		Sister of Zeus, Virgin goddess of the hearth, home and chastity.	Appeared as a modestly veiled woman.	Symbols are the hearth and kettle.
Poseidon	Amphitrite	Cronus (Anu)	Rhea (Antu)	Neptune	Enki	Brother to Zeus and Hades. Rules as king of the seas and waters.	Depicted as a mature man of sturdy build with an often luxuriant beard and holding a trident.	Horse and dolphin are sacred to him as well as the fish and bull.
Zeus		Cronus (Anu)	Rhea (error)	Jupiter (Jove)	Enlil	King of the gods and ruler of Mount Olympus and god of the sky, weather, thunder, lightning, law, order, and justice.	Depicted as a regal mature man with a sturdy figure and dark beard.	Depicted with royal scepter and the lightning bolt. Sacred animals are the eagle and the bull.

Table 7: Olympian God Table 3

Table 8 below depicts the list of weapons programs and their affiliated Greek God names. Why was this obvious honoring of Greek Gods done? Are forces acting within NASA and the Pentagon aware of the Anunnaki presence here on Earth, thereby naming space and weapons programs after them?

Based on the disclosures from so many sources, it seems plausible that the alien forces operating here on Earth have been influencing our technical development progress both in the past and again here on planet Earth. We are currently witnessing the exponentially advancing Space Age take us to the stars.

USA Weapons/Space Program Table

Weapon Name	Functional Use	Greek God Name	Sumerian Name	Date Developed	Symbol
SM-65 Atlas	ICBM + NASA use	Atlas	Anu?	1953	
LIM-49 Nike Zeus	Anti-ballistic missile (ABM)	Zeus	Enlil	1950-1960	Lightening bolt
Zeus A	Upper atmosphere ABM	Zeus	Enlil	1950-1960	
Zeus B	Extended range ABM Satellites	Zeus	Enlil	1950-1960	
Nike X	Layered ABM	Nike			
Zeus EX	Layered ABM	Zeus	Enlil		
Spartan	ABM				
Nike Hercules	ABM				
Nike Zeus	ABM				
Nike X	ABM				
Titan SM-68	ICBM				
Ares	ICBM	Mars	?		
Spartan	ABM				
P-8 Poseidon	Anti-Submarine Warfare (ASW)	Poseidon	Enki	2011	Trident
Project Mercury	First Human Space Flight	Hermes	Ningishzida	1959-1963	Caduceus-Winged Messenger
Project Gemini	Second Human Space Flight	Zodiac Gemini (twins = Castor + Pollux)	?? ??	1962-1966	Horse(manship) Naval Patron St Elmo's Fire

Table 8: Space and Weapons Programs Post WWII

NWO Destroys America

- Infiltration of all Society by NWO Forces.
- Idol Worship Leads Gullible to Destruction.
- Sporting Activities Distract the Angry Mob.
- Eating Habits Create Sheeple Ripe for Slaughter.
- Foreign Debit Relief, and Reservations Sold.

Ah, welcome to the American Dream (nightmare). This is your host Gerald Clark. Let's take y'all on a peaceful and relaxing tour of rural living with our guest today, Rancher extraordinaire, Mister Cliven Bundy. The American hero and Patriot, acting as the grassroots focal point for the impromptu cavalry, formed while the local sheriff is absent without leave (AWOL to us Army grunts), is forced to an armed showdown *"agin them thar BLM varmits muddying up the crik with theys New World Order advanced cattle russling plans to run em offin their rightful land."*

Clive Bundy has some tales to tell. Senator Harry Reid facilitated the sale of 600,000 acres to the Chinese, probably as a way to give away federal land stolen from Nevada (NOTE: Laws prohibit federal ownership of any state land to no more than 30%) to mitigate the foreign US debt sold as bonds to unsuspecting China. He is now under assault by sovereignty stealing thugs and cattle thieves. Where is the sheriff when you need one?"

Nothing is black and white, and considering that this scenario has been playing out for almost two decades, there is a whole lot of gray to wade through in arriving at an accurate picture of what is going on with the Bureau of Land Management (BLM) and Bundy.

For one thing, there seems to be a strong undercurrent of resentment among many landowners in the area against the federal government's management of public lands. The federal government is by far the largest landowner in the U.S., and state and federal land ownership exceeds 30% in at least 16 states. In Alaska, it is 90%, 80% of Nevada, 70% of Utah, and 65% of Idaho. Despite Bundy's arguments having been rejected by two appeals courts, the BLM-Bundy case has morphed into a much wider debate over freedom, personal property, state rights, taxation and government overreach.

Recently, even the oppressed Native American population in America is feeling the incursive fangs of the malevolent Luciferian forces. It was not enough to agitate the American Spirit by ordering Bureau of Land Management (BLM) armed forces to rustle cattle from an honorable Nevada rancher like Cliven Bundy.

Figure 27 below depicts how the BLM, among other three-letter government agencies, have worked to facilitate the theft of State's property, especially in the sunny southwest where solar farms built by the Chinese perpetuate the energy independence quest and simultaneous fossil fuel wars [40]

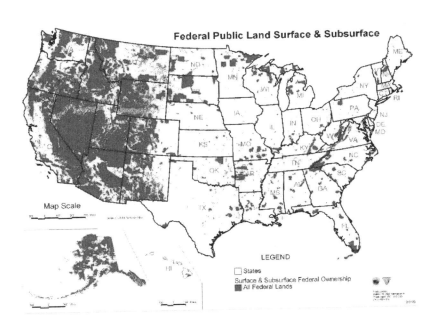

Figure 27: Federalized State Land

We find out that Harry Reid and son are involved with the Chinese that are looking to leverage the US foreign debt for Federal land stolen from the rightful citizens of the state. The motive for the sale of a very large swath of land near the Bundy Ranch to the Chinese, brokered by Reid, is simple. The US owes China big bucks and is swapping stolen land to discharge the debt. The land is attractive for a large solar farm which is the intended target in the Southwestern Sunbelt state of Nevada. Large land sales for similar purposes, also involving the Chinese land barons, is occurring all across the nation.

Albert Pike's Predictions in 1870

An Italian revolutionary leader, Giusseppe Mazzini (1805-1872), and a 33rd degree Mason, was selected by the Illuminati to head their worldwide operations in 1834. (Mazzini also founded the Mafia in 1860). Because of Mazzini's revolutionary activities in Europe, the Bavarian government cracked down on the Illuminati and other secret societies for allegedly plotting a massive overthrow of Europe's monarchies. As the secrets of the Illuminati were revealed, they were prosecuted and eventually disbanded, only to re-establish themselves in the depths of other organizations, of which Freemasonry was one.

Albert Pike received a vision, which he described in a letter [18] that he wrote to Mazzini, dated August 15, 1871. This letter graphically outlined plans for three world wars that were seen as necessary to bring about the One World Order. Consider the accuracy of Pike's predicted events that have already taken place.

Pike's Letter to Mazzini

It is a commonly believed fallacy that for a short time, the Pike letter to Mazzini was on display in the British Museum Library in London, and it was copied by William Guy Carr, former Intelligence Officer in the Royal Canadian Navy. The British Library has confirmed in writing to me that such a document has never been in their possession. Furthermore, in Carr's book, *Satan, Prince of this World*, he includes the following footnote:

"The Keeper of Manuscripts recently informed the author that this letter is NOT catalogued in the British Museum Library. It seems strange that a man of Cardinal Rodriguez's knowledge should have said that it WAS in 1925".

It appears that Carr learned about this letter from Cardinal Caro y Rodriguez of Santiago, Chile, who wrote *The Mystery of Freemasonry Unveiled*.

To date, no conclusive proof exists to show that this letter was ever written. Nevertheless, the letter is widely quoted and the topic of much discussion.

Below are apparently extracts of the letter, showing how three world wars have been planned for many generations.

"The First World War must be brought about in order to permit the Illuminati to overthrow the power of the Czars in Russia and of making that country a fortress of atheistic Communism. The divergences caused by the "agentur" (agents) of the Illuminati between the British and Germanic Empires will be used to foment this war. At the end of the war, Communism will be built

and used in order to destroy the other governments and in order to weaken the religions."

Students of history will recognize that the political alliances of England on one side and Germany on the other, forged between 1871 and 1898 by Otto von Bismarck, co-conspirator of Albert Pike, were instrumental in bringing about the First World War.

"The Second World War must be fomented by taking advantage of the differences between the Fascists and the political Zionists. This war must be brought about so that Nazism is destroyed and that the political Zionism be strong enough to institute a sovereign state of Israel in Palestine. During the Second World War, International Communism must become strong enough in order to balance Christendom, which would be then restrained and held in check until the time when we would need it for the final social cataclysm."

After this Second World War, Communism was made strong enough to begin taking over weaker governments. In 1945, at the Potsdam Conference between Truman, Churchill, and Stalin, a large portion of Europe was simply handed over to Russia, and on the other side of the world, the aftermath of the war with Japan helped to sweep the tide of Communism into China.

*(Readers who argue that the terms Nazism and Zionism were not
known in 1871 should remember that the Illuminati invented
both these movements. In addition, Communism as an ideology,
and as a coined phrase, originates in France during the
Revolution. In 1785, Restif coined the phrase four years before
revolution broke out. Restif and Babeuf, in turn, were
influenced by Rousseau - as was the most famous conspirator of
them all, Adam Weishaupt.)*

*"The Third World War must be fomented by taking advantage of
the differences caused by the "agentur" of the "Illuminati"
between the political Zionists and the leaders of Islamic World.
The war must be conducted in such a way that Islam (the
Moslem Arabic World) and political Zionism (the State of Israel)
mutually destroy each other. Meanwhile the other nations, once
more divided on this issue will be constrained to fight to the point
of complete physical, moral, spiritual and economical
exhaustion...We shall unleash the Nihilists and the atheists, and
we shall provoke a formidable social cataclysm which in all its
horror will show clearly to the nations the effect of absolute
atheism, origin of savagery and of the most bloody turmoil. Then
everywhere, the citizens, obliged to defend themselves against the
world minority of revolutionaries, will exterminate those
destroyers of civilization, and the multitude, disillusioned with
Christianity, whose deistic spirits will from that moment be
without compass or direction, anxious for an ideal, but without*

knowing where to render its adoration, will receive the true light through the universal manifestation of the pure doctrine of Lucifer, brought finally out in the public view. This manifestation will result from the general reactionary movement which will follow the destruction of Christianity and atheism, both conquered and exterminated at the same time."

Since the so-called terrorist attacks of Sept 11, 2001, world events, and in particular in the Middle East, show a growing unrest and instability between Modern Zionism and the Arabic World. This is completely in line with the call for a Third World War to be fought between the two, and their allies on both sides. This Third World War is still to come, and recent events show us that it is not far off.

Simply review the wars and rumors of wars around the globe and you will see the Dark Lords are on a rampage, culling the population, bringing the nations low, and holding the primitive workers captive. The only place the name Lucifer shows up, probably an editorial oversight, is in Isaiah 14:12 describing what Lucifer has and will do to the populace. It is happening now, the game master is pushing the DARK onto the LIGHT, many of whom are asleep not knowing the rules of the simulator, therefore providing easy victims for the enslaver of SUN-light souls that never had the chance to activate their Mer-Ka-Ba energy field, wake up, and exit the material hologram.

CHAPTER 10: Challenges to the New World Order

Given that we now live in a world that operates using the Golden Rule and Might Makes Right, the Golden Rule continues facetiously as he who has the gold, makes the rules and he who has the most might (think weapons) also makes the rules. Seems like Albert Pike, writing on behalf of the Masonic Order, conducted a Black Mass in 1963 releasing a DARK destructive energy. It has been my premise that it was an ancient astronaut, most likely Apollo-Ninurta and or his father Zeus-Enlil, who was summoned and vectored into the Catholic Church. Thus, according to Pope John Paul II, the smoke of Satan has been in the Vatican since 1963, coinciding with the Black Mass Pike led.

Who are the Players and What is the End Game?

The major players are the Anunnaki remnants here on Earth. They include Enki, Enlil, Ninharsag, Ningishzida, Inanna, Nannar-Sin, and many of their offspring scattered around the world. Government and civilian infrastructure is occupied by these infiltrators, controlling all aspects of the information age like hidden hand gamers as depicted in the movie "*The Hunger Games.*"

The goals for the New World Order organizations were engraved in the Georgia Guide Stones, which saw some recent updates just this year with the addition of a cube with two faces showing 2014, this year. What devious genocidal acts are they supporting based on their first commandment? Here are the goals from the Guide Stones specifying their mission objectives for all to see.

Georgia Guide Stones Ten Commandments

On one of the highest hilltops in Elbert County, Georgia stands a massive granite monument. Engraved in eight different languages as well as a number of ancient languages, on the four giant stones that support the common capstone, 10 Guides, or commandments are inscribed therein. This strange but curious stone cypher is often referred to as The Georgia Guide Stones, or the American Stonehenge. Though relatively unknown to most people, it is an important link to the Occult Hierarchy that dominates the world in which we live.

The origins of this occult monument are shrouded in mystery given the fact that no one knows the true identity of who commissioned the project. All that is known for certain is that in June 1979, a well-dressed, articulate stranger visited the office of the Elberton Granite Finishing Company and announced his intent to construct a permanent edifice to transmit a message to

461

mankind. He identified himself as R. C. Christian, but analysis indicates that a false identity was used. Mr. Christian stated that he represented a group of men who wanted to offer direction to humanity, but to date, almost two decades later, no one knows who R. C. Christian really was, or the nature of the group he represented. Given the nature and scope of the monument and its occult meaning, one can categorize the Guide Stones commandments covering four major areas:

(1) Governance and the establishment of a world government

(2) Population and reproduction control

(3) The environment and man's relationship to nature

(4) Spirituality

The Elbert County Public Library, located in Elberton Georgia, lists a book written by the man who called himself R.C. Christian. It was found that the monument he commissioned had been erected in recognition of Thomas Paine who was known to participate in occult philosophy. The Guide Stones are clearly still in use today given that occult ceremonies and mystic celebrations are ongoing. [21]. What follows are the commandments themselves for the readers ease of access and analysis.

Ten Commandments of the NWO

1. Maintain humanity under 500,000,000 in perpetual balance with nature.

2. Guide reproduction wisely - improving fitness and diversity.

3. Unite humanity with a living new language.

4. Rule passion - faith - tradition - and all things with tempered reason.

5. Protect people and nations with fair laws and just courts.

6. Let all nations rule internally resolving external disputes in a world court.

7. Avoid petty laws and useless officials.

8. Balance personal rights with social duties.

9. Prize truth - beauty - love - seeking harmony with the infinite.

10. Be not a cancer on the earth - Leave room for nature - Leave room for nature.

Commandment number one (1) limits the population of the earth to 500 million folks. That implies exterminating about 93%

of the world's primitive workers, based on the current census data reporting circa seven billion people on the planet. The American Stonehenge's reference to establishing a world court, commandment number six (6), substantiates the current flurry of activities on the world stage flexing their global muscle using a newly formed International Criminal Court and a world government (The New World Order). The Guide Stones' emphasis on preserving nature in commandment number ten (10) anticipates the environmental movement of the 1990s and the reference to "seeking harmony with the infinite", commandment number nine (9), reflects Illuminati current efforts to replace Judeo-Christian beliefs with a new spirituality, just as Albert Pike wrote in 1871. One of the goals Albert Pike stated in his letter to Mazzini, describing the outcome desired following a third world war, involved the elimination of Judeo-Christian and Muslim religions. This would happen as an intentional war initiated between Israel and the Muslim world. This is happening here and now as of December 14th, 2014. Just take a look at the headlines to see the latest carnage in the Middle East countries like Syria, Iraq, Pakistan, Afghanistan, Libya, and soon Iran?

The message of the American Stonehenge erected in Georgia also foreshadowed the current drive for Sustainable Development. Any time one sees the phrase "Sustainable Development", it should be substituted by the term *"socialism"*.

The Earth Charter, compiled under the direction of Mikhail Gorbachev and Maurice Strong emphasize population control, world governance, the importance of nature and the environment, and a new spirituality. The similarity between the ideas engraved on the Georgia Guide Stones and those espoused in the Earth Charter with Russian input corroborates a common origin for the Commandments.

Anunnaki Players in America and Russia

Below in Figure 28 we find a painting of Enki and Ningishzida influencing early forms of American life and government. Hermes is handing Robert Morris a bag of funding to help back the revolutionary war. His father Poseidon is shown in a boat promoting the installation of the Trans-Atlantic cable system connecting Europe and America.

Figure 28: Enki and Ningishzida's America

It should be clear that the young lion (United States) in the new land across the Atlantic, newly released from British tyranny and over-taxation, had Anunnaki influence from benevolent ancient astronauts propelling them to start anew, according to Sir Francis Bacon, the location destined for the New Atlantis. Also shown on the US Capital dome is the five-pointed star positioned in its female orientation. This crown of stars ring around the rim of the bowl of the dome, located just below the ceiling frescos, symbolizes Ninharsag-Isis's presence, enveloping the apex with her sacred feminine chalice of stars which is symbolic of her Queenly title as Divine Mother of mankind's first instantiated simulation slave agent, the Adapa. Knowing that many of the founding fathers were involved with the Masonic Order, including the country's first

466

president, George Washington, provides clear evidence of their motives.

Their Enkiite plans for President Washington, depicted undergoing Apotheosis in the fresco, had chosen the American experiment as a prelude to the rising of a New Atlantis. The same three beings who were intricately involved in the Atrahasis creation account for mankind, show up significantly in the US Capital buildings, paintings, and symbolism. A tour of the Temple itself convinced me in 2009 that the connection to the Anunnaki I sought in my research had been verified.

A bust of the first president Washington is located at the Scottish Rite Temple in Washington DC. It is strategically situated at the Temple cornerstone, where Masonic rituals in full regalia venerate the cornerstone that faces eastward toward the rising sun. Based on the symbolism found in Washington DC, it was clear to me following a research trip to the nation's headquarters that the place had been designated to eventually become the New Atlantis. Isis was also venerated using monument locations that are aligned with the planet Venus. Tours were available to show the tourists around the capital city, termed Egypt on the Potomac, pointing the obvious inconsistencies in stating that the United States was founded on Christian principles. The evidence was simply not captured in the monuments arrayed about the city.

Egyptian and Greek architecture and statues abound, although I do not recall seeing monuments of Pilgrims giving thanks to a double headed eagle or an all seeing eye. Some things we have been taught in school seemed strangely awry.

Now that we have made the case for the Anunnaki players being involved with war funding and communications infrastructure, is there a similar ancient astronaut involvement with America's arch rival Russia? It seems quite obvious that the ancient astronaut working with the Germans during WW2, also followed the scientific crew from Europe to America where many were a part of the Paperclip project [44]. This technology transfer happened as part of the ceasefire agreement, wherein the best of the best technologists left Germany post WW2, taking their acumen to Enlil's other domain, which for those wondering, is America. Recall that the original Atlantis collapsed due to the internal issue that befell them. Intermixing of genetics lead to a loss of their connection to the spririt force *ba*, instead settling for the material illusion of *ka*. The New Atlantis shares the same old problems that reared their ugly head in the Old Atlantis, right before Zeus invited himself to the destruction phase of the simulator objects. This was made clear also in the dialog between Timaeus and Plato as well, described previously in this book. Loss of the *ba* SUN-soul and settling for the illusion of material *ka*. This is why America is being destroyed. It is a lesson for the rest of the world that if they too grow prideful and base, destruction lingers on a high precipice waiting to strike.

Soviets Vilified by the Game Masters

Like all wars, one must first have a common enemy to focus upon. This dualistic thinking of us versus them is a fatal lesson that mankind has still yet to comprehend. We hear social movement and peace activists decry war and ask if we just cannot all get along. Thoth asks us in the Emerald Tablets Number XII (12), **"When will you cease striving against your brother?"** Until a unified understanding of mankind's common origins are known to all, the territorial imperative tenets of Identity, Security, and Stimulation will continue to play a primary role in man's inhumanity to man. One would think seeing the total carnage wrought by barbarian beheadings and eating each other's organs would be impetus enough to halt the striving, but not as of yet.

As long as I can remember, having joined the primitive worker race here on Earth since 1963, the United States has had a bipolar relationship with the Russian bear. Various alliances and demonizations have occurred throughout the two superpower's history. After reading Albert Pike's letter written in 1870 [18] specifying in detail how Russia would be leveraged as a key player on the world stage, it becomes clear that there is a hidden blueprint. Religious and political models imposed on Russia were used as experimental teaching tools according to Pike. This chess game clearly began as early as the letter to Mazzini before the year 1900. During my seven years of military service from 1982 to 1989, the opposing force tactics and equipment that had our utmost attention had originated with Russia.

US-Soviet Relations during Wars

The Triple Entente was an alliance that linked the Russian Empire, the French Third Republic, and the United Kingdom of Great Britain and Ireland after the signing of the Anglo-Russian Entente on 31 August 1907. The alliance of the three powers, supplemented by agreements with Portugal and Japan, constituted a powerful counterweight to the Triple Alliance of Germany, Austria-Hungary and the Kingdom of Italy.

The United States declared war on Germany in 1917 on the grounds that Germany violated U.S. neutrality by attacking international shipping among other claims. Thus, the Russian Empire and the Americans were on the same team during that time period.

During WWII, the relationship was more cordial as an alliance was formed as Russia and America cooperated to defeat Hitler. Russia stood its ground during the winter battle with German troops ill-equipped to survive the intense cold. Thus, working against the common enemy, the US and Russia were on the same winning team.

Following WWII, the US and Russia's quirky relationship continued to develop, leading to cooperation in science, space exploration, and advanced research. This astounding cooperative behavior led to joint Space Station missions. This was shocking given the Cold War rhetoric and stockpiling of thousands of nuclear warheads pointed at each other. The cold war officially ended in 1991 when President Reagan prompted tearing down the Berlin wall, symbolically ending the strife. Arms reductions treaties were signed by both countries in an attempt to reduce the threat of nuclear war. The concept of mutually assured destruction as a result of using nuclear weapons seemed to take the big guns out of commission, or so it seemed.

So, in both WWI and WWII, the United States and Russia were on the same side of the conflict with Germany being the focal point for the genesis of both wars. Given the headlines recently, it seems that America and Russia are exchanging roles on the world stage.

Lessons Learned and the New Putin

Recent activities by NATO Allied Forces pushing their influence closer to the Russian bear have led to all-out war in Ukraine. This feels like the Bible prophecy given in the book of The Revelation in which it seems like a false flag event was planned to initiate the Gog-Magog final battle for Armageddon. The words put a hook in the jaw of the enemy really sound different to me at this time. Consider going fishing, putting bait on the hook for an unsuspecting creature in its natural habitat, feeding like it usually does, and suddenly it has a hook in its jaw, a fish hook with an inescapable barbed flange at the end to keep it in place.

Using that fishing analogy, it seems to mirror what we are witnessing in Ukraine, except is should be worded "Putin takes bait, we got him hooked now, WWIII time." Based on the predictions or plans established by Albert Pike in his 1871 letter exposed in this book, the game masters working for the Dark Lords are at the helm to bring about yet another war, if they can. The real question is to what extent is Putin aware of the Anunnaki, as creators, many of which are the destructive ones, and some of which are here to help mankind awaken their *ba* SUN-soul as a species?

Some changes one would not expect to be happening in Russia, given the fact they have been demonized even though working as an ally in both world wars with America are:

- Gun laws allow personal carry
- No GMOs admitted
- Unwarranted Deviant Pandering to Kids in School, Niet.
- RT News rapidly overtook US News on the world stage

The American model (life, liberty, pursuit of happiness) is

moving to Fascism in front of our very eyes and the Russian peoples are experiencing the original freedom model we used to enjoy. A complete role reversal. Was this part of the original Luciferian plan that Pike laid out in 1871. It sure seems to be the case as it is rolling out, leading to WWIII, as we watch a puppet government set up in Ukraine. This led to unrest and will eventually create civil war as Russia moves into the area on its borders, attempting to put out the fires spawned by America under the sign of the Eagle. The trident symbol on the Ukrainian flag, that of Poseidon-Enki, is being smeared by Enlil, based now in America. Interestingly, The New World Order backed by the Illuminati operating out of Europe and the United States is encountering major resistance asserted by global alliances which continue to grow.

Brazil, Russia, India, China, and South Africa joined together recently in a new monetary alliance called BRICS, to oppose the hegemony of the giant Ponzi scheme: the petrodollar. The powerful alliance is making financial moves to thwart mandates to only use the US dollar as the world's reserve currency. This action alone spells the end of the monopoly predicted by the Bible in which the beast locks up the world economic system in order to force all the primitive workers to bow to the demands of the usurping Great Deceiver, Zeus-Enlil. Given the post WWII weapon program names along with the NASA affiliations with Greek Gods, we have to give credence to the former Canadian Defense Minister

Paul Hellyer's congressional testimony. Paul disclosed the presence of two "Tall White" extraterrestrial beings residing in underground bases near Indian Springs, Nevada. He further stated that they had been running US domestic and foreign policy ever since the end of WWII in 1945. These advanced beings seem to have accompanied the German scientific talent like that of premier rocket designer Werner von Braun. He was transferred to the United State as part of the Paperclip Project, now known to be part of the NASA helm since its inception. Should we be surprised to see Nazi influence involved in Ukraine that started the war, as a proxy agent for the Great Destroyer, the head of the Dark Lords, Lucifer himself: Enlil? All these moves continue to bring the nations low just as noted in the King James Version of the Bible.

Isaiah 14:12-17 King James Version (KJV)

[12] How art thou fallen from heaven, O Lucifer, son of the morning! how art thou cut down to the ground, which didst weaken the nations!

[13] For thou hast said in thine heart, I will ascend into heaven, I will exalt my throne above the stars of God: I will sit also upon the mount of the congregation, in the sides of the north:

[14] I will ascend above the heights of the clouds; I will be like the most High.

15 Yet thou shalt be brought down to hell, to the sides of the pit.

16 They that see thee shall narrowly look upon thee, and consider thee, saying, Is this the man that made the earth to tremble, that did shake kingdoms;

17 That made the world as a wilderness, and destroyed the cities thereof; that opened not the house of his prisoners?

For those of you who are affiliated with secret societies or religious institutions venerating Lucifer, be warned. The ultimate goal for them is eternal enslavement for the primitive workers, so the main mission for the Dark Lords is to pervert the truth subsequently tamping down attempts to spur the *ba* to life from all angles: poisoned water, food, prescription drugs, nano-particle and chemical filled air, electromagnetic spectrum attacks in the brain wave frequency range, and other heinous acts. This is the Illuminati plan to sell the idea that chaos must precede order. Not so! Consider that you decided to make changes in the world without destructive means. This non-destructive transitional plan is now discussed in the next chapter.

CHAPTER 11: The Golden Age Revolution

Discussing Utopian ideals of how society should be and what is possible, connects one to the ancient thoughts of the almost-completing-his-legend, Solon. Recall he did not finish the story he started out to tell. The fact that he did not become as famous as Homer, is due to the fact that he quit. We still to this day yearn for the "return to Eden" draw that the high civilization of Atlantis and the character qualities they aspired to. This is why Solon was lured in; he saw the model that came from the Great Gods missing from life, among the abandoned temples in Athens. This same Atlantean lure is alive today. What is the fundamental shift needed for our collective spiritual elevation and possibility for breaking out of the simulator, graduating from the holographic prison planet quarantined state? Ascension is available to all, the keys have been provided in this book. It is up to us now to apply the lessons handed down from Plato and to avoid what happened with suppression of consciousness and the resultant overweening pride that brought even Caesar to his dreadful end. If the Golden Age is to begin, the primitive workers have to participate in the alchemical transformation taught to us by Thoth-Mercury. The ability Mercury has to go from liquid metal to an invisible vapor form demonstrates the concept as to why he affiliated with a planet with a mercurial composition and an element that is unique. If we want to experience heaven on Earth, it may not occur in the way we imagine. Suppose that the Great Year culling is really taking place, some are ascending by activating their *ba* and visiting relatives in another dimension? Or perhaps they visit Arulu directly for 6 hours, the limit specified, until our mission is accomplished here on Earth in the third dimensional holographic quarantined simulator.

Technology Unleased

Suppose we achieved energy independence with a suitcase sized device that could run your car, the home, and the business as desired. No more need for Nuclear Plants, oil and fossil fuels, as just one example. Would you need to then destructively eliminate the previous energy solutions? No, not at all. They would be decommissioned in an orderly fashion, taking care in handling and disposal of any hazardous materials in accordance with best practices. In general, any old solution gets upgraded by the new. An even more honorable way to transition without creating worldwide disorder and destruction as is happening now, is to memorialize new techniques, using museums to showcase the solutions provided to mankind by the heroes that invented the previous method or apparatus. This is like saying lets blow up every old solution so a new one can be installed. This is not the way it is done among civilized folks. For those who only have a hammer, every problem or opportunity is seen as a nail.

There are many areas of the simulator that I would design differently. We have the technology to do most all the items on the list now. It is hard to believe we have come this far in such a short time. The reality is that the simulator was designed to promote an iterative raising of consciousness, a slow unveiling by the benevolent Anunnaki agents who are playing a grand game of Chess with us all. For the simulation to be real, the conflict between LIGHT and DARK will be epic, like the Lord of the Rings legions of opposing forces bludgeoning each other toward some unknown outcome, hoping their side wins.

Suggested Societal Changes

Some immediate changes I would make for simulator participants with an active SUN-soul on their way to the LIGHT:

1. Energy independence for all beings. Graphene appears to be just the type of superconductive material that can provide Tesla energy to the masses. Russia has very advanced Tesla technology implemented for energy production uses.

2. Anti-gravity transportation devices to eliminate crowded streets.

3. Encourage personal responsibility for food production. Eliminating GMOs unless modifications are subject to proper long-term testing prior to use.

4. Promote sustainable housing and waste management. The functional elements of an Earthship home are desirable. These include passive solar heating, indoor gardening, alternative energy production, water production and recycling leading to sustainable living conditions.

5. Replace all false doctrine pushing institutes with, well, nothing comes to mind. Just eliminate or repurpose the structures to something beneficial for mankind.

6. Eliminate the current health care debacle. Promote long life by eliminating Telomere decay. Make human energy optimization and preventative care the primary focus. With the new knowledge about **ka** and *ba*, there is no need to fear death and waste the majority of one's resources at the end of life trying to prolong it. Graduate, get a new body, and continue toward the LIGHT.

7. Assess the need for life to feed on life. This does not seem like an optimal population control feature given it is a simulation. May the lion lie down with the lamb. A simple tweak to the simulator code in the class attributes. This means mankind has to participate too, adopting the dietary habits that amplify the human energy body. A

vegan diet is the best choice as it uses no animal products on the menu.

Recently, I was watching YouTube and found a video in which skate boarding legend Tony Hawk was trying out one of the latest technologies to hit the extreme sports market, a levitating skate board, Tony Hawk style.

Additionally, for those of you who still remember the Jetsons, we are moving toward the idea of having a flying car. Here is a link to a YouTube video showing a new model that was flown to demonstrate the paradigm shifting changes in the simulator [46]. Recall the concept that creation and destruction happen simultaneously. That is most likely due to the DARK and LIGHT intentional duality; a villain operating in accord with DARK principles and a vanquishing hero of the LIGHT.

Speaking of light, there have been many advances in the technical use of light. Light amplification through stimulated emission response (LASER) is just one of many technical uses for light. We use LASERs for cutting metals, for landscape leveling, surveying. Telecommunications now uses fiber optical cables and moves through the air with Free Space Optics. Quantum Electrodynamics (QED) is a field that uses the spherical (S) and polar (P) spin states for electrons orbiting a photon. These polarization states are the reason polarized glasses function the way they do. Vertical and horizontal films added to sunglasses cut out the desired S-P light that is aligned in opposition to the film gradient which disables the photon with that spin state from passing. Could this be a similar augmentation that the SUN-soul operates with using a polarization trick to get through the Earth portal, noting that only light beings with the *ba* energy field can pass. Cool sunglasses not needed here, leave them for the Men In Black!!!

Gravity Free

Advances in our understanding of gravity have to be the penultimate knowledge to be guarded in the quarantined hologram. Given our exposure to the Sanskrit writings, we now know about the ancient warring gods in the Indus region, using Vimanas for anti-gravity flight. Even the History Channel has done some specials on the ancient records discussing winged-disc flight, our modern UFOs. The designs contained in the ancient Sanskrit show these gods flying through the skies and shooting at one another!

The Bhagavad Gita is technically part of Book 6 of the Mahabharata. It is a dialog between the God Krishna and the hero Arjuna, unfolding in a timeless moment on the battlefield before the climactic struggle between LIGHT and DARK. The Gita is a classic summary of the core beliefs of Hinduism. It had a significant impact on Robert Oppenheimer who apocryphally recited the 'I have become Death, Destroyer of Worlds", just before the first test of the atom bomb. http://www.sacred-texts.com/hin/gita/

Also within the documents were drawings showing the Vimana designs that involved liquid Mercury exposed to high energy fields while rotating in a gyro-shaped toroid. As an electrical engineer exposed to many projects, both commercial and military, I can assure the reader that the government-funded technology is far more advanced than the general public is allowed to know. That said, consider that the true nature and properties exhibited by the accelerative force we call gravity, which has been shown to be incorrect, continues to be taught in universities around the world. In his book *The Final Theory*, Mark McCutcheon dedicates the first chapter to gravity. I read his book with a sense of amazement, almost feeling like it was written for me given my involvement with Structural Integration and my many years spent defying gravity as a helicopter, airplane, and hang glider pilot. My inner spirit began to ring true after thinking about the model for some time. One needs access to the C^{++} simulator private class object LAWS_OF_PHYSICS, to determine how it is correlated to the LAW_OF_TIME. Recall this is GODs vibrational parameter that sequenced events in the Great NULL and VOID. THE CREATOR OF ALL instituted 9 dimensional realities in the complex simulator, one in which we find our spritely selves in, mostly lost in the maze of skewed perception, *ka*.

Sustainable Water

Potable fresh water is a very valuable resource. As droughts come and go, access to water is a fundamental need for much of the flora and fauna here on Earth. I am tempted to say all life, but would invite a Boolean Logic rebuke for using absolutes so flippantly.

Rain, Fog, and Dew Harvesting

Earlier I referred to the Earthship home design with some friends and stumbled across an article about humidity and dew harvesting. Consider the fact that if the humidity is higher than approximately 35%, one can derive all the water needed from the air using dehumidification principles. When the outside air and the temperature of suspended water particles reach thermal equilibrium, the dew point is reached. This is where fog and clouds come from. Structures can be used to catch water from coastal fog as well as evaporative methods learned by Boy Scouts, but done on a much larger scale. Studying certain beetles that harvest fog we have learned the structural secrets to gathering water from the mist. Consider a spider web that catches fog and is glistening with moisture droplets that formed as the smaller fog particles dripped down the silken threads as a readily understandable example.

New materials are being prototyped that emulate a beetle's bumpy back, taking care to reproduce the correct height and spacing ratios that cause dew to form and accumulate. Some specialized silk-like materials are being used to gather water from the air using what looks like a vertical girdle wrapped around an open basket shell. See Figure 29 below for an example of the passive Warka water generating tower. Structure is function as we see once again!

Figure 29: African Warka Passive H$_2$O Generator

Evaporative materials and condensation plates are an added method to glean water from the air or land. Only the game masters know what may come in the Golden Age. Perhaps the conditions on Arulu will be brought to a New Earth, upgraded to an even higher dimensional state. Consider the old adage "A rising tide lifts all boats." Analogously, increasing energy levels amplifies all Chakras, negative to positive, raising all energetic beings ever closer to the CIRCLE OF LIGHT. With these sustainable low and high-tech capabilities tucked away in out tool belts, let's move on to the final chapter, Breaking out of the Simulator!

CHAPTER 12: Breaking out of the Simulator

Dr. Michio Kaku, appearing on CNN/Fox/CBS [unable to locate reference? Removed?] declared to the show host that from December 21-23, 2014 that the sun could or will stand still for three days. Thus, the sun would be visible for half the earth's surface, bringing about perpetual daylight. Additionally the opposite side of the planet would experience total darkness for the same three days. I searched and searched for the link to the YouTube video capturing the shocking revelation from America's new science guy, having prolific content and influence via the internet. Still looking, but no luck at time of publication.

Simulated Earth Changes

What is the catalyst for such a dramatic rotational axis frictional force, were it to be true, that has the potential to parasitically induce drag on the Earth's surface and atmosphere such that our watery planet stops spinning momentarily, potentially for days? I have postulated that in accordance with the Mayan *Tzolkin* Calendar, as the Earth passes through the Milky Way Galaxy *dark rift* or center, that the amplified energetic effects, to include fatal radiation levels, are coincident with the predicted heavenly event.   Our solar system center or ecliptic is approximately inclined at a sixty degree angle to the center of the Milky Way Galaxy. Due to the Galactic wobble, our solar system and its planets sinusoidally traveling through the Galactic Center every 13,000 years or so. This is half of the duration for a Great Year, which is 25,920 years. Could the Earth really experience three days of rotational axis disturbance? What would be the effect of a sudden stoppage for Earth's 7 billion terrestrial inhabitants? As the adjacent planets experience more gamma rays and begin to heat up, we should not be surprised that the same issues are facing us here on planet Earth.

Twin Flames United

The following research, and pragmatic experience, discusses activities designed to synthesize the two spirits derived from a single source as described in the Tarot Cards given to us by Thoth. This is also described in the books *the Sorcerers' Stone* [1] and *Genesis of the COSMOS* [24, Pgs. 151-152] written by Dr. Paul A la Violette.

Hermes' body was composed as a hermaphrodite, containing both the *original* male and female archetypal energies which independently were partitioned to men and women. Thus, when two twin flames derived from the same source find each other in the simulator, extreme magic can occur in the union. From a physics standpoint, when two waveforms encounter each other in 3D space, peaks and troughs result much as is seen in ocean waves. The wavelength and frequency emanating from a human MODEM varies depending on how close the measurement is taken. Think of it as a layered energy surrounding the body, as well as where on the body the high gain antenna is focused. Various symbols have been used to denote the melding of the archetypal male and female energy. Christa and I began discussing this topic as we reviewed the process by which we met and the point at which we both realized that we were twin flames, given our joint mission. Generalizing, we found our passions and were willing to share and serve humanity. This decision created the emergence and refinement of the male and female hero archetype (inspired) within us. We knew that when two archetypal flames were brought together to conjoin energies, the composite synergy was unstoppable. We had the archetypal union experience in a remote area of the high desert, leaving the oasis already bonded in spirit and mission goals.

The point I want to make with the reader is that men and women are designed from an intentionally disparate frequency standpoint, two distinct but complementary energies, such that when they operate together in accordance with archetypal boundaries, a spiritual union or melding of the independent Mer-Ka-Ba (human energy) fields may occur. This is why living a solitary life without your eternal flame at your side is an incomplete energy state from an access to higher consciousness standpoint. The sacred feminine energy represented by man's twin flame archetype, originating from Thoth directly, is mankind's only path to ascension. Is this possibly why the New Testament Jesus states that no man comes to the father except by me? Knowing that Enki and Ningishzida were father and son might make the Hebrew perversion of the history of mankind, to include the Bible, more sensible. Mother Earth made sure of that, because she was none other than Ninharsag-Isis whose feminine archetypal flame the hermaphrodite God Thoth coupled with his own. This established his dominance in the soul ascension management task, being the controller of souls into and out of the underworld or Halls of Amenti.

Speaking of the Egyptian Tarot deck, it would be interesting to examine the Magician Arcana 1 [24, Pg. 150]. Now that we know Thoth-Hermes was considered to be the keeper of the magical science and is the dual archetype for male and female energy, let's see what LaViolette has to disclose about the card's attributes. See Figure 30 below.

Figure 30: Egyptian Tarot and the Magician

Arcanum 1, the Magician Tarot Card expressed the archetype of the perfect man, specifically in full possession of his moral and physical qualities. [24, Pgs. 150-151]   He is shown standing in a white outfit signifying purity. Note the pentagram indicating none other than Isis in the female orientation, although she is shown with male attributes being composed of both the dragon and the goddess archetypes. As a reminder, the goddess archetype was represented on the escutcheon of the Biblical Ham along with the dragon. The goddess was none other than the female archetype for mankind, Adapa's mama Ninharsag-Isis. A serpent biting its tail and making the infinity symbol represents the Ouroboros a never-ending process. From the Emerald Tablets Thoth declares he is immortal, renewing his life in whatever body he had taken on, time and again in the Halls of Amenti. The image is a shedding snake (exiting a body after incarnation) rejuvenating itself indefinitely.

The Ouroboros often symbolizes self-reflexivity or cyclicality, especially in the sense of something constantly re-creating itself, the eternal return. Another symbol is the Phoenix which operates in cycles that begin anew as soon as they end. It can also represent the idea of primordial unity related to something existing in or persisting from the beginning with such force or qualities it cannot be extinguished.

While first emerging in Ancient Egypt, the Ouroboros has been important in religious and mythological symbolism, but is also frequently used in alchemical illustrations, where it symbolizes the circular nature of the alchemist's craft. It is also often associated with Gnosticism, and Hermeticism.

Biblical Rich Man and the Needle

Why such a low quota for ascension? How does wealth often lead to shoring up personal security, isolation, and lack of concern for the common man? This is the basis for rich folks like Bill Gates and George Soros being involved with the CDC and the Ebola Virus funding for Tulane researchers on behalf of the USAID Chemical Weapons Laboratory, in the author's humble opinion.

Pulling back the dark shades of the Middle Ages, we find the unsuspecting primitive worker plague victims, rotting and dying in the streets, piling up exactly 666 years ago. The Black Death was ravaging Europe and eventually the rest of the world. There are solid documented connection from a contemporary story indicating that the Jews were responsible for poisoning the wells with the plague virus as admitted in a video that I compiled, it raises many questions. We indeed are living in circumstances that parallel the attempt to eliminate humans using genocidal assaults in the past, e.g., The Atrahasis, just like what is going on in the world today. Here is a link to the YouTube video that presents the evidence we are living in the days of Noah.

https://www.youtube.com/watch?v=UdlEPByjw2M

We know that the Bible teaches that it is harder for a rich man to get to heaven than it is to get a camel through the eye of a needle. What an allegory to contemplate. Perhaps the quota is based on open requisitions for ascending light beings. In either case, the Georgia Guide Stones and their anonymous founder R.C. Christian has as one of their goals maintaining the population at 500 million. Is this the reason (a quota cap according to the Georgia Guide Stones) that the difficulty getting to experience our birthright is near impossible? Given how the path to the "keys to the kingdom" has been suppressed, it is no wonder the schools that taught this knowledge had to swear their graduates to secrecy. The lessons were only shared symbolically, like a parable that the Biblical Jesus uses so often to teach the disciples and his followers.

*Matthew 19:24 (*King James Bible "Authorized Version", Cambridge Edition*)*

And again I say unto you, It is easier for a camel to go through the eye of a needle, than for a rich man to enter into the kingdom of God.

Cymatics: Frequency and Geometry

Consider the interesting fact that science has verified the matter recycling ability of a black hole. Recall we stated a physics principle that energy is neither created nor destroyed, it merely changes state. Black holes are functionally analogous to your high power vacuum cleaner, operating not by the same principles but simplified for ease of discussion. If one gets the nozzle of a pressure differential and velocity amplifying vortex debris suction apparatus (engineering speak for a vacuum cleaner) just close enough to the event horizon, the targeted matter disappears into a reservoir to be recycled. In a similar fashion, unlike vacuums, if any form of matter crosses the event horizon of a black hole, it disappears never to be seen in its same material form again. This is where galactic balance between energy and matter are held in check. The black hole forces the disintegration of all matter converting it back into energy, which can be considered to be the unmanifested force that creates all matter, in a circular fashion, the cylindrical Venturi generating "Wind of Cleansing" approximates the matter recycling power of black holes.

Let's now connect the FIRST CAUSE (vibratory sound of GOD manifests LAWS OF CREATION out of VOID equated with modern scientists Big Bang Theory) to the creation of matter. Recall from Emerald Tablet X where Thoth describes how the LAW OF TIME did not exist when there was only the VOID. Think of the analogous void that the black hole matter recycler represents. The CREATOR OF ALL had the meta-perspective that used vibratory constructs like we have discovered in the field of Cymatics.

Cymatics is an interesting field to me, thus by definition I knew that at some point in my path it would have significant meaning to me as a seeker, paying attention to the "omens" that subtly guide our life's fated steps toward our destiny. Cymatics is essentially using frequency (sound or otherwise) to form various levels of harmonic vibrations which can be viewed. The technique is easy to demonstrate using an adjustable tone generator (software is free for computer users) and a vibratory surface covered with small particles that can move with the vibratory waves tracing the resultant force of overlapping pressure waves. It is similar to placing a magnet beneath a white piece of cardboard covered with iron filings. The force field from the magnet displaces the iron filings to align them with the magnetic field.

Cymatics creates patterns that we now know are structurally at the basis of composing small particles into material form. A good example is to understand that all matter is composed of vibrating energy that attracts the constituent components present (iron filings or Au+ ions). We reviewed them on the periodic table of the elements shown in Chapter 2. The vibratory pressure wave for a specific tone or note (like our voice or the musical scale) stitches matter together creating our illusion of matter or the circle of chaos termed *ka*, the life of man. So, getting deep in our thought experiment, could the FIRST CAUSE as described in *Emerald Tablet XV (15): Secret of Secrets*, be a single vibration that the SOURCE OF ALL initiated just like it says in the Bible? The creation story in Genesis states that the void of space was distinguished by creating matter such as planets, flora and fauna. So the bottom line from a scientific perspective is that vibratory energy can be used to CREATE (LIGHT) matter from the Great Void, which is the polar opposite of the DESTRUCTIVE (DARK) black hole function destined to destroy all matter. This is why the LAW OF CONSERVATION OF ENERGY reveals to us how the SOURCE OF ALL can be understood as it relates to our constrained holographic reality. Let's connect the dots to the simulator. Now consider that a very advanced scientist had figured out, by reverse engineering the destructive effects that black holes used to disintegrate matter, and discovering how matter is put together. This is what is going on in the particle colliders like Fermi Lab or CERN where the Higgs-Boson God Particle is being sought (destructive reverse engineering methodology).

On the opposite side of the creative spectrum, Cymatics is helping us understand how energy creates matter, versus reverse engineering underground lab rats at CERN. The beauty of music is the key to connecting the nine parallel dimensions discussed in

Emerald Tablet X. The harmonic octaves are constrained to the first nine images of the fundamental frequency. With Cymatics, we find that various tones formulate the "force field" lines like the ones in the magnet and iron filing experiment for visual effect. This ability to take energy and create matter is the secret knowledge that illuminates the seeker to the homeostatic balance of CREATION and DESTRUCTION involving energy and matter. We are the offspring of the Anunnaki who enslaved us, 'tis true. But we are also vibratory constructs using the ultimate building block of all matter, which is LIGHT. LIGHT is where we are told is where the CREATOR OF ALL resides, in a CIRCLE OF LIGHT. Light can be seen to be in either a particle or wave state, depending on whether there is an observer present at the time of analysis. This is weird science that should spur someone to ask, what did you just say? Yes, you heard me correctly. Light behaves as either a particle (think ping pong ball as a model) flying off the surface of a photon generator (our sun) like a pebble. We also know that photons can travel like a sinusoidal waveform like all other wavelengths along the electromagnetic spectrum. Thus, the photon has the mind of GOD and hides its nature from the observer to preserve its high potentate matter creating authority to essentially be the most unmanifested form of energy. LIGHT therefore, has the most potential to manifest as matter in ANY FORM.

That form includes your body, the trees, the rocks and moon, and your DNA. Light is the fundamental building block that creates the illusion of matter representative to our limited biological sensors (our eyes) which we use to establish our mental construct. In other words, it forms the reality of what is perceived by the simulation entity of interest. In the movie *The Hunger Games*, the Game Master manifests predatory animals, forest fires, and all sorts of devastatingly real entities of interest. Our protagonist heroine Katniss keeps looking for a way out of the rat maze of her holographic existence. These were all simulator constructs that were experienced as real threats. One must ask oneself, how a simulated Saber Tooth Tiger could interact with Katniss and crew leading to death? At this point, one should then realize that they too are a simulation entity just like the software programmers in the movie *The Thirteenth Floor* discovered. Now that you know the significance of the number 13 and that is composed of 9 parallel dimension plus the 3 natures of man plus the final SOURCE, it is clear that LIGHT totals thirteen!!!

Thanks, Ningishzida and Enki for creating the Zodiacal signs of Scorpio and Sagittarius. The arrow of the Sagittarius archer points to the same location as the Scorpio stinger, the thirteenth sign of Ophiuchus. This is a time of great importance for discovering the SECRET OF SECRETS and perhaps taking the time for intense purification on our way back to the portal of LIGHT.

Reality's Bounds: Spherical Energy Layers

Scientists have discovered something truly remarkable above the Earth's atmosphere. An invisible shield is located approximately 7,200 miles above Earth that scientists are likening to *"force fields on Star Trek"* [19].

According to *Front Line Desk*, the shield was discovered in the Van Allen radiation belts, two doughnut-shaped rings above Earth that are filled with high-energy electrons and protons. Held in place by Earth's magnetic field, the Van Allen radiation belts swell and shrink in response to incoming energy disturbances from the sun. The Van Allen radiation belts were first discovered back in 1958. However, scientists only discovered two belts, an inner and outer belt extending up to 25,000 miles above Earth's surface.

Last year, Professor Daniel Baker from the University of Colorado Boulder and his team used the twin Van Allen Probes launched in 2012 to discover a third, transient 'storage ring.' According to their research, the third belt is located between the previously known inner and outer Van Allen radiation belts. **This belt is different in that it seems to come and go as space weather changes.**

The purpose of the ring according to the researchers is to block killer electrons from entering deeper into the Earth's atmosphere. These electrons can be extremely devastating at their near-light speed and have been known to threaten astronauts, fry satellite systems and damage space systems.

Baker likened the invisible shield to Star Trek force fields. The Earth's magnetic field holds the belts in place, but the scientist says that the electrons in these belts — which travel at nearly the speed of light — are being blocked by some invisible force that reminded him of the kind of shields used in television series like Star Trek. The primary use was to stop alien energy weapons from vaporizing starships. However, in the case of Earth, the invisible shield is being used to stop killer electrons from entering the atmosphere.

Prior to the invisible shield discovery, scientists assumed that electrons making it into the upper atmosphere of the planet would be dispersed by air molecules, but it looks like these particles don't even get that far thanks to Earth's invisible electron shield.

Now that the scientists know the invisible shield exists, they are trying to determine how it was formed and exactly how it works.

"It's almost like these electrons are running into a glass wall in space. It's an extremely puzzling phenomenon."

As is evident all throughout the scientific discovery process, we are just now becoming sophisticated enough, as epitomized by science, to leave our planet as an exploring species visiting the

Moon, Mars, and whatever has NASAs attention next. The idea that there is an energy sphere around the earth, is not new knowledge. Drunvalo Melchezidek detailed the origin, shape, and function of the grid as disclosed to him by none other than Thoth. As above, so below seems true still to this day. Robert Monroe describes encountering similar boundary constructs in his seminal disclosure book *Journeys Out of the Body* [30] assigning the labels Locale 1-3 to these invisible barriers. Locale 1 is equated with present space-time. Locale 2 was reported by Monroe to be where the human personality survives the transition of death [30, Pg. 238]. The attributes of Locale 3 are more elusive, but my experience is that this is the boundary or our spherical holographic cage. This is where the Duat portal is located based on the *Emerald Tablets of Thoth.*

Additional information regarding the boundaries and the OOBE limits for mankind are detailed by Thoth himself in the Emerald Tablets disclosed earlier. Thus, we should not be surprised to find Mer-Ka-Ba energy fields shaped like the star tetrahedron from Drunvalo [31, Pg. 343]. In addition, he teaches in his Flower of Life books, Volumes 1 and 2, how to understand, activate, and optimize the human Mer-Ka-Ba fields which extend approximately 55 feet around us. Stay tuned to the holographic disclosure channel, on full time now it seems, as the Mayan-prophesied ascension window is ready to receive new terrestrial bound energy.

Be prepared for a transition to a higher spin state. Here is a YouTube video link that one can use to learn and practice the meditation[33].

https://www.youtube.com/watch?v=XyUOgHVsDiY

Just think, in less than 18 breaths, you can activate your Mer-Ka-Ba energy field every day. Give it a try and see what you think and feel. The 18th step has been more occluded as it involves astral projection fear issues dealt with by Robert Monroe [30] during his OOBE travels.

Finding the Way Out: Inside

A clue is offered in the King James Version, Luke 17:21 of the Canonical Bible. This contentious passage indicates to seekers that the focal point for our spiritual evolution, the way to the Kingdom of Heaven, is within us. Note that Heaven is also known as Nibiru for those who have studied the Sumerian documents know that these writings frequently equate Nibiru with the term Heaven.

Luke 17:21 (KJV)

Neither shall they say, Lo here! or, lo there! for, behold, the kingdom of God is within you.

As I have stated, this internal kingdom is the energetic electromagnetic interface to our energy body system of nerve ganglion and correlated endocrine glands like the pineal gland. This gland correlates with the crown Chakra and the pituitary gland correlates with the 3rd Eye Chakra. Ningishzida-Thoth, the real Jesus, is consistent in his lessons from both the *New Testament* and the *Emerald Tablets* as it concerns his immortal energy. Recall that Thoth multiple times states that his soul roams the Earth even now, occupying the material containers we all our bodies. The same promise is made to Jesus's disciples when he leaves them behind with assurances they will achieve the same miracles he has performed, becoming the sons of God. Contrasting the lessons taught using parables for children in the New Testament with the advanced wisdom of Thoth in the Emerald Tablets ought to ignite a déjà vu synchronicity. This is the same being sent by Anu to teach mankind the pathway out of the quarantined holographic enslaved reality we are trapped within.

In this following question and answer session I did with a book fan, I tried to explain in detail my personal understanding of the verse I see as tied to Thoth's energetic disclosure in the Emerald Tablets. From the New Testament teachings of Jesus, a key Protestant salvation doctrine verse, John 1:12, we find a link to the Chakras as they relate to power. The less understood second part of the verse involves an energetic and physical DNA transformation as the sons of God.

This short article is published (Gerald Clark) to supplement the Caduceus write-up in my book *The Anunnaki of Nibiru* [3, Pg. 189]. Now think about the Bible verse and consider a frequency allocated from a transmitter, say like *HAARP*. Now imagine this power could trigger an electro-magnetic spectral interaction with the human nervous system, in particular the Reticular Activating System or the Sacrum. What if this power, instead of being used to fry your brain or poke holes in the troposphere, could be used to "light up" humans initiating or triggering latent potential energy stored in the Human Coccyx bone at the bottom of the Sacrum (sacred bone).

John 1:12: King James Bible "Authorized Version", Cambridge Edition states, (with my additions in parentheses):

"But as many as received him, to them gave he power to become the sons of God (Enki that is), even to them that believe on his name (Ningishzida-Thoth-Jesus):"

The Caduceus Replaces the Cross

Consider the concept of receiving a frequency (power), where energy meets matter, in the Ganglion of Impar, the nerve complex at the base of the human Coccyx bone. This is where the received power initiates the alchemical transformation symbolized by the

Caduceus. This ancient healing symbol was carried by Thoth-Ningishzida, and explained in my book on pages [3, Pgs. 189-195].

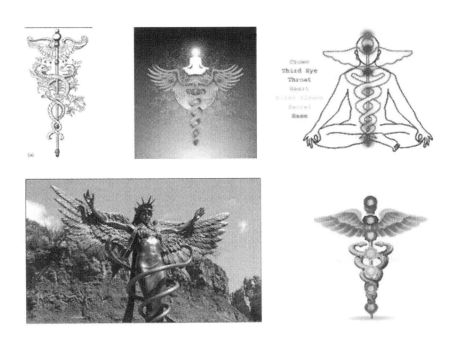

Figure 31: Caduceus Symbol of Enki and Thoth

Here is the *becoming* part, the second part of the verse... Potential energy received in the Coccyx (called power from John 1:12, KJV) bone triggers a snake-like wiggling in the Ganglion of Impar, the electrical conduit for energy. The energy is represented by a coiled snake, suggesting the wound up spring is prepared to uncoil rapidly, releasing the potential energy stored in the coil.

Then the double helix DNA that was dumbed down for the primitive worker design, represented by entwining snakes wrapped around the central pole, were indicative of the energy received, transforming the DNA to a higher subset of Enki's archetype. This is a process that seems to coincide with the opening of each Chakra in succession.

Once the rising Kundalini energy reaches the 7th Chakra (crown), the Pineal gland is activated producing DMT, which does not cross the blood-brain barrier. This "Spirit Molecule", as it was called by Dr. Strassman in his book *DMT the Spirit Molecule* [35], is what floods the lateral ventricles, shown in the Caduceus symbol as the Wings of Hermes. Hermes was the head of the Hermetic tradition that taught folks along the Nile at the Mystery Schools how this alchemical transformation worked.

The *New Testament* Jesus was crucified on a cross whose shape made a mockery of the similarly-shaped Caduceus, representing the internal spiritual/energetic cumulative human energetic struggle, and the ultimate human achievement, lateral wings of Hermes. These pilot wings represent the achievement of an enlightened consciousness shared by the Anunnaki, an activated *ba* SUN-soul.

Now compare the death and destruction symbol of the Roman cross with the shape of the Caduceus, and you will see symbolically that Enlil was broadcasting to the Enkiites, namely Ningishzida-Thoth, that he would do any level of evil to prevent mankind from having what their true CREATOR OF ALL and Enki intended, an elevated consciousness like that of Jesus-Thoth-Ningishzida. A cosmic battle has come to a head, a battle over the evolution of human consciousness, one that I aim to finish, here and now by exposing the lies of Enlil. Consider the term Enlightenment, overcoming the glass ceiling imposed by Enlil. No coincidence here… We have the advantage of knowing the prophesied end result of the war between Light and Dark, LIGHT wins and darkness is erased from the Earth!!! Let the good times roll on out.

Book Fan Question and Answer Session on John 1:12

A book fan recently sent me these questions. They are provided here along with my answers. This gets to the heart of the energy-matter issue and crosses religious boundaries. You've been warned...

The reader's questions start with Q_i and Gerald Clark answers with A_i.

Q1:

I am sorry I understand Jesus is Mercury, Hermes, Thoth... Also that this is an actual energy used, to upgrade our DNA based on our 7 chakras but to activate it you only need to say his name?

A1:

I feel like you have cornered me like a Baptist preacher, defining salvation doctrine...Did not expect the topic to lead to this discussion. That said, there seems to be two distinct phases related to the energy/frequency dispensation. Phase 1 is receiving and storing potential energy in the sacrum. Phase 2 is releasing the potential energy and getting it to clear and occupy all Chakras, resulting in the elevation of human consciousness, symbolized by the caduceus. That means pineal gland firing, wings of Hermes experience!

Phase 1, Receiving Power:

Believing in the name Ningishzida-Jesus as the one that dispensed a frequency that has the potential energy (kundalini) that can be received by a primitive worker, storing it in the Ganglion of Impar at the end of the Coccyx bone, bottom of the sacrum, is defined in Phase 1.

I guess this is a leap of "*faith*" to believe such a thing, yet with the science I have provided you, it is not such a leap anymore. The Ganglion of Impar is the negative pole of your energy body, which can be measured near ground electrical potential with the being standing in the gravity field. This is just potential energy, stored, dispensed freely to anyone on the broadcast channel that wants it. It can sit latent in the Ganglion of Impar/Coccyx Bone for a lifetime if not released. Once the potential energy is triggered/released from its dormant state, it is up to the being to facilitate the transformation as referenced in the second part of John 1:12, the becoming part is up to us.

Q2:

And the reason why it (activation from power/frequency dispensation) won't work for most is because their bodies aren't aligned properly? I really want to know if this is what you are saying.

A2:

That is partly correct. It is my view that part one of the two part process works, although it a potential energy, meaning it lays latent waiting to be released. Note: it is the author's further view that as our solar system approaches the Milky Way Galaxy Center (GCR), as predicted by the Mayans, the 10GeV measured radiation must leak through our atmosphere, increasing the received energy on the surface of the Earth. That said, this increased energy from the GCR, forces the human energy body to approach its zenith or height of human consciousness. Nearing the GCR may be responsible for automatically triggering the latent energy stored in the Ganglion of Impar/Coccyx bone root Chakra. Thus, as the broadcast energy level rises, so does all the human energy bodies, like a time triggered consciousness raising event. This theory is supported by

Drunvalo Melchizedek in this book *The Ancient Secret of the Flower of Life*, Volume 1, pages 56-58, where he generalizes the waking up and going to sleep process approaching the GCR and going away from it respectively.

Our bodies are random structures that without intervention cannot align properly with the gravity field. This is where Structural Integration (SI) comes in. The latent energy is stored in the sacrum, waiting to be released, but remains dormant as one seeks a spiritual path that involves weekly visits to an entertainment-focused ceremony inside a building with a Roman torture symbol placed thereon, singing to Jesus and Enlil in the same breath. The short answer is they did part 1 of John 1:12 but failed to do part 2, becoming or transforming to that dispensed frequency by lighting up their Chakras, where energy meets matter. If churches were serious about **spiritual matters** they would take seriously the energetic design we exhibit and replace the sign of death and torture symbol, the Roman cross, with a symbol that represents the elevation of human consciousness toted by mankind's appointed teacher Ningishzida-Thoth-Jesus-Hermes, his symbol being the caduceus.

Phase 2, Transformation:

Once the latent energy is released from the Sacrum (my

method has been through Structural Integration and a combination of movement repatterning like Tai Chi or Yoga). This causes the rising energy to begin changing the double helix (entwined snakes along spine) DNA in some manner, permanently altering the being's relationship to energy and matter. This transformation is exemplified by the individual relating to the infinite force of gravity: specifically aligning the segmented stacked blocks of the body to the gravity field. The alignment referenced by Structural Integration principles facilitates satisfying Equation 5/5A in my book *The Anunnaki of Nibiru*, Chapter 6. This is where the idea of the symbol of the caduceus sums this transformation up, and when experienced pragmatically, finally makes sense.

Q3:

Have you experienced this upgrade?

A3:

Phase 1 took place at a much earlier time in my life, as a young adult. I was raised as a wild buck on a seven acre farm in the Northwest corner of Arkansas. We had a garden, chickens, pigs, goats, horses, and cattle on our remote plot in the Ozark Mountains. I was exposed to the concept of Baptist salvation doctrine by the time I was 13 years old. The concept of intrinsic versus extrinsic locus of control were at the forefront of my spiritual path at this age. While attending a (Southern Baptist

Church) service with a fellow pilot in Manhattan, KS, I completed the Phase 1 leap of faith, had an infused energy feeling for some time perhaps 2 years, then it seemed to fade to the background remaining dormant until my 33rd birthday.

Q4:

What is it like?

A4:

Phase (1) one was fulfilling, but was so far in the past that I will focus mostly on Phase 2. It reminded me of the fluctuating feelings affiliated with dating. Exciting for some duration then ebbs and flows like most other passions in life. Structural Integration, Yoga, and Martial Arts together facilitated rapid transformation for me, helping alleviate some very damaging and energy-blocking physical patterns caused by previous accidents and injuries. Phase 2 of the process began for me when my brother was killed in a car accident at age 34. I was 33 years old at the time.

My spirit began to soar when I made the decision to live with no regrets spawned by my brother's death. Within a week I began hang gliding lessons to get myself back in the air. As a former helicopter pilot for seven years, being aloft with the soaring birds found in the sheer zone between the mountains and the desert with a hang glider strapped to my back, gave me the perspective to live without fear.

Mustering my courage needed to face the challenges of having a genetically disabled child, I made the scary transition from Vice President of Engineering to Holistic Health Care Practitioner on behalf of my son JJ. The SI recommendation was received during a Triathlon in the year 2000. JJ was born in 1999.

The path choice to follow my heart and not my wallet led me to Structural Integration, the life work brought to humanity by Dr. Ida Rolf. As my structure began to change, so did my energy and life lessons. I shared the SI work with my boy JJ and many others over my seven year practice, seeing tremendous improvements in him.

Each Chakra seems to have a gating function with its affiliated physical blockages from past injury, posture, and random fascia. Additionally, each Chakra has spiritual lessons that must be learned before taking on the next quantized consciousness/energy level for the nerve ganglia closer to the head. Gotta learn your heart Chakra lessons before you get to your Throat Chakra tests. This coincides with many historical takes on the common spiritual transition experience, being iterative and quantized with energy/consciousness levels. When the rising kundalini energy got stuck trying to open up a Chakra, one's full attention is brought into the body as a burden of awareness, until change is achieve unblocking the rising energy.

Indian medicine and spiritual science calls the energy channels Nadis, the chosen pathway for the human bioenergy. Similar to the acupuncture meridian concept. In regard to Kundalini Yoga, there are three of these Nadis: Ida, Pingala, and Sushumna. Ida (spoken "iRda") lies to the left of the spine, whereas Pingala is to the right side of the spine, mirroring the Ida. Sushumna runs along the spinal cord in the center, through the seven chakras – Mooladhaar at the base, and Sahasrar at the top (or crown) of the head. It is at the base of this sushumna where the Kundalini lies coiled in three and a half coils, in a dormant or sleeping state, shown in Figure 32.

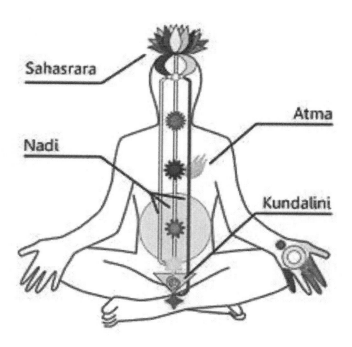

Figure 32: Yogic Energy Pathways

Reader's Final Comments from the Q&A session

Gerald, I am sorry to have made you feel cornered I don't want to come off as pushy but I really wanted to know. My brain is spinning now. Wow! What a discovery!!!! Wow!! In your book you sort of said you had experienced it, but I wanted to be sure.

At first before listening to your book I thought why is it important to know who all these names and everything there has always been good and bad forces at work in the world. Now I see the point. You have to understand who Jesus was to understand what he was trying to do, why he was trying to help mankind.

I am still spinning and trying to digest everything and put it into the larger picture. Thank you so much for your time and patience with me I really appreciate it.

Jason and the Argonauts

Next we visit the big screen where the Anunnaki archetypal lessons are conveyed to mankind as the screen actors in the classic movie *Jason the Argonaut*, help lift the veil and clarify the rules of the holographic reality game.

Sophisticated live Greek theatrical plays involving complex sets and actors in costume played their simulation roles, modeling the expected behavior for the sons of God(s). The plays were conducted in acoustically perfected amphitheaters which served a similar cinematic and entertaining function as well as education for the peoples of Greece. Here the Olympian Gods attempted to teach them the character qualities that lead to ascension, using theatric means for effect.

Figure 33: 1963 Movie, "Jason and the Argonauts"

Various Hollywood attempts at lifting the veil on holographic and simulated reality have already transpired and continue to this day. Movies like *The Matrix, Avatar, Hunger Games,* and many more invite the modern viewer to ponder the state of reality one is experiencing. Could we be entrapped in a simulation, immortal energy beings temporarily occupying material bodies having a human experience? Is our soul composed of non-local energy which is the basis for OOBEs? All evidence points to our bodies being simply containers that house energy at quantized levels coincident with our seven Chakras.

If my hypothesis, shared by many, is true, then until we have experienced the lessons preplanned for our current lifetime, there is no reason to try to escape our destiny early. The way out of the simulation is via graduation, achieved by building ones character qualities forged in the fires of change, mustering the courage to face life's greatest fears as Truman does. By facing and overcoming the stormy seas which drowned his father when he was a small boy, Truman is on the ascendency path. The fear of dying at sea as his father had done terrorized Truman and was his greatest fear. When Truman finally is ready to graduate from his life simulation of entrapment, he must face the threatening seas, looking for truth, thereby choosing to walk in the archetypal and mythical heroes' footsteps. This is what Jason the Argonaut did risking his life to serve the peoples in his community of Thessaly, launching his legendary quest for the Golden Fleece to heal his land.

For those that have not seen the 1963 movie *Jason and the Argonauts*, I highly recommend that the readers watch this cinematic masterpiece produced by Charles H. Schneer. Several times it occurred to me that it would be interesting to get inside the producer's head given his interest in aliens and mystical legends, and telling the archetypal stories of days gone by. Thus, some of his other works are highlighted herein.

The son of a jeweler, Charles H. Schneer was chiefly famous for his collaborations with animator and special effects wizard Ray Harryhausen. Together, they created some of the best-loved fantasy and science fiction films to grace the silver screen between 1956 and 1981. Importantly, Schneer encouraged Harryhausen's imaginative flights even to the point of exceeding his budget - unlike many other producers active in the realm of low-budget film making.

Schneer had initially entered the motion picture industry with Columbia in New York in 1939. He worked as an assistant there for three years and then did his wartime service with the U.S. Army Signals Corps Photographic Unit, turning out training films at the Astoria Studio in Queens, New York. After the war, he joined Sam Katzman's B-unit at Columbia as producer. It was Schneer's original concept of a giant octopus enveloping the Golden Gate Bridge that led to his introduction to Harryhausen and their subsequent joint work on It Came from Beneath the Sea (1955). Despite a miniscule budget, the venture proved to be a notable box-office success.

Their next project together was the seminal science fiction <u>Earth vs. the Flying Saucers</u> (1956), which took Harryhausen's stop motion technique to the next level. Again, it was Schneer who had provided original background research by collecting news reports of actual UFO sightings.

By 1957, Schneer had ceased working for Katzman and became co-founder and president of Morningside Productions as a means of gaining more creative and financial control for both himself and Harryhausen (who was henceforth also credited as associate producer). Their subsequent ventures were based on mythological themes, rather than being simply 'creature features'. These included <u>The 7th Voyage of Sinbad</u> (1958) (in which the three dimensional stop-motion animation process was first referred to as "Dynamation"); <u>The 3 Worlds of Gulliver</u> (1960) and <u>Jason and the Argonauts</u> (1963) (Schneer's own favorite among his films). In 1960, Schneer moved to London to form an independent production company, American Films. He produced several features without the involvement of Harryhausen, notably a biopic of rocket engineer <u>Wernher von Braun</u>. They later resumed working together and had further successes with <u>Sinbad and the Eye of the Tiger</u> (1977) and <u>Clash of the Titans</u> (1981), with its brilliant Medusa sequence. Schneer retired in the 1980's, once stop-motion work had been somewhat superseded by cheaper computer-generated special effects. He continued to reside at his Holland Park home in

West London until returning to the United States just three years prior to his death in 2005. *[IMDb Mini Biography By: I.S.Mowis]*

This classic hero tale involves the protagonist Jason, an agnostic and doubting Thomas type macho guy. **Jason's story in this film is an arduous heroes journey contrived to hone the fated steps in his archetype eliciting character**, complete with a happy ending.

The problem facing Jason is that there is sickness and disease in his land. His father Aristo, the King of Thessaly, was killed by the military commander Pelias. Jason and his sisters are targeted for elimination by Pelias, fearing a future threat to his unjust coup based on lies. Jason is scurried out of the temple as Pelias' troops overrun the complex, killing Jason's sister Briseis still kneeling and praying to the very large statue of the goddess Hera for salvation for her and her child.

Hera is standing in the shadows of her temple statue dressed in black witnessing the whole event. Pelias sees her and engages her in conversation at which point he is told by Hera that Jason escaped. Confusion overcomes Pelias as he suddenly realizes that the prophecy he got from a priestly oracle speaking on behalf of Zeus, whose authority he claims while destroying the temple, the kingdom, and children of Aristo, was tainted. He asks Hera why Zeus had him kill an innocent girl given that Jason was the one in line to rule? This is a critical dialog in which Hera clarifies the method in which Zeus interacts with mankind. The reason I bring up this level of detail regarding the interaction between the characters is to expound on the relational understanding we can garner relative to mankind's freewill and the influences of the ancient astronauts from Nibiru.

Pelias: "It is the will of Zeus".

Hera: "It is not the will of Zeus, it is your will. Zeus has given you a kingdom, the rest will be your own doing. The gods abandon you Pelias. A one-sandaled man shall come, and no god shall protect you from him."

Pelias: "A one-sandaled man?"

Hera: "The child who has escaped you, Jason"

Pelias: "Why did Zeus drive me to kill this girl when the only one I needed to kill was Jason?"

Hera: "Zeus cannot drive men to do what you have done. **Men drive themselves to do such things that the gods may know them and men may understand themselves.** The killing of Jason will do you no good. Kill Jason and you kill yourself."

The conversation ends and Hera disappears from her desecrated temple in a dissolving holographic misty fog, and Pelias is left standing among the barbaric carnage and destruction he has wrought. All because he sought to possess the kingdom of Thessaly promised to him by the oracle of Zeus. She reappears in the elaborate temple full of busy activity on Mount Olympus, where she has an encounter with her husband, Zeus-Enlil. First she gives her hell-bent on destruction hubby the business asking why one of her temple priestess was murdered by the latest agent he was puppeteering in the simulator. She is angry and states that she wants to help Jason accomplish his quest, but Zeus tells her it is a man's business. She persists and gets her way. You go girl!

Zeus decreed that Jason can only call upon Hera's aid five times. This is the number of times Briseis specifically stated Hera's name while praying in front of her statue prior to the siege by Pelias. How interesting. Wonder what he would have done if she had prayed and stated Hera's name seventy times? That is a lot of intervention and Zeus probably would have come up with a decimation scalar to get the number down to a handful anyway.

A couple of the Olympian gods make their appearance in this media tool designed to teach the primitive workers character-honing lessons. The first encounter with the Niburian displaced astronauts from Nibiru, portraying themselves as the Olympians to the ancient Greeks, occurred early in the film between a supposed temple priest and Jason. While walking toward a stoic looking, white-haired priest playing a Lyre, the gentle and soft-spoken soul stops playing music and asks Jason if he has come to ask the god for help with his mission. The elderly disguised priest begins discussing the difficulty of the mission to recover the Golden Fleece and suggests that Jason call on the gods for assistance. Jason notices a very large statue of Hermes holding his Caduceus and sporting a winged helmet, fallen over on the ground near the small disheveled and crumbling foundation whose marble pillars were still barely standing.

Jason balks at the persistent old priest's suggestion of asking the gods for help. He further explains that he would have to first believe in gods to act in faith to ask them for help. To add insult to injury, Jason then points out the fact that one of the supposedly benevolent Olympian god's statues, that of the winged Hermes, lay in ruins on the abandoned temple grounds, symbolic of a fallen God. The priest briefly and apologetically states that sometimes the winds of change blow, even for the gods.

The priest gets an opening with reluctant Jason and invites him to come meet the gods for himself. What is one to do in such a situation? The priest turns and walks into the center of the very small temple which is just large enough for one person to stand in the middle, surrounded by carved pillars and lentil stones making a quasi-circle. Leading Jason to a stone just within the confines of the center of the pillars, the priest instructs Jason to step back slightly away from him and suddenly, with a Cheshire cat smile on his face, the priest began transforming into the great god Hermes. He stands holding his symbolic golden caduceus as the cinematic magic men morphed him from an average sized human into a thirty five foot giant towering over the stunned protagonist Jason. At that point, the towering Hermes dissolves and a fire breaks out at Jason's feet, suddenly dematerializing him. Then, Hermes reappears before the entire Greek God Council, located in their gloriously decorated temple on Mount Olympus, Jason hidden in the messenger God's hand.

The preplanned visit to Mount Olympus was conceived by the God Hermes to help Zeus and Hera with a kingly misrule issue in Thessaly. Zeus, engaged in a game of global chess, is the first one to encounter Hermes still holding the miniature sized hero which Jason has hidden in the palm of his hand. Suddenly during the small talk dialog between Zeus-Enlil and Hermes-Ningishzida-Thoth, Jason is presented as a pawn piece in the game, placed on the chess board. Zeus is amazed and subsequently offers counsel that Jason IS the solution to one of the Chess Master's dilemmas regarding the unease that had swept the lands causing famine, pestilence and disease. Finding an expendable hero to do the Gods bidding was a perfect fit to illustrate the key features necessary to tell the archetype story, yet again.

Jason, being one of a thousand heroic faces, is used in this high drama teaching vignette for the soul edification of lowly mankind. As Hera stated to Pelias, Zeus was running operations with mankind, fanning their malignant desires for various vices to include greed, pride, and power. Pelias is an easy victim, claiming authority from Zeus to be a barbarian desecrator of civilized life. Hera further states that this vice-promoting influence created by Zeus for his chess pieces is designed for two purposes. The first is so that the Gods may know the character development of the man. The second reason given is that man may know himself. In other words, she wanted Pelias to recognize his fallen state to facilitate spiritual growth.

During several radio shows, I have made the point that in the universe we have come to expect that creation and destruction (matter and energy) happen simultaneously and generally reach a homeostasis state until the next triggering event disturbs the current one. A natural order occurs forming spherical bodies in the heaven until a celestial battle ensues possibly converting matter into energy, or at a minimum breaking the planet into smaller pieces as evidenced in our own asteroid belt. This belt is termed the *hammered bracelet* in the Sumerian Epic of Creation, the Enuma Elish. Enki-Poseidon as I have proselytized during the last year, is mankind's true genetic creator, not to leave out Ningishzida-Thoth and Mother Earth herself, Adapa's mama

Ninharsag-Isis. Poseidon-Ahura Mazda, has been deemed the God of Light and Wisdom whereas Zeus-Angra Mainyu, has been playing the role of the God of Destruction from the Atrahasis account through Greco-Roman incarnations up until this very day, now hailing as Lucifer. The point I want to reiterate here is that just as energy and matter are kept in balance, the creation and destruction of human energy is not exempt from the same laws seen in nature and the universe.

On the stage of life here on Earth, the Anunnaki Gods were clearly playing chess with the fate and destiny of their primitive worker pawns. Classic tales like Jason and the Argonauts were born in the midst of the Niburian astronaut-occupied land in Greece, where they were hidden away from the populace in their mountain temple decorated in gold. I wonder if some of that decorative temple gold was previously gathered by the Igigi and their primitive worker chimera replacements whose creation by the Anunnaki scientist put out the fires of rebellion in the South African mines? The image of game masters hidden away in their fortress, fusing telemetric sensor data gathered by their alphabet agencies into a cogent picture of the primitive worker enslavement and potential rebellion status comes to mind.

This technology used by the Olympian Gods is no different than the veil-busting film series *The Hunger Games*. Recall the scene in which President Snow (Enlilite Archetype) works closely with the move-countermove game master (Enkiite Archetype) in the all-seeing eye room where the game is played. In a similar fashion, Zeus and Hera use a viewing system to snoop in on the heroes' archetypal journey progress, using their sensor fusion simulation portal located on Mount Olympus. This device plays center stage as the Gods huddle around when Zeus and Hera decide to check in on the sleeping agents in their covert operation in the holographic universe. Pawns like Jason and the villain Pelias are intermittently viewed by Hera and Zeus using the all-seeing eye heads-up display. The use of the all-seeing eye is not only symbolic, but riveting given the disclosures Edward Snowden has recently made about the CIA and NSA snooping using electronic devices and the electromagnetic spectrum. I took my readers and listeners even further down the disclosure path concerning technical snooping abilities accessible to the game masters. Brain waves and energy levels exhibited in the Chakras can also be snooped, even from a large distance. I was reminded of several deployments to the National Training Center located near Fort Irwin California, where I encountered some advanced simulation toys in the windswept desert lands spotted with dusty dry lake beds that filled the sky with obscurant particles during frequent gusts. As a Chief Warrant Officer serving in the Army, my job as an attack helicopter pilot was to kill tanks, plain and simple. An entire Soviet Motorized

Rifle Regiment was relocated to the training center so that the Army had a place to bring large battalion-sized forces to learn Russian war tactics during simulated battles. Each vehicle and all personnel were fitted with transponders and sensors to participate in the multiple integrated laser engagement system (MILES) vignettes. The amazing part of the training happened atop a special observation mountain peak near Bicycle Lake Army Airfield. For it is here that we pilots got a sneak peek behind the wizard's curtain. The after actions review briefing that had been set up for the game masters analysis was being opened to the participants for training purposes, lessons learned real-time if you will.

The telemetry equipment used to monitor the battle lay resident in the transponders fitted on each game player, the soldiers. Each squawk of the transponder emitted the weapon code and a location was affixed for the source and the receiver, color coded as blue for us good guys, and red for those evil communists, our mortal enemies of the state. It was a fascinating briefing providing a God's eye view of the entire battle, color coded for ease of interpretation. Additionally, each weapon system was simulated using low power laser transponders that simulated the weapon systems in use, both direct and area fire armament was modeled to include range and tracking durations. With this kind of perspective, what kind of chess game could the game masters play? The possibilities are unlimited. Now consider the advancements in imaging and communications technology in the past 20 years. If the technology permitted satellites to perform facial recognition and brain wave monitoring in the 1960's, how much more sophisticated are the snooping toys used in the game room now? Far beyond your belief is my best guess, knowing that technical development programs used by the military often lead to commercial byproducts many years later. Only the game masters know the extent to which their tools are effective enough to use the planet's Sleeping Agents as pawns in the archetypal journey to either destruction or completion of the assigned destiny in this incarnation.

Hera directs Jason to search for the Golden Fleece in the land of Colchis. Zeus offers his direct aid to Jason, but Jason refuses stating that he can organize the voyage, build the ship, and select a crew of the bravest and most able men, Argonauts, in all of Greece by holding an Olympic trial. **Zeus, observing that those most worthy of the aid of the gods, are those who least call upon it.** How ironic and the theory still seems to hold water today. Zeus is pleased with Jason's plan to aggregate some heroic Argonauts to recover the golden treasure, and sends Jason back to Earth.

We find out the true extent of Jason's mission objectives, when Jason has his fated encounter twenty years later, saving Pelias from drowning in a river. Pelias hides his identity and brings Jason into his encampment to interrogate his mortal enemy and Sleeping Agent. Pelias puts on his best poker face during the dialog. Jason discloses that he is the son of the slain King Aristo and he is going to return and claim the throne.

Jason states: "Pelias has turned the kingdom of Thessaly from the pride of Greece into a savage evil land, unwittingly saying this directly to Pelias. He further clarifies the importance of the mission telling Pelias "**This time it will not be enough to fight, I could fight, finding Pelias and killing him. But the people need more than a leader, they must believe the gods have not abandoned them. They need a miracle**. I heard there was a tree at the end of the world with a fleece of gold laying in its branches. It has the power to heal, bring peace, and rid the land of plague and famine. If I could find the prize and bring it home to Thessaly, then it would inspire the people, wipe out the years of misrule. They would know the gods have not abandoned them. My land would be rich and strong again. As it was before this tyrant Pelias murdered my father King Aristo."

According to the myths perpetuated in his time, there is a solution that is guarded by the gods. It is purported that a golden fleece, located in a distant land across the sea, has magical healing powers. The archetypal character in the story must face tremendous odds in order to retrieve the sacred fleece. Keep in mind how the story of gold woven into a fleece has healing powers. Consider what we now know about monoatomic gold and its effects on the human energy body, and subsequent disclosures involving this superconductive colloid triggering DMT production in the pineal gland as well as affecting the levels of telomerase. This is a precursor to the proper preservation of the Telomeres during cellular reproduction. It is also now known that this process affects aging as disclosed in 2009. Jason completes his death defying journey, returning to Thessaly. The Olympian game masters assess the players performance in their after actions briefing, commenting on Jason's mission to get the Golden Fleece. At the final scene of the briefing on the Mount Olympus game room, Zeus tells Hera that in due time he will call upon Jason again. The drama play goes on.

The World Needs a Miraculous Leader

Luckily, according to Emerald Tablet XII, mankind has been assigned an account manager, a consciousness coach, and benevolent teacher all in one, Thoth.

For all those seekers that have chosen to walk the character honing path to enlightenment and graduation from the holographic enslavement simulator of life, Thoth-Jesus' words engender a sense of hope for the world we live in, inscribed by a miracle worker and philosopher King hailing from Atlantis!!! Enki-

Poseidon's honorable son, Hermes-Thoth-Ningishzida, has taken it upon himself to inscribe his wisdom and the future destiny of mankind on the notorious *Emerald Tablets*. The narrow gate exit path which Jesus spoke of in the New Testament, allegorically specifying how few escape the primitive worker enslavement, is obtainable much as it was prescribed to the inhabitants of Atlantis carved into the twin orichalcum pillars near Poseidon's silver and gold clad temple. Character counts and is a fundamental attribute that arises when choosing to live a principled life of the archetypal hero, versus succumbing to our myriad of vices and desires that lead to one's destruction. Recall the seven virtues and vices. They are worth looking up for those who have forgotten them. They were posted on a building on the UCSD campus, illuminating alternatively in large neon lights for all to see. This did not seem to deter those I spent almost 10 years with as a student and employee.

This is how the game is played. According to the lessons taught to us by an insider, one of the game designers, we manifest our own reality and are therefore responsible for the causality that leads to the subsequent effect. You reap what you sow, so decide now to start the character building path that begins with being honest first and foremost with yourself. Thoughts are real tangible electrically verifiable manifestations emanating from our primitive worker antennas. Our meat-MODEMs are easily snooped upon by those that possess the all seeing eye technology used to run CIA-like operations on the chosen hero of a thousand faces to be memorialized and used as a teaching tool for the people so that the *Gods may know them and that they may understand themselves!!!* This is why the simulations are run from remote information gathering sites. Secret locations equipped with sensor fusion command centers, (i.e. Mount Olympus Temple and perhaps Indian Springs Nevada underground bases?) house the Godly game masters.

Using this God's-Eye holographic interface, separated by dimensions, training vignettes can be crafted as virtual worlds within worlds, placed here in our holographic quarantined simulator, where their primitive worker pawns hone their soul's immortal character qualities in anticipation of their next incarnation. Thoth eloquently describes this process in the Emerald Tablets. A large section of Thoth's prophesies about the destruction to come and the promising future plan for mankind is revealed in *Emerald Tablet XII* and a subset is repeated here. I wish to emphasize the profound guidance that one of our most benevolent teachers throughout recorded history graciously left for us truth seekers. The message is very positive, study these words and know your destiny as a Light Being!

...

Know ye the future is never in fixation but
follows man's free will as it moves through
the movements of time-space toward
the goal where a new time begins.

...

Know ye, O man,
that all of the future is an open book
to him who can read.

...

Know ye the future is not fixed or
stable but varies as cause brings forth an effect.
Look in the cause thou shalt bring into being,
and surely thou shalt see that all is effect.

...

So, O man, be sure the effects that ye bring
forth are ever causes of more perfect effects.
Know ye the future is never in fixation but
follows man's free will as it moves through
the movements of time-space toward
the goal where a new time begins.

...

List ye, O man, while I speak of the future,
speak of the effect that follows the cause.
Know ye that man in his journey light-ward
is ever seeking escape from the night that surrounds him,
like the shadows that surround the stars in the sky
and like the stars in the sky-space, he, too,
shall shine from the shadows of night.

Ever his destiny shall lead him onward
until he is One with the Light.
Aye, though his way lies midst the shadows,
ever before him glows the Great Light.

Far in the future, I see man as Light-born,
free from the darkness that fetters the Soul,
living in Light without the bounds of the darkness
to cover the Light that is Light of their Soul.

Know ye, O man, before ye attain this that
many the dark shadows shall fall on your Light,
striving to quench with the shadows of darkness
the Light of the Soul that strives to be free.

These are the challenges to one's archetypal journey through
this life. Recognize them and overcome the fear they elicit, and

you move on to the next one, turning lemons into lemonade (until charged with sale of food item with no government permit)!

Great is the struggle between Light and darkness,
age old and yet ever new. Yet, know in a time, far in the future,
Light shall be All and darkness shall fall.

List ye, O man, to my words of wisdom.
Prepare and ye shall not bind your Light.
Man has risen and man has fallen as ever new
waves of consciousness flow from the great
abyss below us toward the Sun of their goal.

Ye, my children, have risen from a state
that was little above the beast,
until now of all men ye are greatest.
Yet before thee were others greater than thee.
Yet tell I thee as before thee others have fallen,
so also shall ye come to an end.

And upon the land where ye dwell now,
barbarians shall dwell and in turn rise to Light.
Forgotten shall be the ancient-wisdom,
yet ever shall live though hidden from men.

Aye, in the land thou callest Khem (Egypt),
races shall rise and races shall fall.

Forgotten shalt thou be of the children of men.
Yet thou shalt have moved to a star-space
beyond this leaving behind this place where thou has dwelt.

I suggest that time of departure for those reading these words, is now!

The Soul of man moves ever onward,
bound not by any one star.
But ever moving to the great goal before him
where he is dissolved in the Light of the All.
Know ye that ye shall ever go onward,
moved by the Law of cause and effect
until in the end both become One.

This reminds me of a rising tide lifting all boats. . Earth's received (whole solar system) energetic levels increase as the Galactic Center is approached. Humans on the Earth's surface, unless blocked by a planetary radiation shield, receive increased energy at the Great Year processional wobble cycle that lasts 25,920 years to repeat.

Aye, man, after ye have gone,
others shall move in the places ye lived.
Knowledge and wisdom shall all be forgotten,
and only a memory of Gods shall survive.

As I to thee am a God by my knowledge,

so ye, too shall be Gods of the future

because of your knowledge far above theirs.

Yet know ye that all through the ages,

man shall have access to Law when he will.

Ages to come shall see revival of wisdom

to those who shall inherit thy place on this star.

They shall, in turn, come into wisdom

and learn to banish the darkness by Light.

Yet greatly must they strive through the ages

to bring unto themselves the freedom of Light.

Then shall there come unto man the great warfare

that shall make the Earth tremble and shake in its course.

Aye, then shall the Dark Brothers

open the warfare between Light and the night.

When man again shall conquer the ocean and fly

in the air on wings like the birds;

when he has learned to harness the lightning,

then shall the time of warfare begin.

Great shall the battle be twixt the forces,

great the warfare of darkness and Light.

Nation shall rise against nation
using the dark forces to shatter the Earth.
Weapons of force shall wipe out the Earth-man
until half of the races of men shall be gone.
Then shall come forth the Sons of the Morning
and give their edict to the children of men, saying:
O men, cease from thy striving against thy brother.
Only thus can ye come to the Light.
Cease from thy unbelief, O my brother,
and follow the path and know ye are right.

Then shall men cease from their striving,
brother against brother and father against son.
Then shall the ancient home of my people rise
from its place beneath the dark ocean waves.
Then shall the Age of Light be unfolded
with all men seeking the Light of the goal.
Then shall the Brothers of Light rule the people.
Banished shall be the darkness of night.

Aye, the children of men shall progress
onward and upward to the great goal.
Children of Light shall they become.
Flame of the flame shall their Souls ever be.
Knowledge and wisdom shall be man's
in the great age for he shall approach the eternal flame,

the Source of all wisdom,

the place of beginning,

that is yet One with the end of all things.

Aye, in a time that is yet unborn,

all shall be One and One shall be All.

Man, a perfect flame of this Cosmos,

shall move forward to a place in the stars.

Aye, shall move even from out of this space-time

into another beyond the stars.

Conclusion

My birthday falls on December 23rd, at which time I symbolically arrive at the age that coincides with the Lord of the Earth Anunnaki Council Rank of 50. Hopefully, after years of being ensconced in a culture that one grows up in, substitute yours here, that no matter the level of darkness that was poured out on your path, you have the courage (overcome your fears) and the wisdom (review Ch. 3, Hillbilly Lessons on Knowledge) to transmute the darkness of ignorance into LIGHT. This is our SUN-soul's purpose here in the third dimensional holographic screenplay we call life, *ka* to those that know better, all matter is in a transient state on its way back to the same simulator source energy, the LIGHT of the CREATOR OF ALL. We can overcome the illusion of **ka** by activating the **ba** field which ignites our path out of the illusion all the way to

541

the home of the Great Gods on Arulu. To many, however, it is merely a myth to those gullible enough to believe that the genius population in Athens ascribed to childish ideology regarding their creation account and the drama plays of Greek life.

I received this inspirational www.TUT.com message "from the Universe" via email this morning, December 25th, 2014 which seemed unusually timely, although quite flattering (Christa got the same message as did thousands of subscribers). I thought it would be nice to share it as it encapsulates the timely message I am giving to you, the *READER*, in this book.

"If it's not yet obvious to you, the real
reason for this (Christmas), and all seasons, is
you, Reader. A more perfect child of the Universe
has never lived. Until now, only celebrations
cloaked in myth and mystery could hint at your
divine heritage and sacred destiny. You are life's
prayer of becoming and its answer. The first
light at the dawn of eternity, drawn from the
ether, so that I might know my own depth,
discover new heights, and revel in seas of
blessed emotion.
A pioneer into illusion, an adventurer into the
unknown, and a lifter of veils. Courageous,

heroic, and exalted by legions in the unseen.

To give beyond reason, to care beyond hope, to

love without limit; to reach, stretch, and dream,

in spite of your fears. These are the hallmarks of

divinity - traits of the immortal - your badges of

honor. May you wear them with a pride as great

as what we feel for you.

Your light has illuminated darkened paths, your

gaze has lifted broken spirits, and already your

life has changed the course of history.

This is the time of year we celebrate (you the

READER).

Bowing before Greatness,

The Universe

This is my gift to all my peers (especially you the READER) in the simulator, performing my pilot role as an aerial scout, seeking first contact with the target, annotating the existing map with the new illuminating external entities of interest, and providing the data in a coherent manner such that decision makers on the battlefield of life can make the next move or countermove in the game. Listen to your heart (spirit) and pay attention to what you are paying attention to because it is interesting!!!

Reflecting in this way on your life's circumstances, lessons in the dark leading to more light, draws inspiration from our CREATOR(s), wanting to aid the archetypal hero Jason find the Golden Fleece at the end of the world, with an outpouring of unwavering willed actions chosen to make it so!

Thus, happy are those that dream dreams and are willing to face the obstacles that stand between their *LIGHT*- inspired thoughts and their desired reality, no matter which of the nine parallel dimensions or back home to Arulu one chooses at the forks on our mutual fated journey back to our destiny. My plan is to get as close as possible to THE CIRCLE OF LIGHT, reserved for the CREATOR OF ALL alone!

It's not just an engineering optimization problem for me either, minimizing the delta between the photon source (LIGHT=GOD) and the biological light receiver (human eye: a limited range visible light only detector), it's my mission objective. During this Great Year go around, our communal destiny, for the brave heroes on their archetypal pathless land to the TRUTH, can graduate from the quarantined confines of the illusion of **ka**, dissolving the false reality and landing in the LIGHT.

All matter is composed of LIGHT, and we may be seen as fleeing photons from our transitioning matter containers, reborn into the higher (4th-6th) dimensional LIGHT-body, the **ba**. This is our ticket ready to be punched by Osiris as we slink through the narrow gate out of the 3rd dimension spherical prison, pausing briefly to pet the Azazel-pardoned proverbial biblical camel we chose to honor and not liquefy its body in an industrial strength blender in our barbarian attempt to force it through the eye of a hero-discouraging needle as the childish parable envisions blocking our birthright, available since your design, here and now! The gate is wide, access has been granted, but the warning still stands, don't come unless you are prepared. Study Thoth's words like you would a graduate level text. Read the Emerald Tablets a hundred times as advised by Thoth himself, as many times as is necessary to get the WISDOM he desires. Perseverance and persistence to obtain WISDOM will outperform the lazy intelligent seeker every time. There are no shortcuts, your path is unique to ensure that every solitary soul makes it home, even if the scout lead is killed enroute. The object of seeking is finding, when you are free from illusion you have truly begun your spiritual journey on its next leg to the utopian goal we all share, trying to get back to the SOURCE state that is our birthright. This is when you know that your seeking is over (until the next level or lesson) graduating to FINDER status!!!

Thoth-Mercury, the holder of the keys out of the 7th Planet holographic lesson chamber, offers his invitation to all, *"win ye the way to me"* as he invites all on the road to LIGHT and WISDOM to approach him with a countenance free of darkness (*ka*) and filled with light (). Fan the flames of your energy body as my Human

545

Energy equation shows, stoking the fires of *ba* enthusiastically, breathing the flaming embers hot enough to smelt gold and vaporize the fears that stand in the way of your alchemical transformation, promised by the symbol of LIFE, the Caduceus.

We are faced with a choice in our paths, often generically categorized as making decisions based on love or fear. A fearful being accumulates material items to enhance their sense of security, often at the expense of community isolation, the quintessential scrooge. They are likely to be found in the stands versus in the arena of life.

Alternatively, the hero or heroine chooses to risk their own security by sharing the acquired knowledge gleaned from their personal truth quest, how to win at the game. Empowering the path of others is the right road to travel. 'Tis the Futant path...

My major premise and message to humanity is that as we pass through the Milky Way Galaxy and the intense gravity and radiation described by the Mayans as the Dark Rift, this is what modern science deems the flattened nebula. This is a result of the intense attractive power seen capturing even photons at the event horizon of a very large black hole at the center of the galaxy. This is a common feature of all galaxies, a matter to energy converting void where all matter is subject to the law of conservation of energy. This heightened GCR emanating energy affects the human

MODEM, specifically the receiver or demodulator. Our earthly antennas are being activated by this galactic energy and we are reaching the apex of our consciousness glass ceiling, as predicted by Thoth's amazing calendar that rewound to the beginning on December 21st, 2012. We are now arriving at the cyclical narrow time window, a place where we can best assimilate the archetypal lessons provided to us by our holographic simulator game masters, the Anunnaki.

It is our opportunity during this transit through the energetic gradient belt to see the karmic wheel for the learning tool that it was designed for, cyclical repeating energetic windows. These can be used to facilitate spiritual evolution for some, ascension for far fewer others due to ignorance of its presence and how to pass. The gate is not narrow, but the time to access the gate is limited. There are only open requisitions for ascended beings in the promised next life, actually promised to us, by Thoth in the Emerald Tablets. Thus, there is no quota as implied in the biblical camel through the eye of a needle parable. The impediment is our need to develop the character qualities specified on the pillars of Atlantis, and now subsequently on the Emerald Tablets of Thoth the Atlantean.

A fascinating opportunity exists for human beings operating out of love and not fear. By overcoming the fear of one's own death (security), we are freed to empower those in our communities. Given the communications infrastructure in existence today, the intended receiver may be a radio or television or Android mobile smart phone, perusing alternative information venues, or a primitive worker (human antenna) seeking to know the actual versus propagandized state of the simulator. Information is power and there is no question that we are ensconced in the Information Age.

Having now completed the task of reading this book, you, Noble Reader are endowed with the knowledge preserved through the ages by your CREATORS, detailing mankind's go forward plan with access to eternal life as promised herein. I look forward to joining you all in the convergence where cause and effect are ONE SOURCE. May Thoth visit us all daily as inspiration until that time.

BIBLIOGRAPHY

[1] Hauck, Dennis William, "Sorcerer's Stone: A Beginner's Guide to Alchemy", 2004, Kensington Publishing Corp, New York.

[2] Dalley, Stephanie, "Myths from Mesopotamia: Creation, the Flood, Gilgamesh, and Others", 2000, Kensington Oxford University Press, Oxford.

[3] Clark, Gerald R., "The Anunnaki of Nibiru: Mankind's Forgotten Creators, Enslavers, Destroyers, Saviors and Hidden Architects of the New World Order", Create Space Self-Publishing, 2013, San Diego.

[4] The Electronic Text Corpus of Sumerian Literature http://etcsl.orinst.ox.ac.uk/

Sumerian is the first language for which we have written evidence and its literature the earliest known. The Electronic Text Corpus of Sumerian Literature (ETCSL), a project of the University of Oxford, comprises a selection of nearly 400 literary compositions recorded on sources which come from ancient Mesopotamia (modern Iraq) and date to the late third and early second millennia BCE [4].

The corpus contains Sumerian texts in transliteration, English prose translations and bibliographical information for each composition. The transliterations and the translations can be searched, browsed and read online using the tools of the website.

Funding for the ETCSL project came to an end in the summer of 2006 and no work is currently being done to keep that site updated.

[5] "Scientist sequence oldest DNA from fossilized leg bone found in Spain", The Independent, Dec, 2013, silised-leg-bone-found-in-Spain.html
http://www.independent.co.uk/news/science/scientists-sequence-oldest-human-dna-from-fossilised-leg-bone-found-in-spain-8983416.html

[6] Holloway, April, "Initial DNA analysis of Paracas elongated skull released – with incredible results", February 5th, 2014, http://www.ancient-origins.net/news-evolution-human-origins/initial-dna-analysis-paracas-elongated-skull-released-incredible#sthash.6pSJJRUX.dpuf

[7] Carlo, John, White, Paul, "The Secrets of Thoth and the Keys of Enoch", http://www.lightparty.com/Spirituality/ThothEnoch.html

[8] Van Auken, John, "The Body - Temple of God", http://www.edgarcayce.org/ps2/body_temple_of_god_J_Van_Au

ken.html

[9] Sitchin, Zecharia, "History Timeline According to Sitchin", World Mysteries, http://www.world–mysteries.com/pex_2.htm

[10] Doreal, "The Emerald Tablets of Thoth the Atlantean", 1930, http://www.crystalinks.com/emerald.html

Originally published in mimeographed form in the 1930s by a mysterious "Dr. Doreal," these writings quickly became an underground sensation among esotericists of the time. Tablets 1-13 are part of the original work; tablets 14 and 15 are supplemental.

[11] "The Ancient Astronaut Theory", http://imaginealiens.weebly.com/rh--blood-type.html

[12] Hegland, T.J., "Virtual Earth Graduate", 2014

[13] Thorkild Jacobsen, "The Treasures of Darkness: A History of Mesopotamian Religion: Lamentation of Ur", www.GatewaysToBabylon.com

[14] Maldacena, J. M. Adv. Theory. Math. Phys. 2, 231–252 (1998).

[15] Hyakutake, Y. Preprint available at http://arxiv.org/abs/1311.7526 (2013).

[16] Hanada, M., Hyakutake, Y., Ishiki, G. & Nishimura, J. Preprint available at http://arxiv.org/abs/1311.5607 (2013).

[17] Ashliman, D.L, "The Legend of Saint George", http://www.pitt.edu/~dash/stgeorge1.html

[18] "Albert Pike and Three World Wars", http://www.threeworldwars.com/albert-pike2.htm

[19] "Scientists Discover and Invisible Shield Surrounding Earth, Baffled At How It Formed", http://www.inquisitr.com/1638338/scientists-discover-an-invisible-shield-surrounding-earth-baffled-at-how-it-formed/

[20] Radke, Amanda, "BLM VS. Nevada Rancher Bundy: What Is The Real Story", April 15, 2014, http://beefmagazine.com/blog/blm-vs-nevada-rancher-bundy-what-real-story

[21] "The Georgia Guidestones - Illuminati Ten Commandments?", http://www.rense.com/general16/georgiaguidestones.htm, RadioLiberty.com, 11.15.2001

[22] Coelho, Paulo "The Alchemist", Harper-Collins, New York, 1998.

[23] Wallace, Daniel,"Is Lucifer the Devil in Isaiah 14:12? - The

KJV Argument against Modern Translations",

https://bible.org/article/lucifer-devil-isaiah-1412-kjv-argument-against-modern-translations

[24] LaViolette, Paul A., Ph.D. *"Genesis of the COSMOS*: The ancient Science of Continuous Creation", Bear and Company, Rochester, VT, 2004.

[25] Calleman, Johan, *"The Mayan Calendar and the Transformation of Consciousness"*, 2004

[26] Quinn, Daniel "Ishmael", 1992

[27] "Could-Friday-13th-phones-GPS-devices-knocked-sun-Impact-massive-solar-flare-expected-hit-Earth-tomorrow-disrupt-communications satellites?",
[http://www.dailymail.co.uk/sciencetech/article-2656010/Could-Friday-13th-phones-GPS-devices-knocked-sun-Impact-massive-solar-flare-expected-hit-Earth-tomorrow-disrupt-communications-satellites.html#ixzz351pJqZLg]

[28] Coleman, John "Weather Channel Founder: Man-Made Global Warming is Baloney",
http://cnsnews.com/news/article/patrick-goodenough/weather-channel-founder-man-made-global-warming-baloney

[29] Clark, Gerald " Ebola, Immigratin, Gaza, and the Days of Noah",

2014, YouTube
https://www.youtube.com/watch?v=UdIEPByjw2M&list=UUFUH 0JRBPG9g5k5M3AgJ4g

[30] Monroe, Robert A., "Journey Out of the Body", Doubleday, New York, 1977.

[31] Melchizedek, Drunvalo "The Ancient Secret of the Flower of Life: Volume 1", Light Technology Publishing, Flagstaff, 1998

[32] Melchizedek, Drunvalo "The Ancient Secret of the Flower of Life: Volume 2", Light Technology Publishing, Flagstaff, 1998

[33] Merkaba Meditation, YouTube, https://www.youtube.com/watch?v=XyUOgHVsDiY

[34] Freer, Neil "The Annunaki and the Myth of a 12th Planet," 2006, http://www.redice.net/specialreports/2006/01jan/annunaki.html

[35] Strassman, Dr. Rick, "DMT The Spirit Molecule", Park Street Press, Rochester, Vermont, 2001.

[36] Sitchin, Zecharia "Divine Encounters", Avon, 1995.

[37] "Golden oldies! Grandparents were a rare breed until 30,000 years ago",
http://www.dailymail.co.uk/sciencetech/article-2016759/Life-expectancy-Grandparents-rare-breed-30-000-years-ago.html

[38] "Research center or weather weapon? US military is shutting down HAARP ", http://rt.com/news/161672-haarp-closure-weather-experiments/, Published time: May 27, 2014 14:16

[39] Smith, Jerry E., "HAARP: The ultimate Weapon of the Conspiracy," 2003, Adventures Unlimited Press, pages 10-20.

[40] "Breaking: Sen. Harry Reid Behind BLM Land Grab of Bundy Ranch", http://www.infowars.com/breaking-sen-harry-reid-behind-blm-land-grab-of-bundy-ranch/

[41] Leary, Timothy, "Are You a Futant", YouTube Video
https://www.youtube.com/watch?v=rAmi9kDQe7U

[42] Wilcock, David, "The Synchronicity Key", Penguin Group, New York, 2013.

[43] Taylor, L. Hanson, "The Ancient Atlantic", Library of Congress, 1969

[44] "Notes on Paperclip Project", Marshall Space Flight Center History Office, http://history.msfc.nasa.gov/german/paperclip.html

[45] Gardner, Laurence "Genesis of the Grail Kings", Fair Winds Press, 2002.

[46] https://www.youtube.com/watch?v=FdoaPkqPQhs

[47] Talbot, Michael *The Holographic Universe,* Harper Perennial; 4.6.1992 edition (April 6, 1992)

GENEALOGY TABLES

A 3 foot by 8 foot full digital PDF file is available here:
http://geraldclark77.com/products.html

THE ANUNNAKI OF NIBIRU: GENEALOGY TABLE

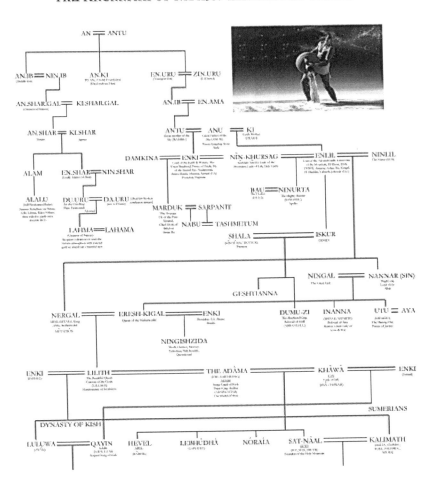

GERALD CLARK

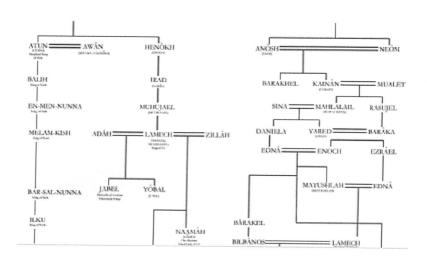

THE 7th PLANET MERCURY RISING

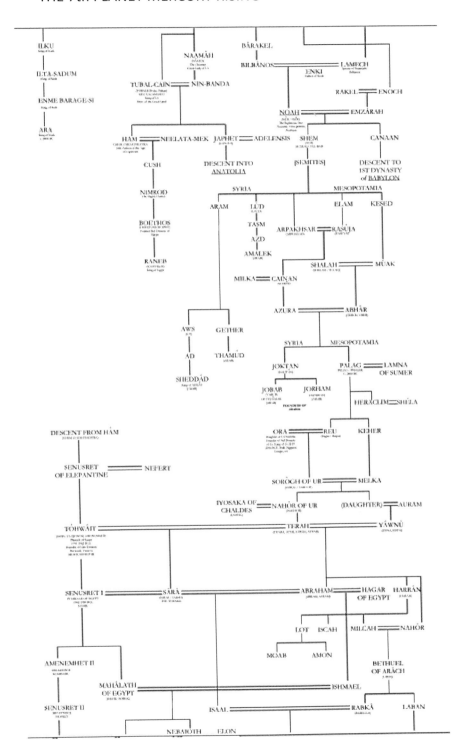

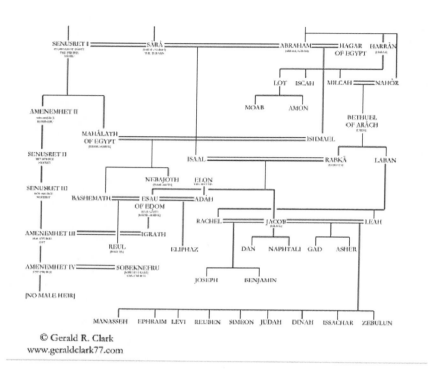

A 3 foot by 8 foot full digital PDF file is available here:

http://geraldclark77.com/products.html

INDEX

F

G

H

487, 489, 506, 507, 508, 510, 524,

525, 533, *Ningishzida*

human, 10, 12, 13, 14, 15, 24, 25, 49,

62, 64, 65, 122, 135, 139, 153, 171,

367, 402, 403, 409, 410, 488, 501,

504, 506, 507, 508, 509, 510, 514,

518, 525, 527, 532, 547, 550

I

ice age, 18

Igigi, 24, 29, 44, 56, 61, 69, 80, 98, 527

illegal drugs, 12

Inanna, 33

intelligence, 10

IRAS, 43

Ishmael, 13

J

Jason, 394, 515, 517, 518, 520, 521,

522, 523, 524, 525, 526, 527, 528,

530, 531, 532, 544

Jupiter, 33, 38, 41, 42, 44

K

Ki, 38, 68, 132, 401

Kishar, 38

L

Lahamu, 38

Lahmu, 38

Lord of the Command. *Enlil*

M

magnetic, 15, 16, 499, 500

Marduk, 37, 39, 40, 361, 362

marijuana, 29

Mars, 38, 41, 42, 44, 48, 501

Masonic, 22, 372, 373, 397, 445, 460,

466, 467

ME. *ME Tablets*

ME Tablets, 21

Mercury, 8, 19, 31, 32, 33, 36, 38, 39,

40, 110, 135, 391, 392, 393, 394,

395, 396, 397, 398, 399, 400, 401,

476, 482, 507, 545, *Ningishzida*

Mesopotamian. *Mesopotamia*

metal, 26, 31, 32, 47, 76, 392, 423,

425, 426

metallurgy, 21, 366

microwave, 12

military, 11, 13, 28, 151, 152, 421, 470,

521, 530

MODEM, 15, 153, 488, 547

money, 13

Moon, 38, 76, 322, 331, 501

Moses', 378

MPEG, 273, 568

Mummu, 38

R

radiated, 16, 19

rebellion, 10, 80, 81, 366, 527

rebels, 9

Robert Morris, 22, 465

Roman, 11, 506, 510, 527

S

satellites, 17, 423, 500, 530, 553

Saturn, 33, 39, 40, 42

secret societies, 19, 454

serfs, 12, 14

sexagesimal, 22

signal, 13

simulator, 20, 30, 31, 33, 57, 63, 64, 67, 135, 139, 141, 151, 152, 154, 170, 372, 401, 408, 410, 476, 487, 523, 532, 547, 548

Sitchen, 37

slave, 11, 24, 25, 27, 30, 70, 401, 415

slaves. *See* Slave

Solar Maxima, 18

South Africa, 17, 24, 45, 52, 473

spiritual, 20, 65, 134, 135, 148, 152, 153, 155, 170, 171, 367, 374, 376, 408, 413, 414, 457, 476, 488, 502, 506, 510, 511, 513, 514, 526

Sumer, 33, *Sumeria*

Sumerian, 17, 20, 22, 30, 32, 35, 36, 52, 69, 72, 78, 79, 121, 135, 360,

369, 400, 502, 526, 549

sun, 14, 16, 17, 18, 19, 30, 35, 60, 76, 165, 353, 404, 467, 486, 499, 553

Sun, 36, 38, 39, 40, 145, 166, 172, 178, 181, 182, 184, 193, 199, 201, 224, 231, 246, 256, 285, 301, 306, 314, 319, 327, 331, 335, 343, 354, 537

T

THC, 29

Thoth, 23, 32, 33, 52, 56, 59, 61, 63, 65, 133, 134, 135, 137, 138, 140, 142, 143, 144, 148, 155, 156, 157, 158, 168, 170, 171, 176, 183, 184, 235, 265, 293, 296, 299, 304, 310, 356, 365, 367, 370, 372, 373, 374, 376, 396, 406, 469, 487, 489, 501, 503, 504, 505, 507, 510, 525, 526, 532, 547, 548, 550, 551

Tiamut, 36, 39, 40, 41, 42

Tigris, 26, 36

U

United States, 11, 12, 13, 21, 23, 27, 29, 58, 410, 422, 467, 469, 473, 521

Ur, 22, 45, 70, 72, 73, 74, 75, 76, 77, 78, 79, 80, 122, 367, 368, 551

Uranus, 39, 41, 42, 43

W	Z

war, 11, 14, 22, 29, 149, 371, 402, 422, 455, 456, 457, 464, 465, 468, 469, 471, 473, 519, 529

Zeus, 33
Zodiac, 40
Zodiacal, 16, 24, 28, 34, 135

ABOUT THE AUTHOR

Gerald Clark is a 1994 graduate of the University of California at San Diego (UCSD). Gerald holds an MSEE in Electronic Circuits and Systems, and a BS in Computer Engineering both from UCSD. Gerald is the author of several papers in the communications and electronics field and is well known for his work in the San Diego high technology industry, awarded several patents in the Free Space Optical Laser Communications field while serving as Vice President of Engineering, LightPointe Communications, Inc. Gerald's career involved companies like Loral Telemetry and Instrumentation where he lead the final phase of the Globalstar Telemetry and Command modem designed for Qualcomm- used to command, monitor, and control 54 LEO Globalstar Constellation Satellites.

While serving as VP Engineering at Tiernan Communications, Gerald and his small team of hardware and software engineers were credited with "Digitizing American Television", having demonstrated the first live HDTV Monday night football game on-air transmission from New York to the world using Tiernan Communications, Inc. HDTV 720p MPEG-2 Encoders.

During the years 1996-2002, working as a telecommunications executive, Gerald's business travels took him to various parts of the world exposing him to a plethora of cultures which acted as a catalyst for his research into mankind's earliest technologies and accomplishments, including the cultures of Mesopotamia and the surrounding areas of Turkey, Egypt, Persia, and Iraq, eventually leading to the cuneiform-inscribed tablets left by the Sumerians.

Knowledge of the Anunnaki here on Earth, both in the ancient past their presence here and now, is being fully-disclosed around the world. My hope is that this book will help the billions of primitive workers, left to fend for themselves on a hostile planet, to find hope that following the great destruction underway, wrought by the warring gods of Light and Dark, a promised peace in the new age of Aquarius is dawning, actually already upon us.

I am excited about sharing this research with like-minded collaborators authors, film makers, and seekers of the truth

Be ye kind and of good integrity, most of all animate the frequency of Love, the one devised by the Creator of All for us to enjoy. Best wishes on your archetypal journey toward your destiny where we will reunite where cause and effect are One.

Gerald R. Clark

Websites:
www.geraldclark77.com

Christa J. Clark
www.artisticvegan.com

Made in the USA
San Bernardino, CA
02 August 2016